IMAGES
of America

YORK

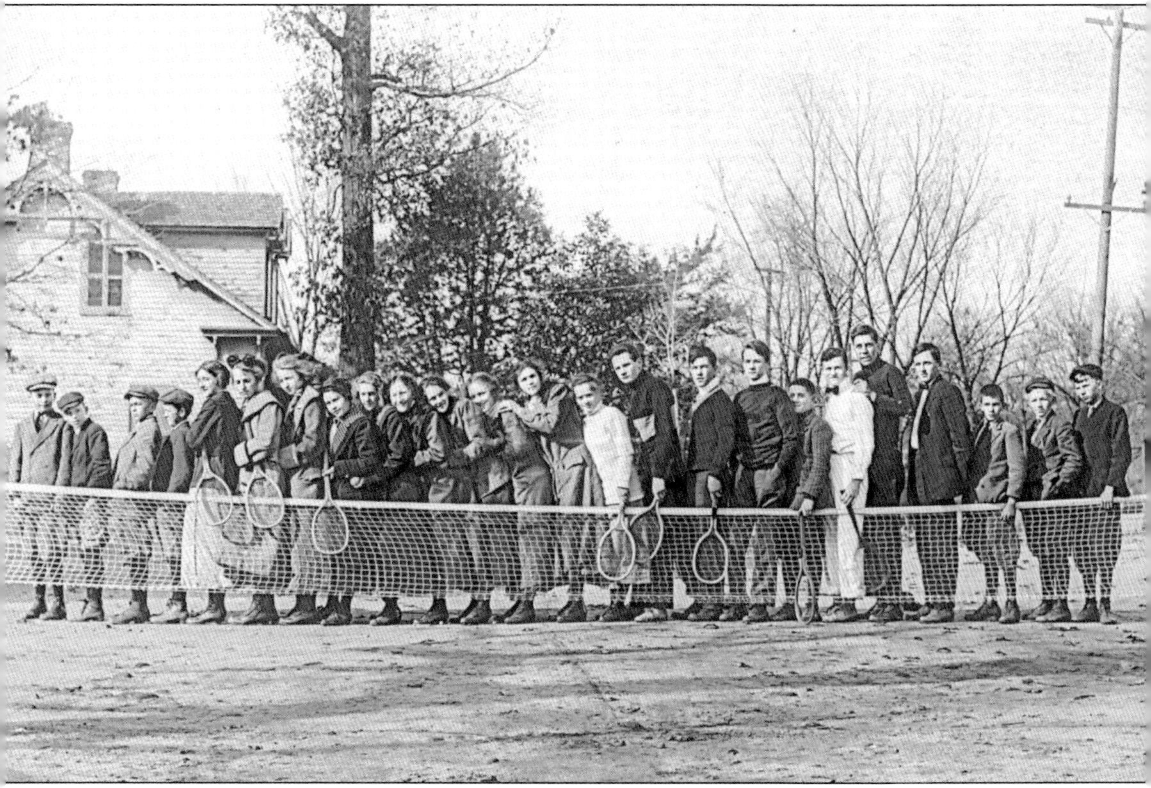

ON THE COVER: The Yorkville Graded School tennis team poses for this photograph on a windy winter day in 1912. The photograph was taken on the west side of the old Graded School building (now the McCelvey Center) on Jefferson Street and originally appeared in the Yorkville Graded School Annual Report for 1912–1913. (Courtesy Culture and Heritage Museums.)

IMAGES
of America

YORK

Michael C. Scoggins and Nancy Sambets

ARCADIA
PUBLISHING

ISBN 978-0-7385-4413-7

Published by Arcadia Publishing
Charleston SC, Chicago IL, Portsmouth NH, San Francisco CA

Printed in the United States of America

Library of Congress Catalog Card Number: 2006937456

For all general information contact Arcadia Publishing at:
Telephone 843-853-2070
Fax 843-853-0044
E-mail sales@arcadiapublishing.com
For customer service and orders:
Toll-Free 1-888-313-2665

Visit us on the Internet at www.arcadiapublishing.com

To the city of York, past, present, and future.

Contents

ACKNOWLEDGMENTS

The authors would like to acknowledge the following individuals who assisted in the preparation of this book. First and foremost, we would like to thank Andrea Rice and Denise Jensen of the Culture and Heritage Museums (CHM) archives staff for investing many hours in scanning photographs and researching the information for the captions in this book. We would also like to acknowledge the hard work and dedication of two of our volunteers, Anna Bortner and Angela Adams, who spent many hours of their own time scanning these images and recording source documentation.

The majority of the images in this book came from the archival collections of the Historical Center of York County, based at the McCelvey Center in York. Over the years, this historic building has functioned as the Yorkville Graded School, York High School, York Elementary School, and McCelvey Elementary School, and there are several photographs included in this book documenting the building's appearance in former times. Archival photograph and document collections housed at the Historical Center used in the preparation of this volume include the Hart Family Collection, the J. R. Schorb Photograph Collection, the Francis Lewis Collection, the Hanks Family Papers Collection, the Lowry Family Papers Collection, the Scott Collection, the Boggs-Carroll Collection, the Glenn Collection, and the CHM Archives' Photograph and Postcard Collections. The historical scrapbooks and photograph albums donated to the archives by the York National Guard Armory were another invaluable source, as was the Yorkville Graded School Annual Report for 1911–1912, which contains a wealth of photographs of old houses, businesses, factories, and people from the first decade of the 20th century.

The Yorkville Historical Society's dedicated work in preserving and documenting the history of York, including the city's historic houses and buildings, has been an invaluable reference for the material in this book, and we acknowledge our debt to their efforts.

Finally, we would like to acknowledge the contributions of several individuals who loaned us photographs, postcards, and other documents for inclusion in this book. They include Pat Guerry Hodnett, Diane Roberts, and Frank Coleman. Unless otherwise noted, all images in this book are from the collections of the Culture and Heritage Museums.

INTRODUCTION

Situated halfway between the Broad River and the Catawba River in the foothills or Piedmont region of upstate South Carolina, the area now known as York was inhabited by Native Americans for several thousand years before the first emigrants from the British Isles began arriving in the 18th century. Tribes like the Cherokee and Catawba Indians left their marks on the landscape by creating trails and paths linking their villages and river crossings throughout the southeastern United States. As European settlers began filtering into the region in the late 1740s and early 1750s, they settled along these trading paths and turned them into wagon roads. The points where these old wagon roads intersected frequently became the sites for early trading posts and settlements, and in the 19th century, many of these crossroads evolved into towns and cities. The city of York, situated in the center of York County, South Carolina, can trace its origins to the intersection of two of these Colonial wagon roads, one running north-south and the other running east-west.

For much of the Colonial period, the region between the Broad and Catawba Rivers, now called York County, was claimed by both North and South Carolina. Following the border survey west of the Catawba River in 1772, the York County area officially became part of South Carolina and was christened the "New Acquisition." Throughout this period, the intersection that would later become the basis for the city of York was known as Fergus Crossroads after a family that lived nearby.

As the name "Fergus" indicates, most of York's early Colonial settlers were of Scottish ancestry. Some came directly from Lowland Scotland, some came from the Scottish colonies in Northern Ireland, and some were second- or third-generation settlers from the frontiers of Virginia and Pennsylvania. These hardy folk referred to themselves as Scotch-Irish to differentiate themselves from the native Irish, and unlike the Catholic Irish, the Scotch-Irish were predominantly Protestant, mostly Presbyterian.

When the American Revolution began, these Scotch-Irish Presbyterians almost overwhelmingly supported independence, and two important Patriot victories—the Battles of Williamson's Plantation (Huck's Defeat) and Kings Mountain—were fought in the New Acquisition in 1780. York County (named for York County, Pennsylvania) officially came into existence in 1785, and the town of Yorkville was laid out and established as the county seat at the site of Fergus Crossroads. Agriculture, primarily cotton and corn cultivation, made up much of the area's economy in the years that followed, and the invention of the cotton gin in 1793 accelerated the importance of cotton as a cash crop and the dominance of African American slave labor in its cultivation.

The Kings Mountain Railroad came to Yorkville in 1852 and helped spark economic growth for the town, giving farmers an easy method of getting their crops to market. The Kings Mountain Military School opened in 1855 and made Yorkville an educational center for the Upcountry. Yorkville's cotton planters and slave owners overwhelmingly supported the Confederacy during the Civil War, and the town furnished troops for at least four different companies of the 5th, 12th, 17th, and 18th South Carolina Infantry Regiments, as well as several cavalry and artillery units. York County and Yorkville were hotbeds of activity for the Ku Klux Klan following the end of the war, and Yorkville was occupied by Federal troops for several years during Reconstruction. Gradually the county's large population of former slaves were enfranchised and given equal rights, although the process took many years and was bitterly opposed by many of Yorkville's white citizens.

In 1873, the Kings Mountain Railroad was finally extended into North Carolina and became the Chester and Lenoir Railroad, which in turn became the Carolina and Northwestern Railway in 1897. This north-south rail line was then crossed by the Southern Railway running from the Broad River through Yorkville and east to Rock Hill. Cotton planting continued to be important to Yorkville's economy, and in the late 19th century, several textile mills were established to process raw cotton into yarn, cloth, cottonseed oil, and other products, providing stable employment for both whites and blacks. By the end of the century, Yorkville had recovered sufficiently from the devastation of the Civil War to earn the descriptive titles of "Queen City of the Hills" and "the Charleston of the Upcountry."

The early 20th century saw textile manufacturing become Yorkville's dominant industry, with no fewer than four cotton mills located within the one-mile radius of the town limits. As a concession to the changing times, in 1915, Yorkville changed its name to York, gaining in the process a new nickname, "the White Rose City," which it borrowed from its namesake, the city of York, England. By this time, the city boasted a brand-new courthouse, water and sewage system, electrical power system and electric streetlights, telephone system, fire department, two railroads, an efficient postal system, and a plethora of shops, stores, and hotels. The city also had a graded school system with 11 grades for both whites and blacks. Many of the photographs in this book date to this period, providing a glimpse of life in Yorkville when agriculture and textile mills were still the dominant livelihood for most of the area's citizens.

The city of York survived two world wars, the Great Depression, the Korean War, and Vietnam, with many of her sons fighting (and sometimes dying) in Europe, Asia, and the Far East. The period of the 1950s and 1960s brought renewed prosperity to the town and the county. In the early 1980s, however, the textile industry began suffering from foreign competition, and York made a concerted effort to recruit new, high-technology industries and to place more emphasis on business, tourism, and its rich historical heritage. Today York stands as a model of growth and development in the upstate, with continued emphasis on highway improvement, educational advancement, and economic progress. Although it has long since ceased to be the largest city in the county, York is still the county seat and still has an important and exciting role to play as a leader in the history and development of York County and upstate South Carolina.

One

Streets and Buildings

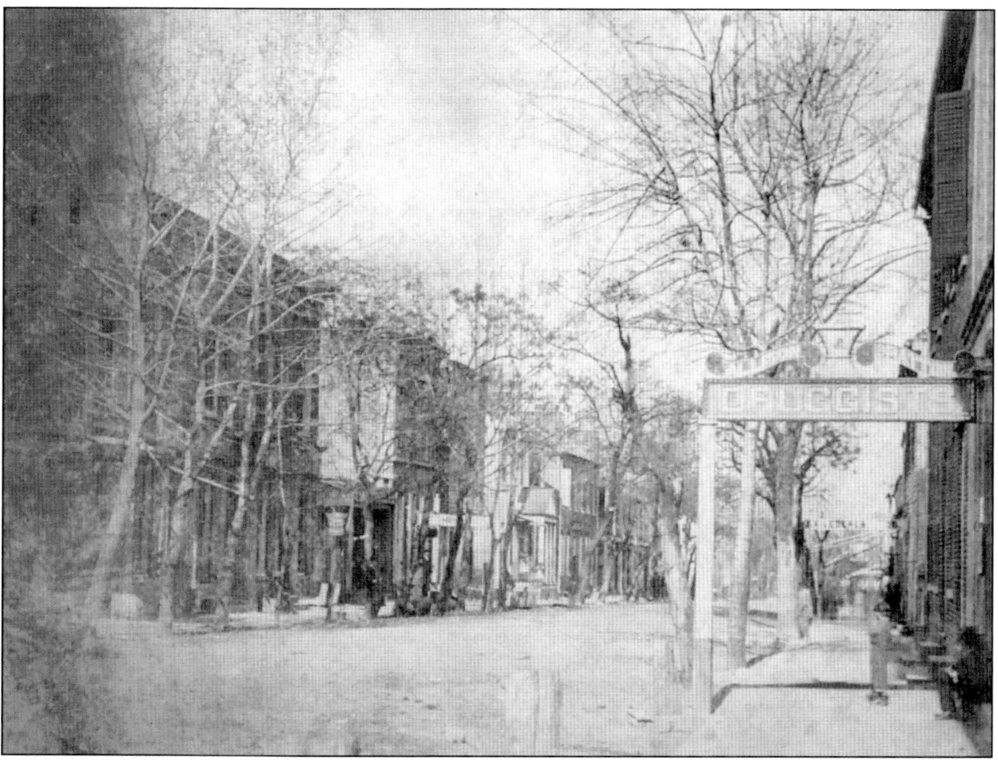

Congress Street is the "main street" running north to south through York. It has always been the principal business street of the city and the dividing line between streets running east and west. Taken *c.* 1870, this is one of the earliest photographic images of North Congress Street facing north. On the right of the photograph is Allison and Bratton, Druggists, and farther up the street, J. A. Lederer. Across the street are the signs for F. M. Dobson's millinery and the York Drug Store. A small herd of pigs is just visible in front of the York Drug Store, rummaging through street trash as a nearby dog watches them.

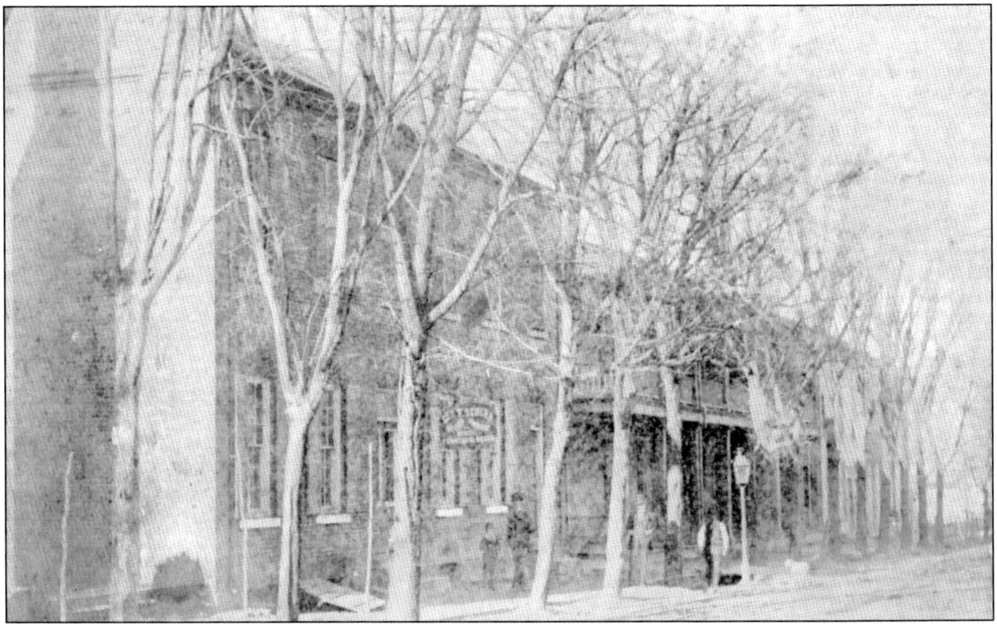

Taken 1880–1890, this is another early image of North Congress Street facing north. Visible in the foreground is the sign for the establishment of George T. Schorb, who sold "Stoves, Tinware and House Furnishing Goods." The building with the veranda next to Schorb's is the Parish Hotel, originally known as the Kings Mountain Hotel, operated by C. G. Parish. In front of the hotel is a gaslight.

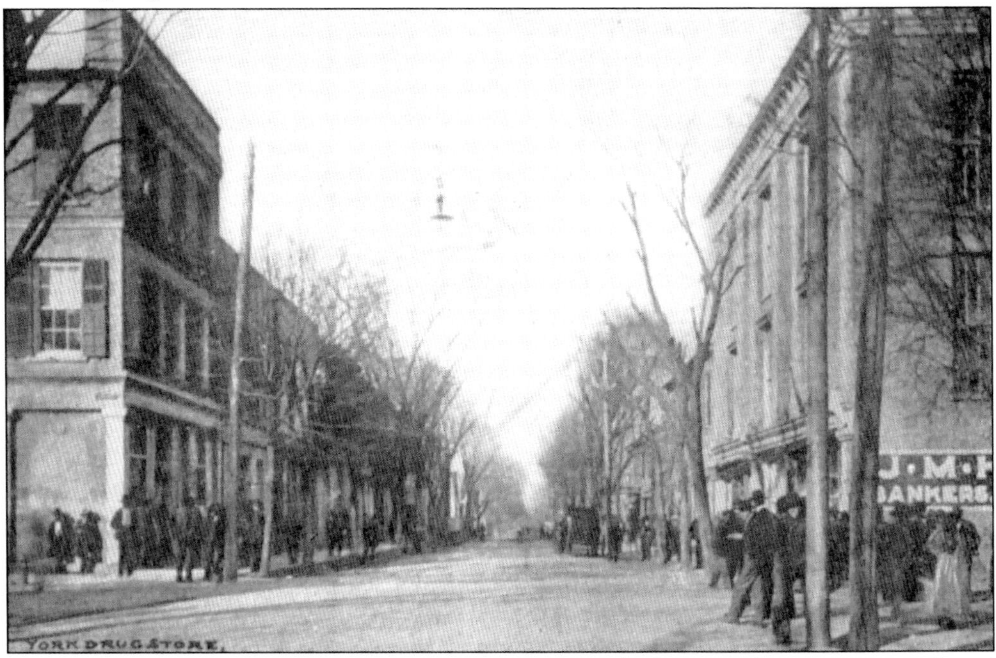

This photograph is another view of North Congress Street looking north *c.* 1900. A number of horse-drawn wagons are visible on the right-hand (east) side of the street, along with early utility poles on both sides of the street. J. B. Bowen was listed as one of the proprietors of the York Drug Store in the 1908–1909 Yorkville City Directory.

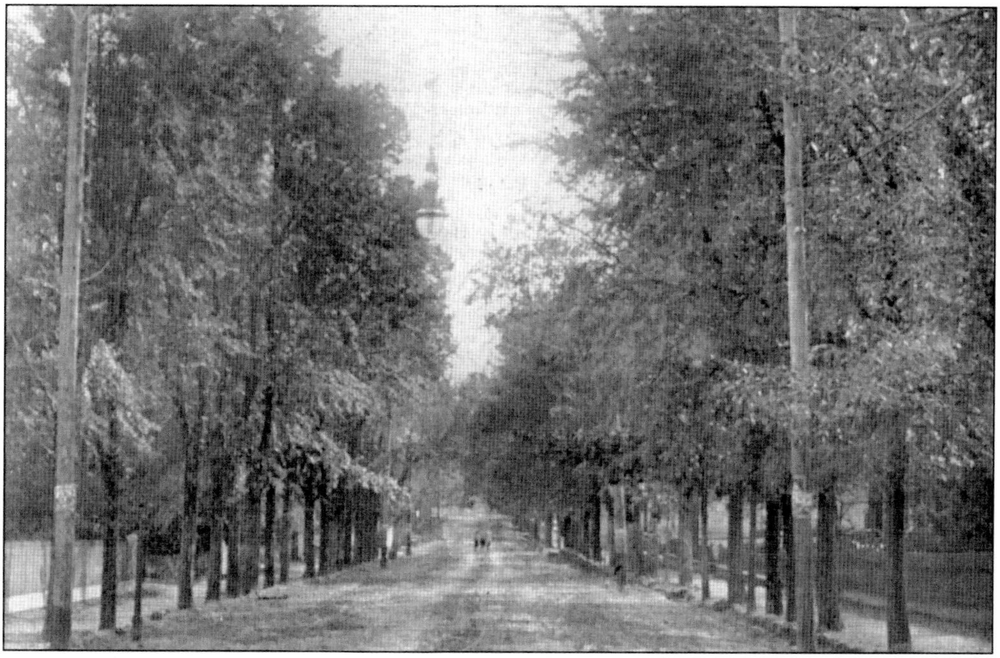

Taken from a York Drug Store postcard, this *Yorkville Enquirer* print shows the view from North Congress Street looking south towards the downtown area *c.* 1905. Note the electric street light suspended from the two utility poles on opposite sides of the street.

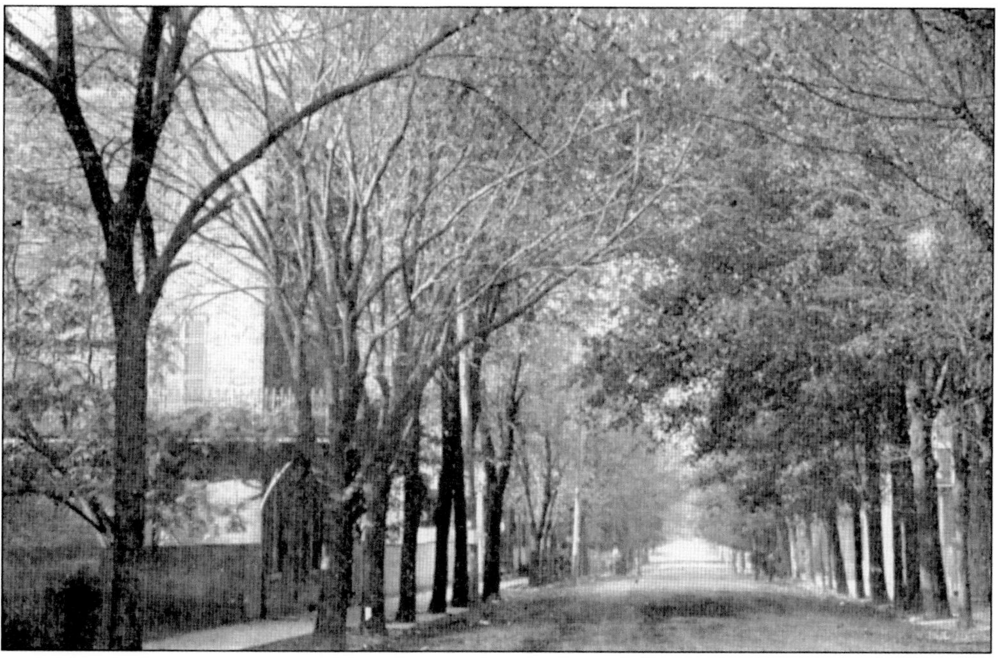

This photograph is another *Yorkville Enquirer* print from a postcard sold by the York Drug Store. It shows the downtown area of Yorkville facing south on Congress Street from the intersection of Liberty and Congress Streets, *c.* 1910. The large building on the left is the Latta House, built by Robert Latta about 1827. Note the increase in tree growth along Congress Street, which was substantial by this time.

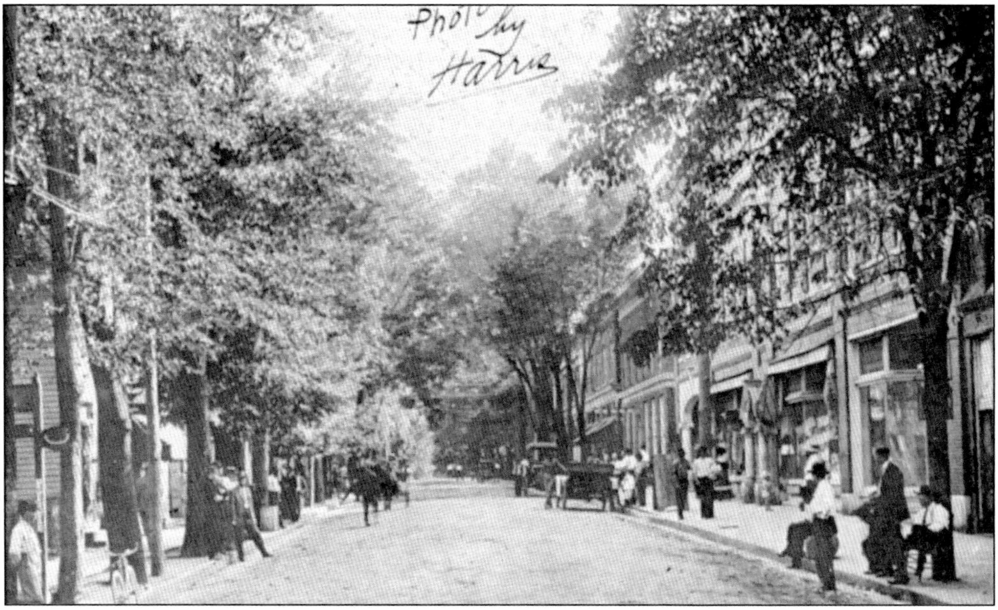

The heavy tree cover, numerous electric lines running overhead, and early automobiles date this photograph to about 1910. In this picture, the view is looking south from North Congress Street towards Chester.

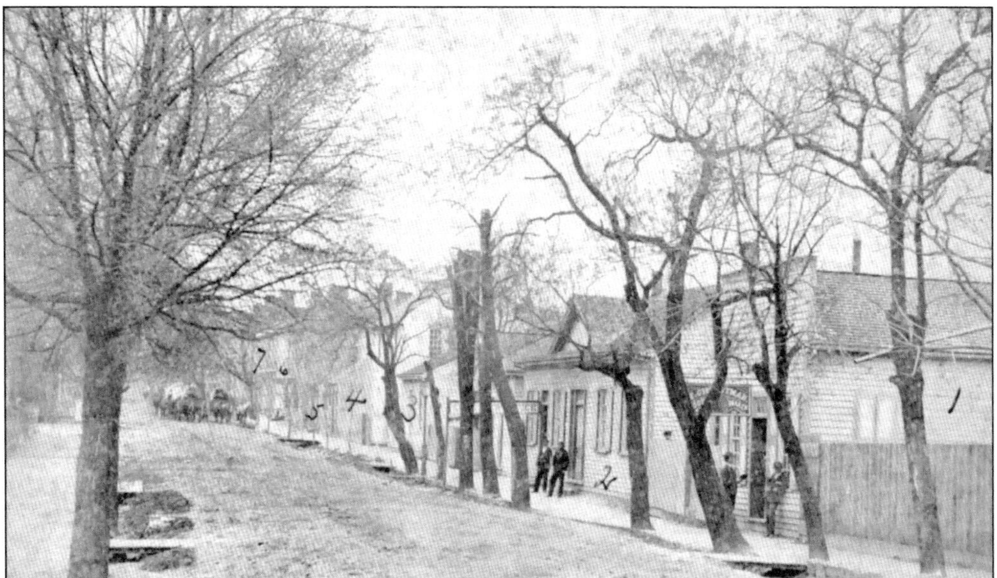

Looking south down Congress Street from the business section of town, this photograph dates from the 1870s. Note the horses and wagons in the street and the various businesses, which are numbered as follows: (1) Ferdinand Christman's shoe shop (the sign reads "F. Christman, Boot Maker"); (2) the *Yorkville Enquirer* newspaper office, which burned on November 23, 1890; (3) the residence of L. M. Grist, editor and publisher of the *Enquirer*; (4) the office of Dr. William Millard Walker, dentist; (5) Dr. William M. Walker's residence; (6) Maurice Strauss and Son's store; and (7) the Kings Mountain Hotel, later known as the Parish Hotel, which burned in October 1901.

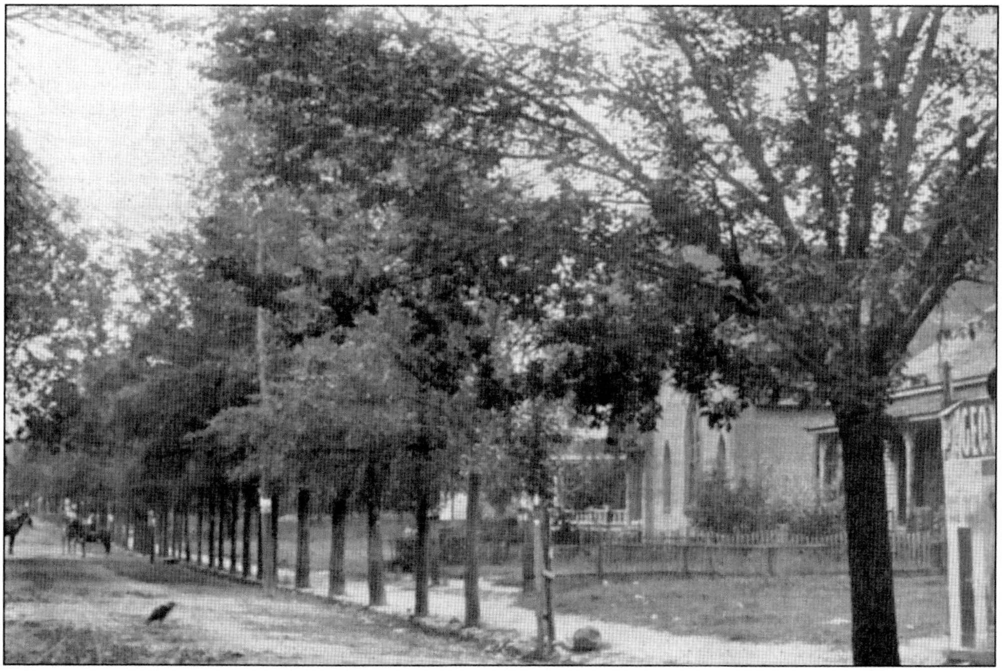

The view south from Congress Street *c.* 1905 is shown in this postcard from the York Drug Store, taken from a *Yorkville Enquirer* photographic print. The First Baptist Church is visible on the right, while a buzzard and a group of men on horseback can be seen in the street.

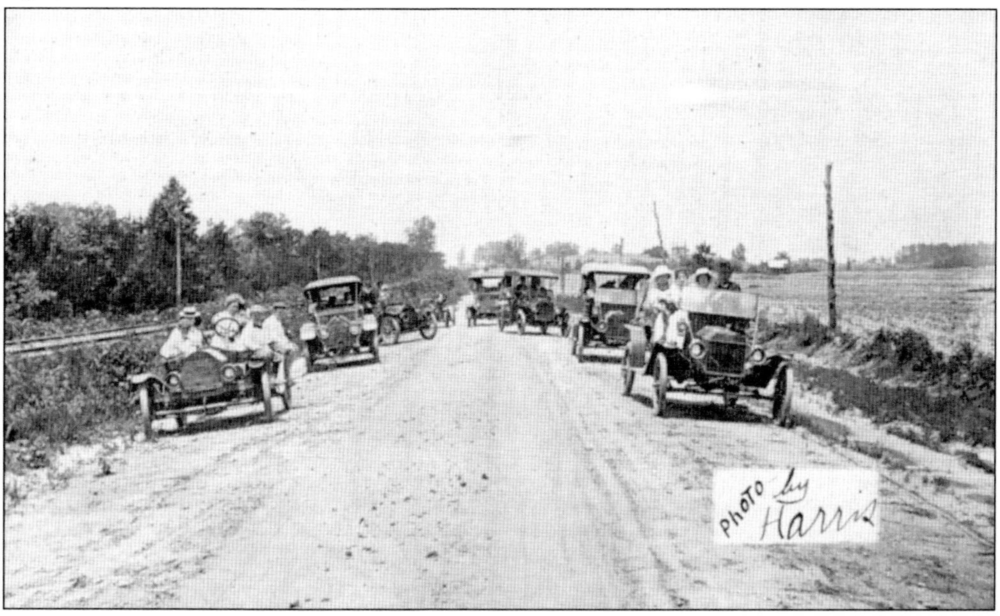

The Chester Road (now Highway 321) runs due south from York to Chester and has always been one of York's most important highways. This photograph, taken c. 1910, shows the unpaved Chester Road just outside of town with a number of early-20th-century automobiles present. The Carolina and Northwestern (C&NW) Railway line can be seen on the left-hand (eastern) side of the road, while the wooden poles on the right-hand (western) side of the road carried the first telephone line from York to Chester.

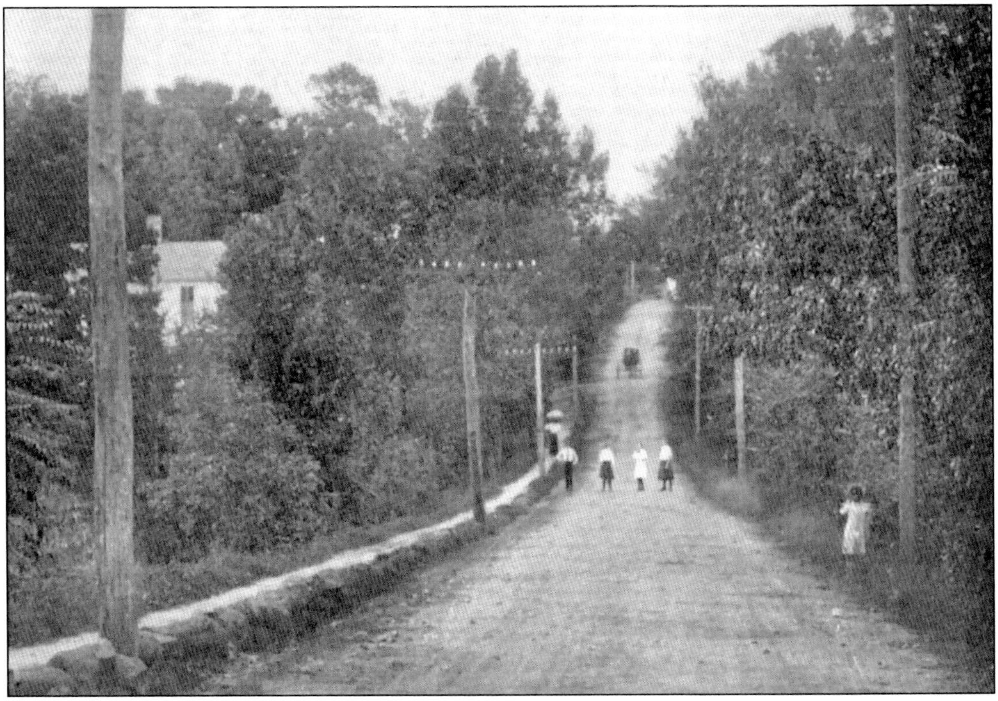

Another *Yorkville Enquirer* postcard print from the York Drug Store, this view shows the Liberty Street extension east of the Southern Railway track looking towards Rock Hill *c.* 1905. Early utility poles and a horse-drawn carriage are both clearly visible in this photograph, dramatizing the transition from 19th century to 20th century.

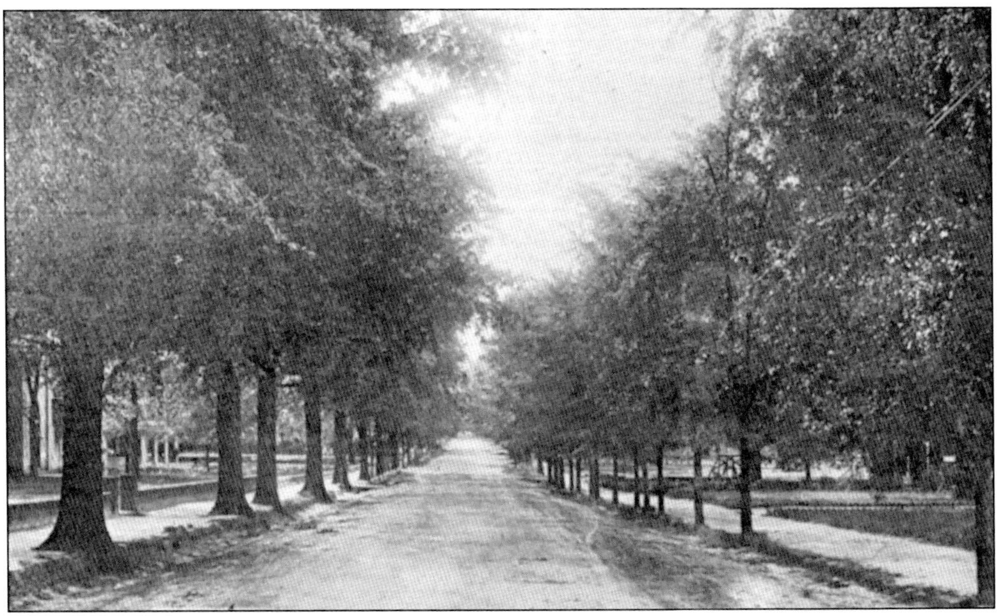

This view shows East Liberty Street heading west from the intersection with Church Street, also from the early 1900s.

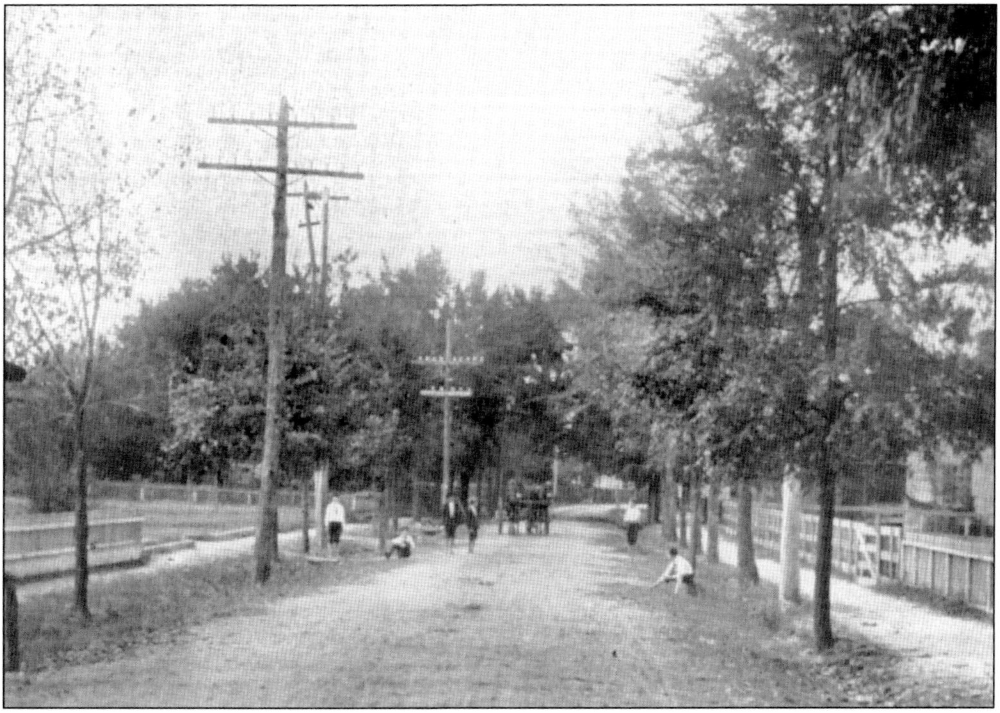

Kings Mountain Street runs from York to the mountain and the Revolutionary War battle site of the same name and dates to the Colonial era. Taken *c.* 1910, this photograph shows Kings Mountain Street looking northwest, near the Episcopal Church Home Orphanage.

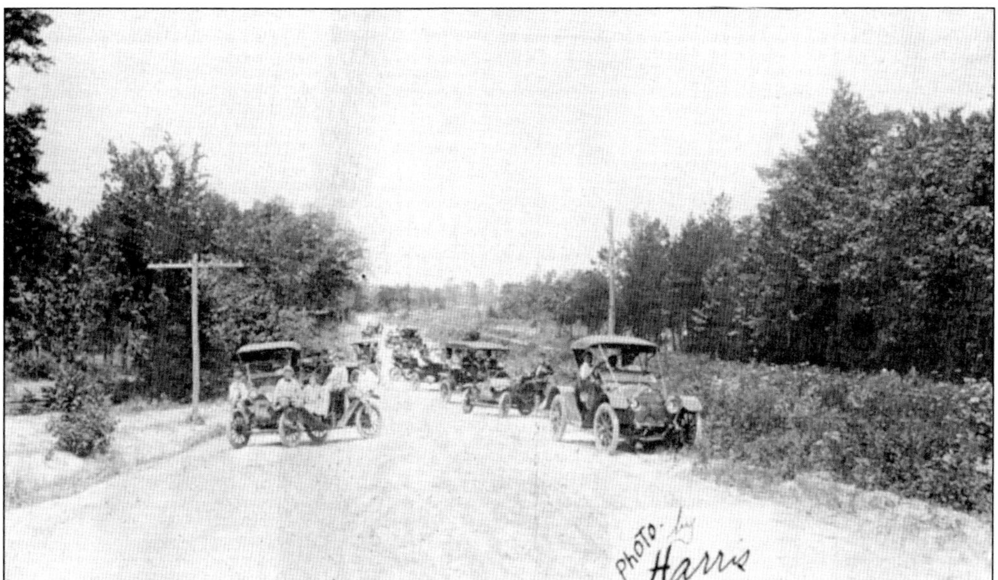

This photograph was taken *c.* 1910 on the Kings Mountain Road running northwest from Yorkville to Kings Mountain. Note the large variety of early-20th-century automobiles present in the picture.

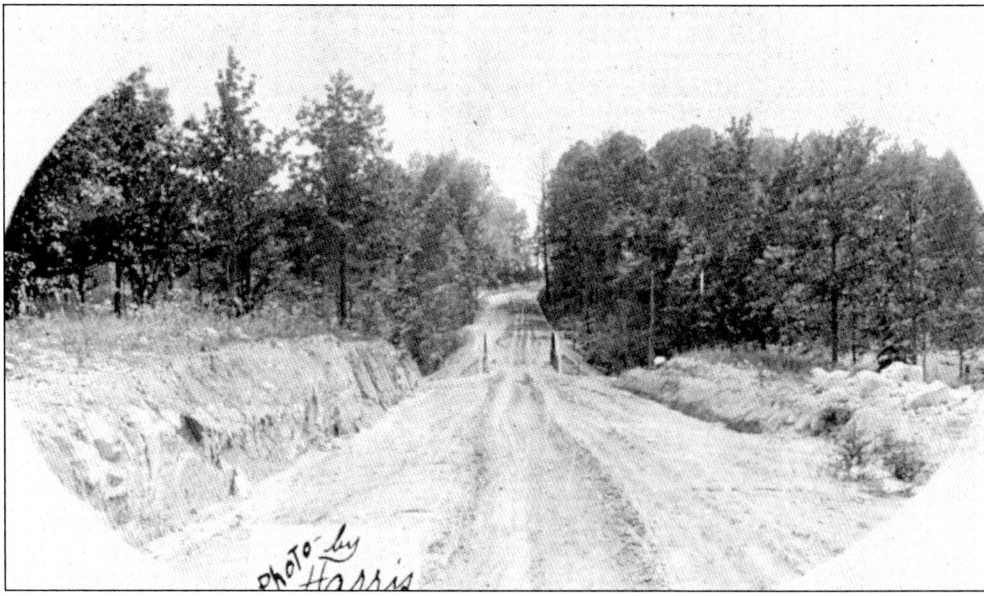

The Lincoln Road, shown in this photograph taken around 1910, is another of York's earliest roads and runs due north to Lincoln, North Carolina. During the Colonial period, it was called the Armour's Ford Road and the Armstrong Ford Road after two heavily used fords on the Catawba River. It became known as the Lincoln Road after the establishment of Lincoln County, North Carolina, in 1779.

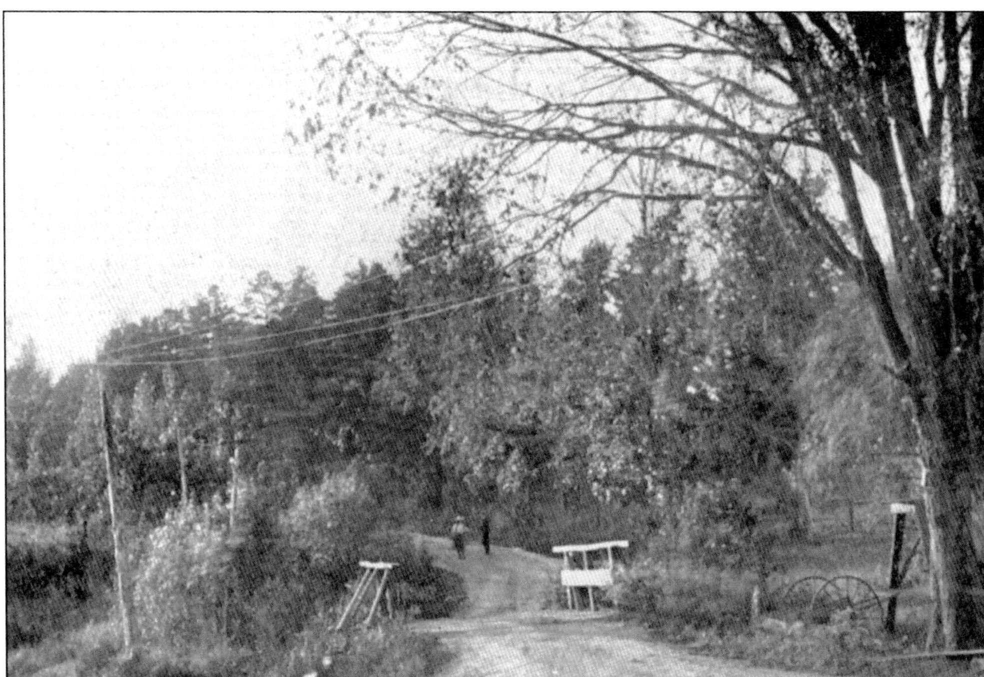

Another early photograph taken c. 1910 shows the area near the Yorkville Water Works, located on the road leading west out of York (now South Carolina Highway 5) towards Blacksburg.

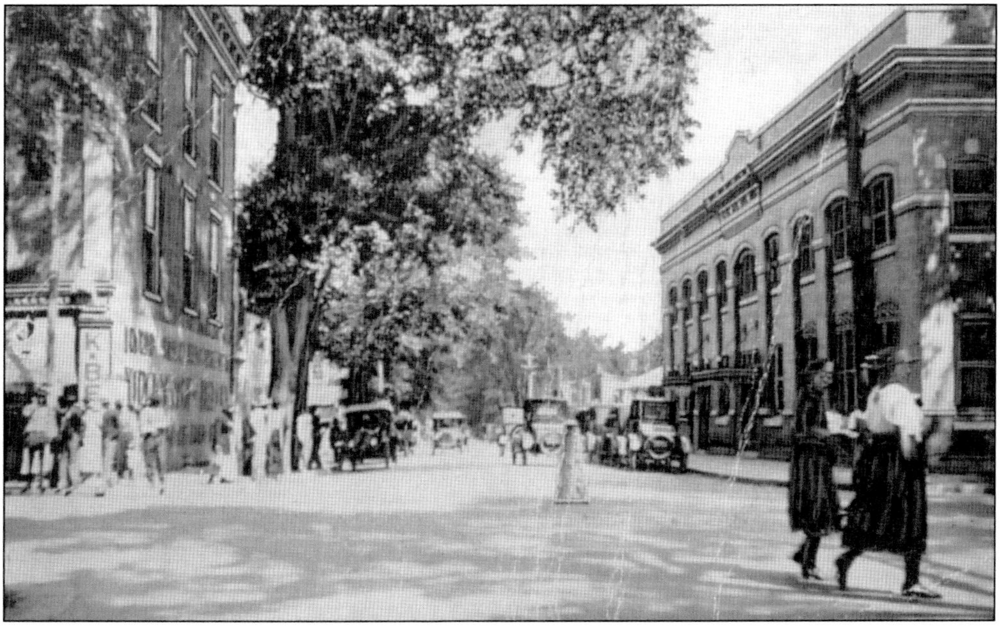

The busy intersection of Congress and Liberty Streets is highlighted in this postcard from c. 1920. The view is looking east on Liberty Street toward Rock Hill. The building on the left is the Nichols Block.

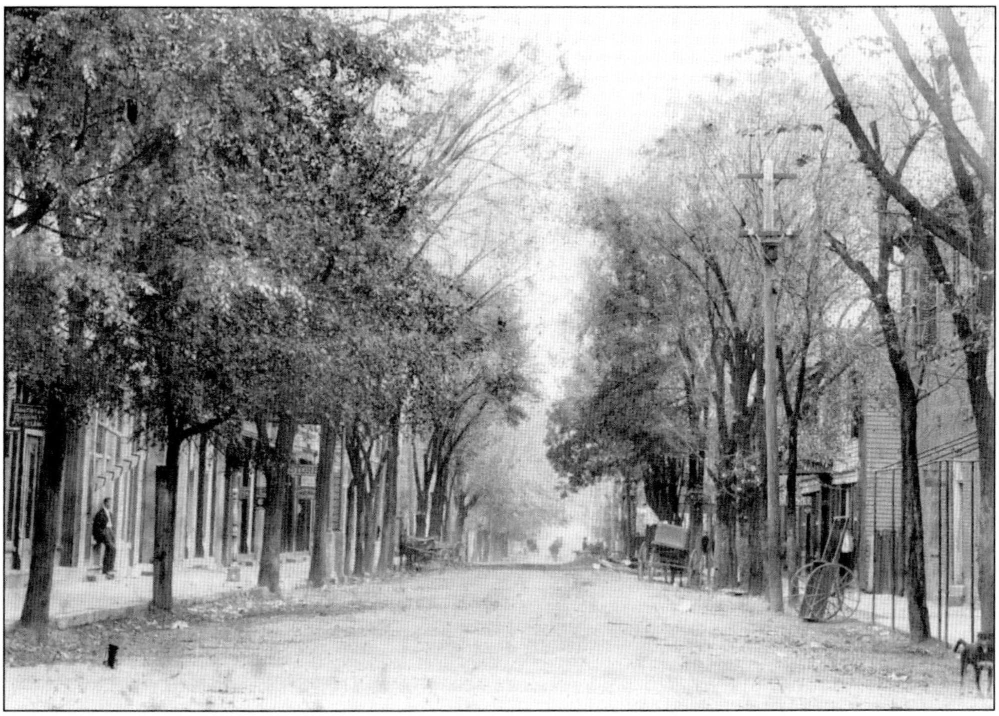

Among the business signs visible in this photograph of Congress Street looking north from Liberty Street are those of Frank P. McCain, attorney-at-law; Greene and Company, tailors; and F. C. Black. Taken c. 1900, the picture reveals a number of horse-drawn wagons and an early utility pole.

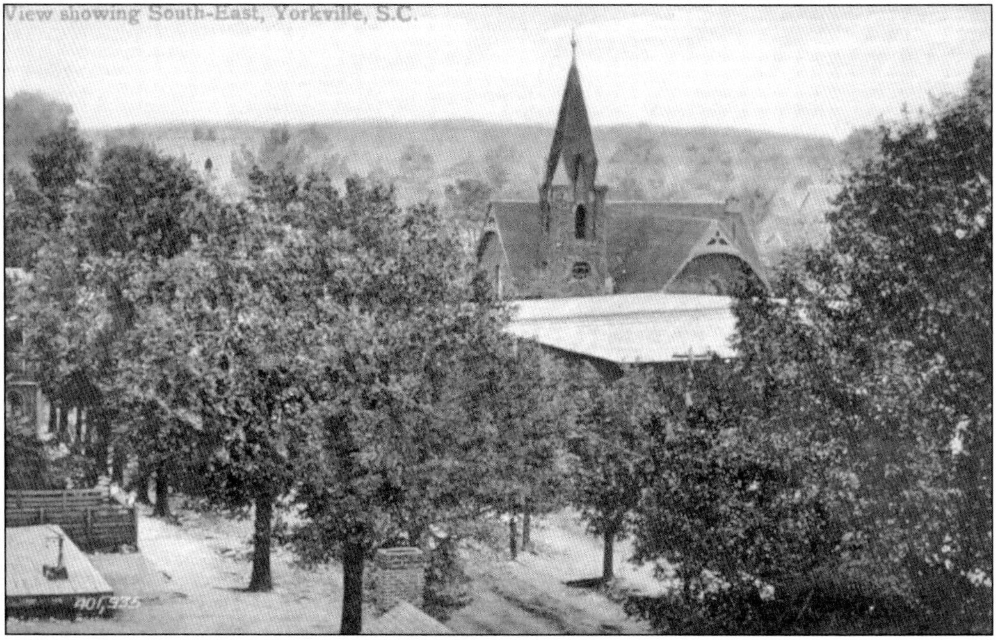

This pre-1915 York Drug Store postcard shows the view from the roof of a building on Liberty Street facing southeast. The building in the foreground is Trinity Methodist Episcopal Church.

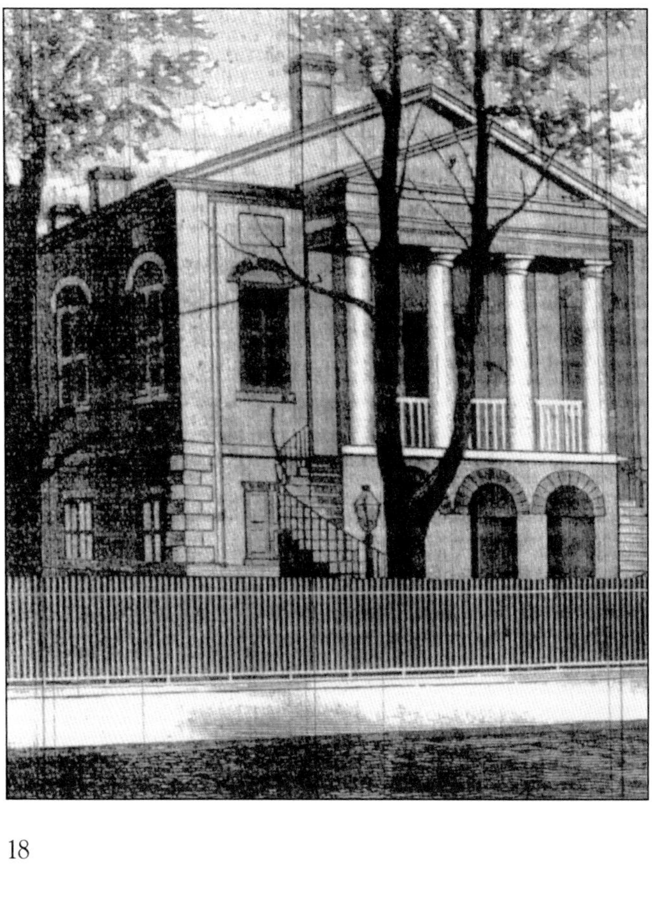

York County's first courthouse was a wooden frame building erected in Yorkville when the county was created in 1786. The second courthouse was a one-story brick building erected about 15 years later. The third courthouse, shown here in a drawing from the *Yorkville Enquirer* of February 27, 1889, was designed and constructed by Scottish architect Robert Leckie, although it may have been based on a design by Robert Mills, the famous architect of the Washington Monument, the United States Treasury Building, and numerous courthouses throughout South Carolina. Constructed in 1825, this third courthouse was in the Classical Revival style with a double curved wrought-iron stairway leading to the front doors.

In November 1892, the second floor of the York County Court House caught fire and burned, and over the course of the next two years, the building underwent extensive repairs and renovations. A bell tower and new steps were added to the front of the building, and two wings were added to the rear of the building at that time.

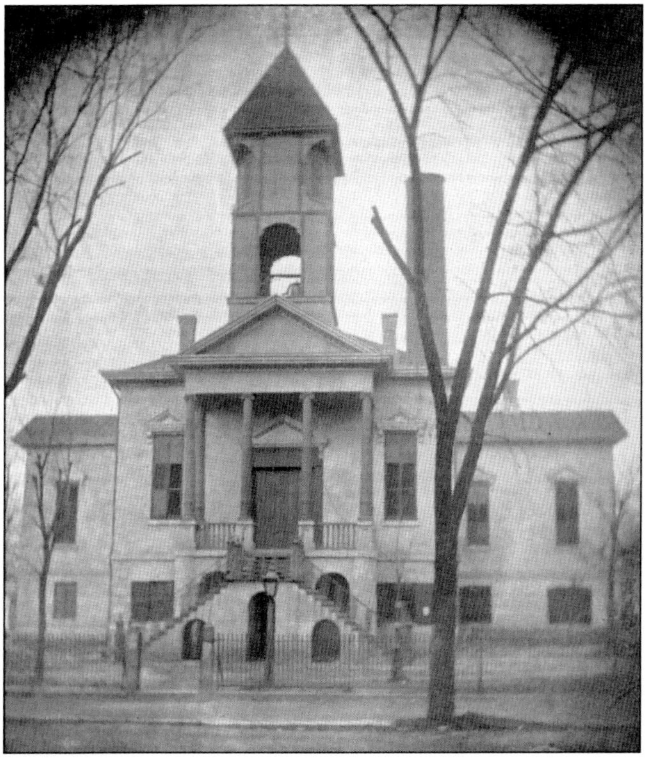

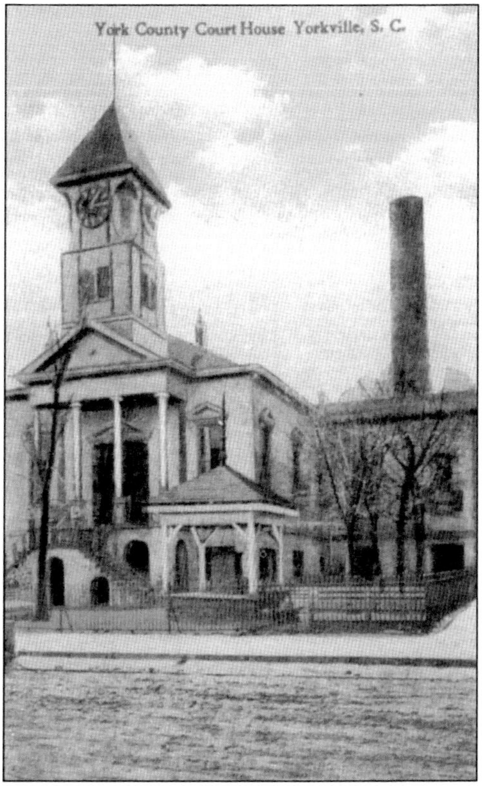

In June 1894, the county purchased a bell for the remodeled courthouse. The bell weighed 838 pounds and cost $160.76. In May 1896, an eight-day clock was installed in the top of the bell tower, as shown in this postcard published by the York Drug Store. Eight-day clocks were very popular during this era; their name derived from the fact that they required winding only once a week.

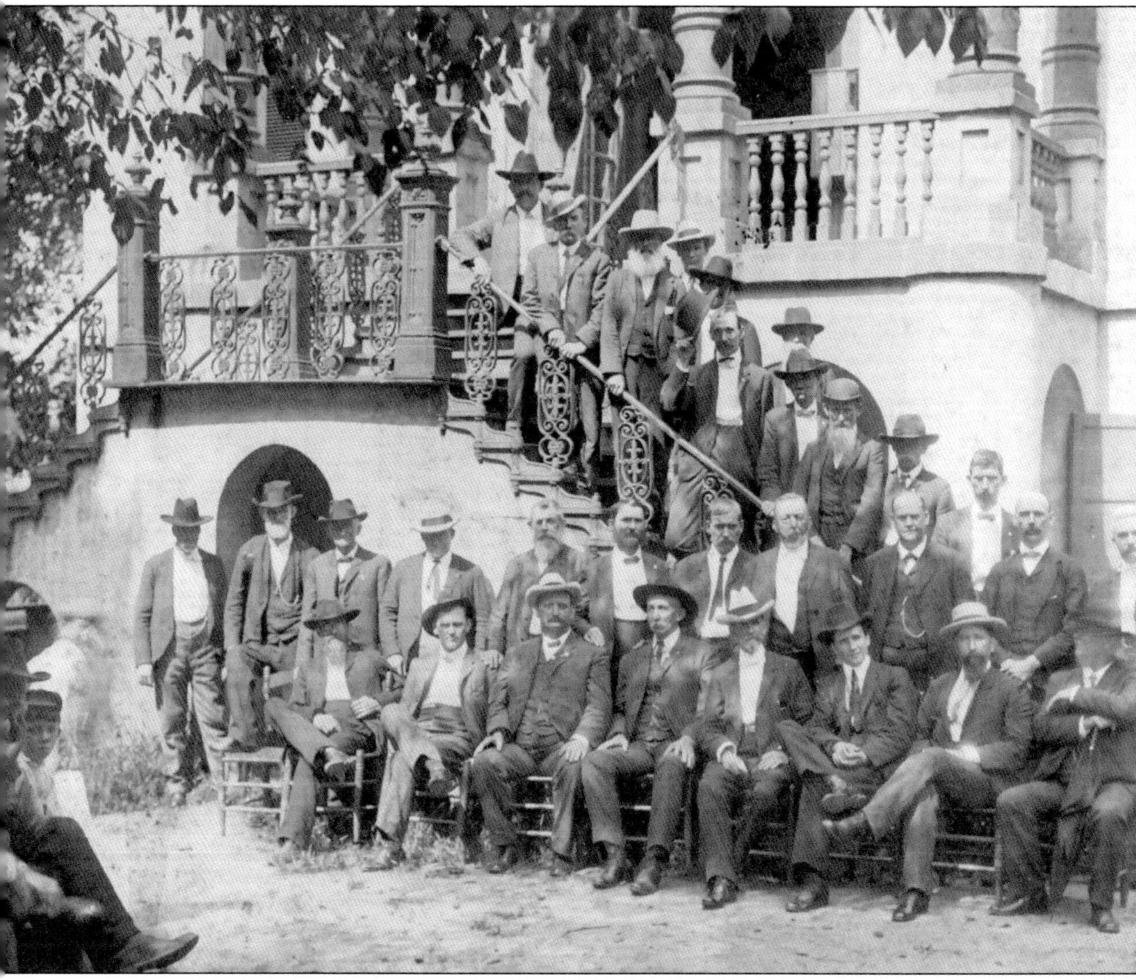

In 1901, a group of York's leading citizens, including a number of Civil War veterans, assembled in front of the remodeled York County Court House for this photograph.

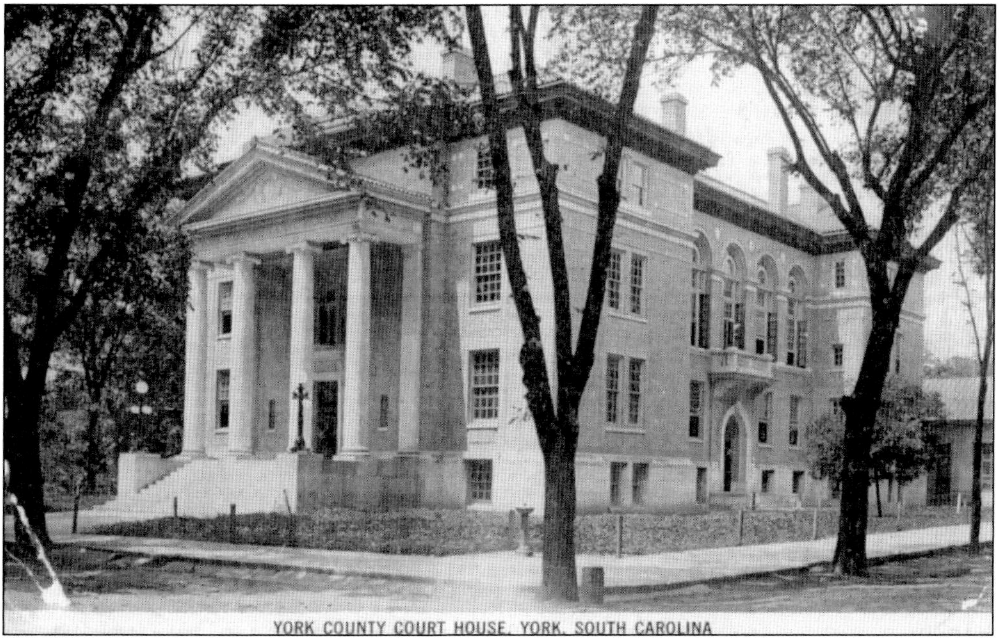

In 1913, the York County government decided to demolish the 1825 courthouse and replace it with a more modern design created by architect William Augustus Edwards. The Travers-Wood Company of Richmond, Virginia, received the general construction contract, and Rock Hill Heating and Plumbing Company contracted for the utilities. Work was begun on the building in February 1914, and the new courthouse was officially dedicated on July 13, 1915.

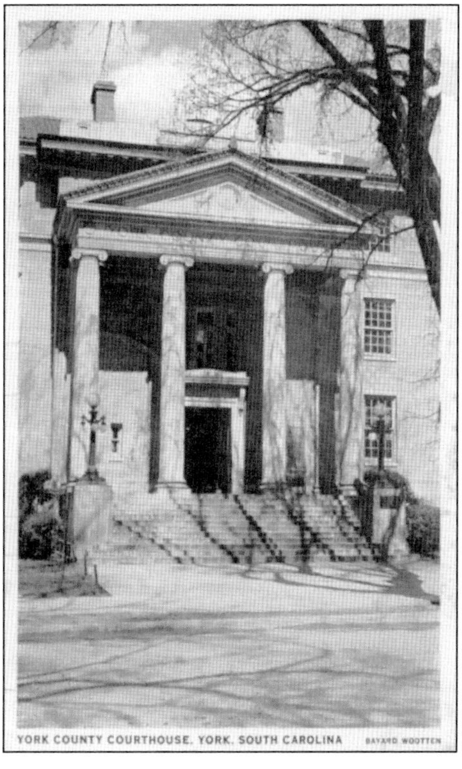

Another view of the fourth York County Court House is shown in this 1915 postcard.

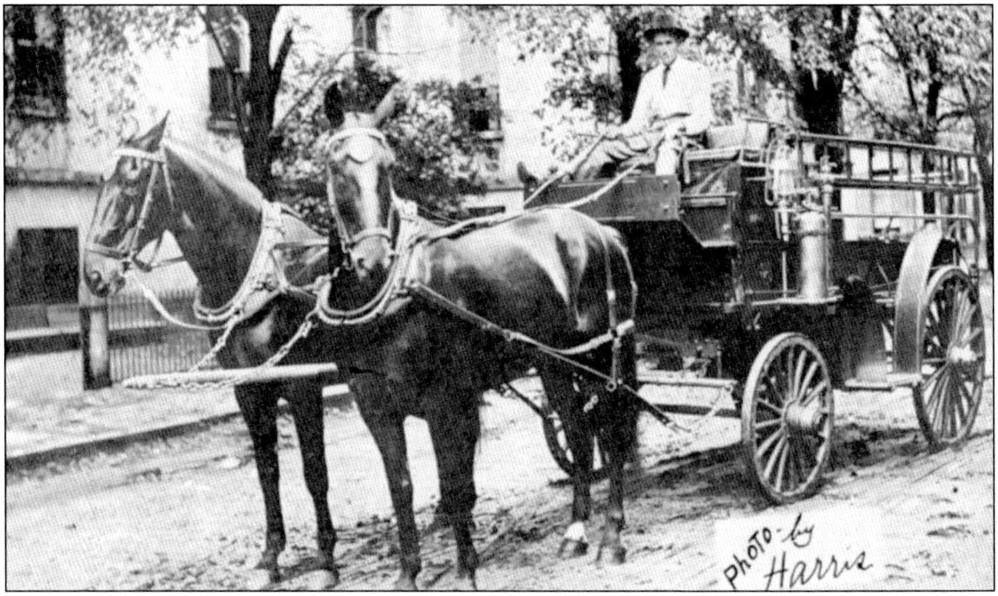

Fires were an ever-present danger to the numerous old wooden buildings in early Yorkville. The town's fire department in the early 1900s included this "state-of-the-art" hose wagon and horse team.

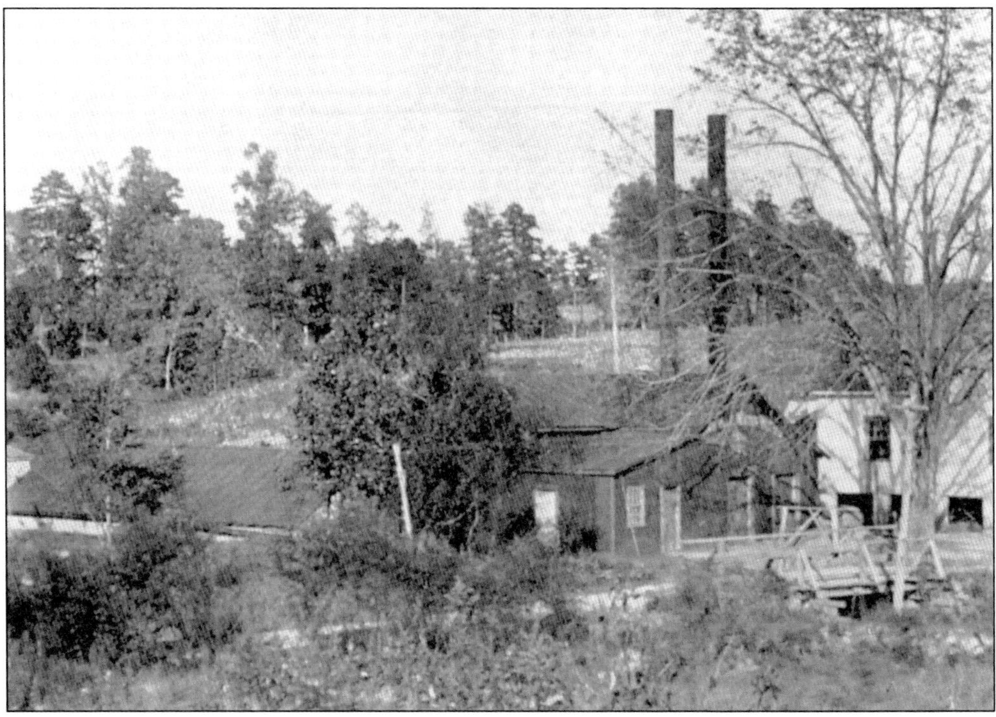
Following the courthouse fire of 1892, the city government of Yorkville decided that the town needed a public waterworks. Established one mile west of the courthouse on West Liberty Street, the city waterworks and pump station made pressurized water available throughout the city for the first time. Originally powered by two coal-fired steam pumps, by 1910, the pumping station ran off electrical power.

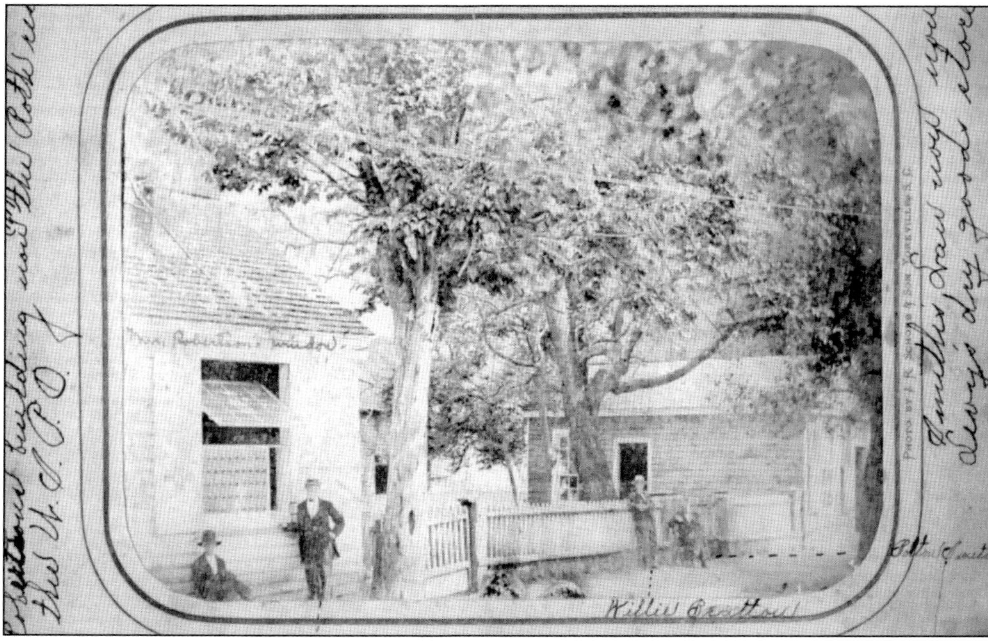

The first post office in York was officially established at York County Court House in 1802. It became the Yorkville Post Office in 1833 and the York Post Office in 1915. This photograph by J. R. Schorb shows the post office in the late 1800s, when it was located on Congress Street. Note the post office boxes visible in the window on the left side of the picture. The gentlemen in the photograph are, from left to right, unidentified; John Wallace, postmaster; Willie Bratton; and Polton Smith.

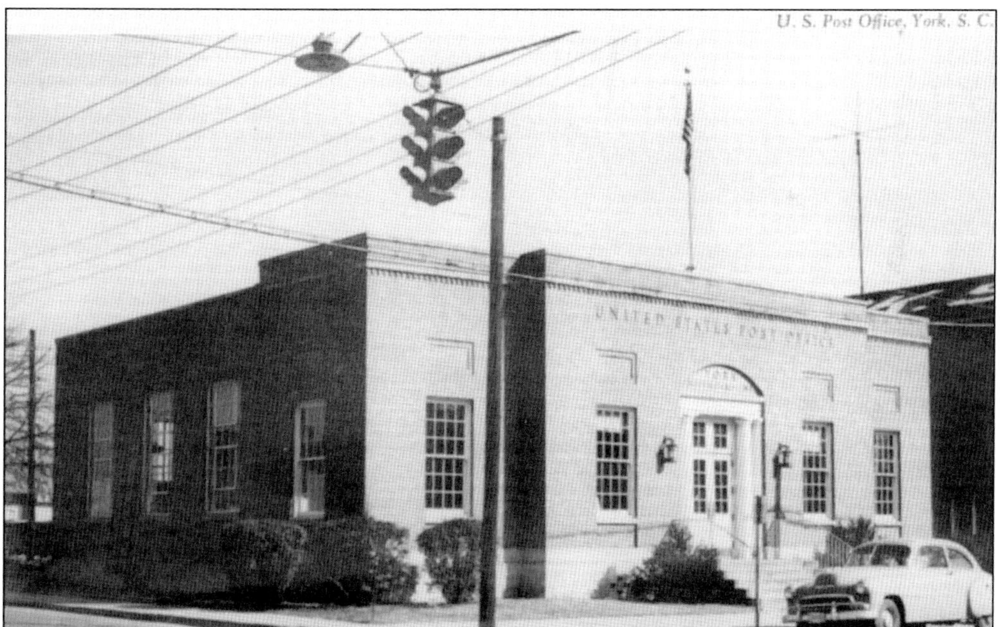

A modern building for the York Post Office was erected on East Liberty Street in the spot once occupied by the York Clock Tower. Finished in August 1935, the post office is shown here in a postcard image from the late 1950s.

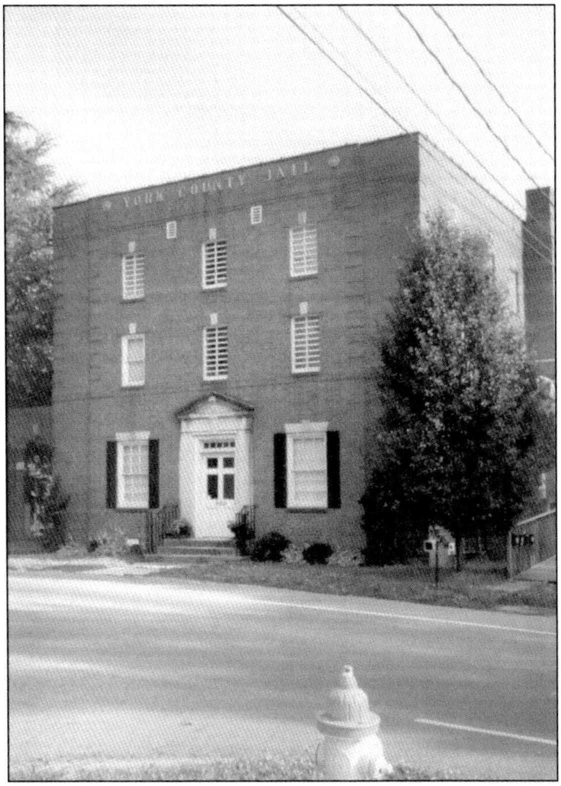

The old York County jail on West Liberty Street was built c. 1932 and replaced an earlier brick jail building on South Congress Street located directly across from the courthouse. The sheriff's family lived on the bottom floor, and female inmates would cook meals for the other inmates and the sheriff's family. This jail continued in service until the Moss Justice Center was completed in 1994. (Courtesy Pat Guerry Hodnett.)

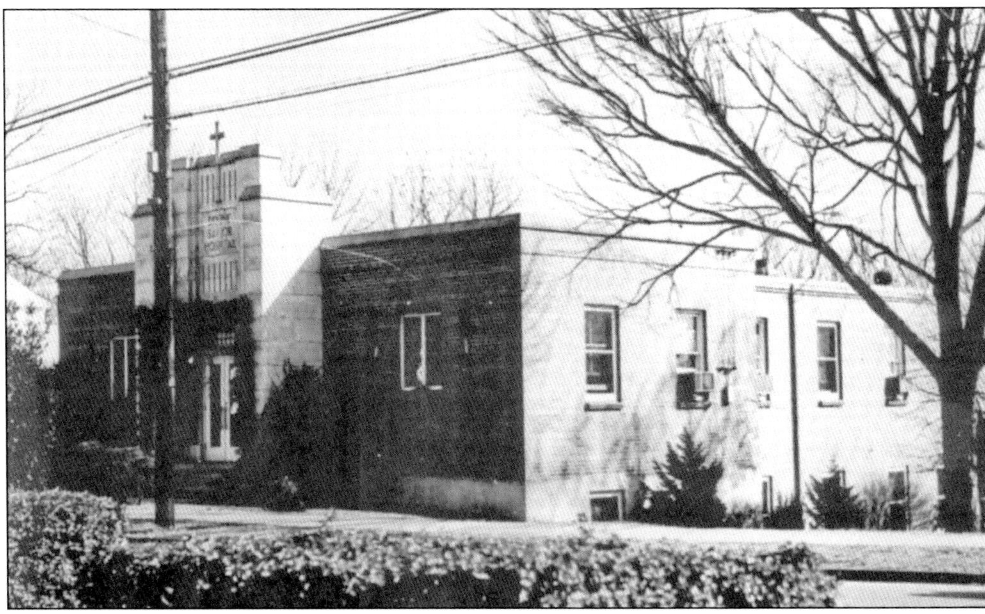

Divine Savior Hospital was established on South Congress Street by the Roman Catholic Church in 1938 and was administered by the Sisters of Charity of Our Lady of Mercy from Charleston. It operated out of the Carroll House until 1942, when this brick building was constructed. The hospital closed in October 1991 and was purchased by White Oak Manor in December 1991. It is now a nursing home.

Two

BUSINESSES

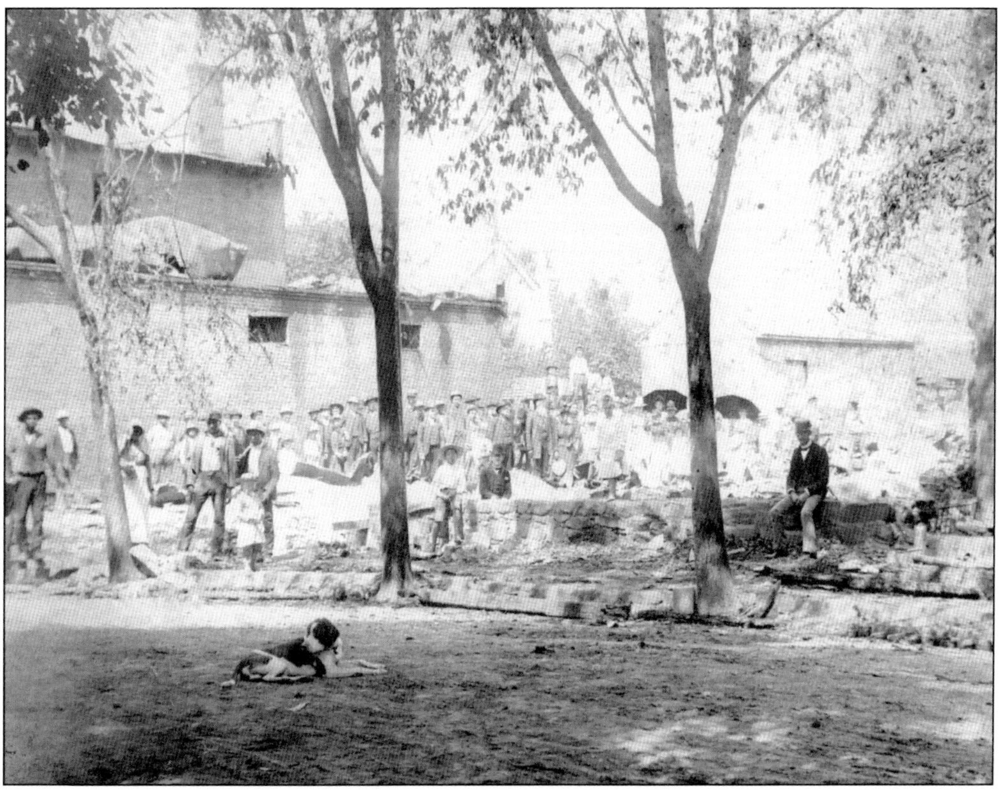

Fire was a continual threat to the wooden buildings in downtown York for many years. In 1891, the Hunter and Oates Store on North Congress Street caught fire and burned. The aftermath and cleanup was documented in this photograph taken by Thomas Baxter McClain.

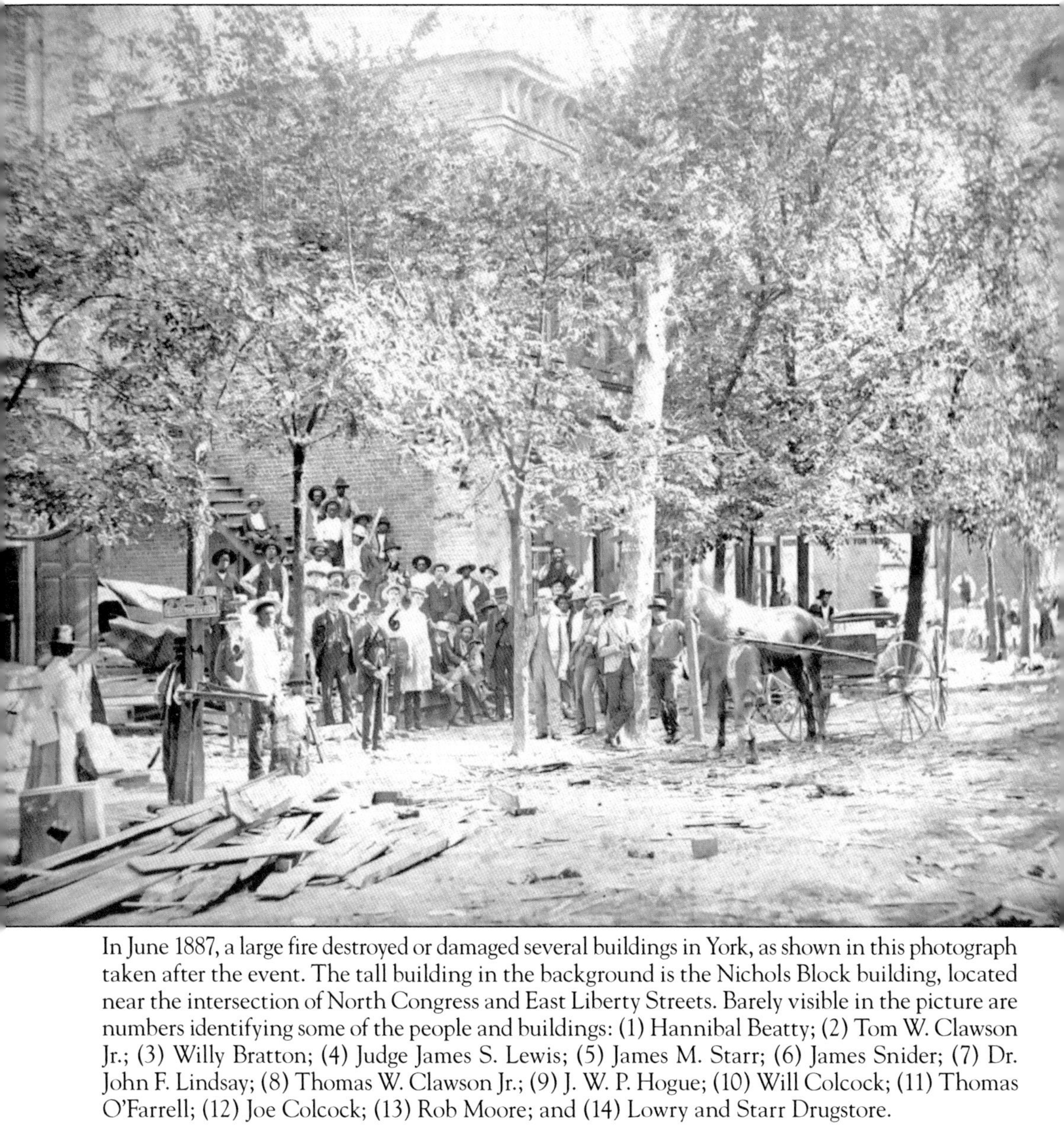

In June 1887, a large fire destroyed or damaged several buildings in York, as shown in this photograph taken after the event. The tall building in the background is the Nichols Block building, located near the intersection of North Congress and East Liberty Streets. Barely visible in the picture are numbers identifying some of the people and buildings: (1) Hannibal Beatty; (2) Tom W. Clawson Jr.; (3) Willy Bratton; (4) Judge James S. Lewis; (5) James M. Starr; (6) James Snider; (7) Dr. John F. Lindsay; (8) Thomas W. Clawson Jr.; (9) J. W. P. Hogue; (10) Will Colcock; (11) Thomas O'Farrell; (12) Joe Colcock; (13) Rob Moore; and (14) Lowry and Starr Drugstore.

The Loan and Savings Bank, Inc., was located on North Congress Street near the intersection with Liberty Street. The bank flourished in the early 1900s under the presidency of Samuel M. McNeel, who also owned Tavora Cotton Mill, but it did not survive the Great Depression.

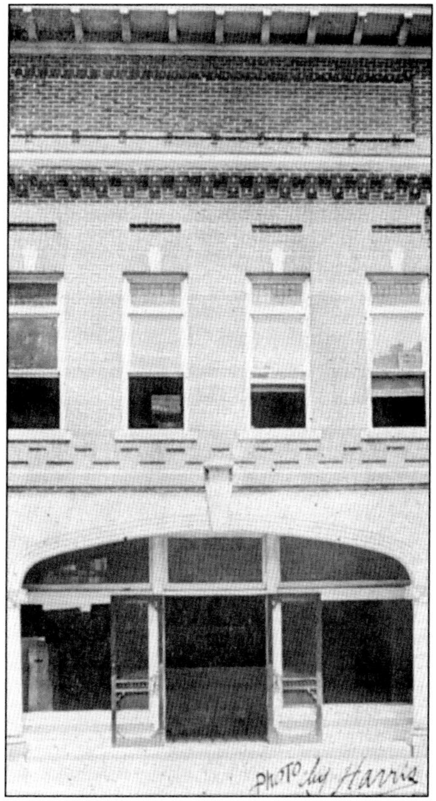

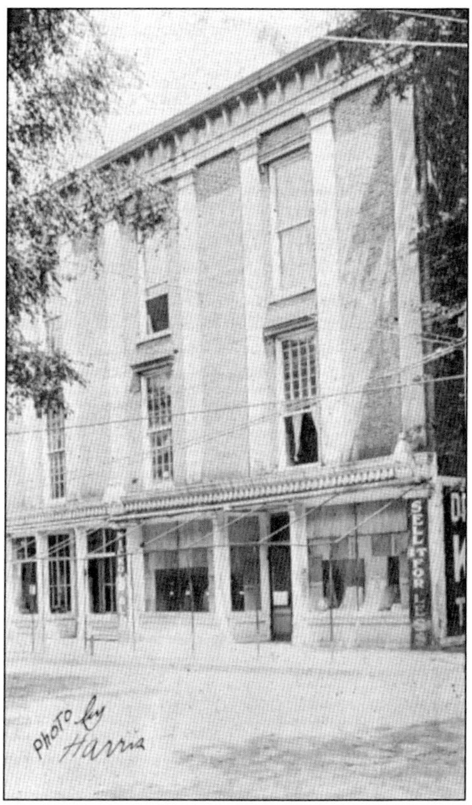

The Nichols Block building, depicted in this early-1900s photograph, was located at the corner of North Congress and East Liberty Streets.

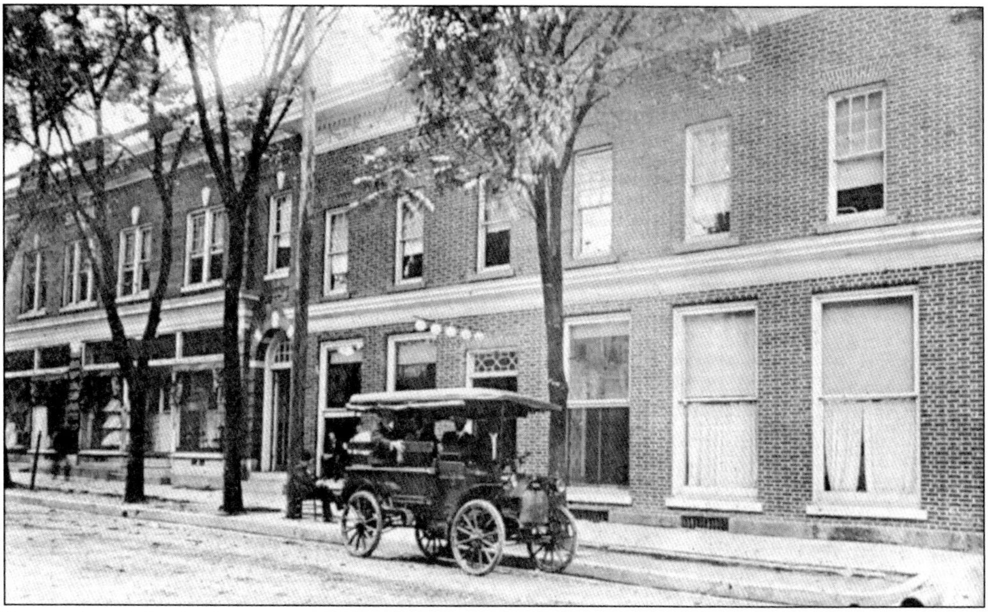

Located on North Congress Street, the O'Leary Block of buildings was owned by George H. O'Leary in the early 1900s. This block included George O'Leary's store, which sold furniture, stoves, and harnesses.

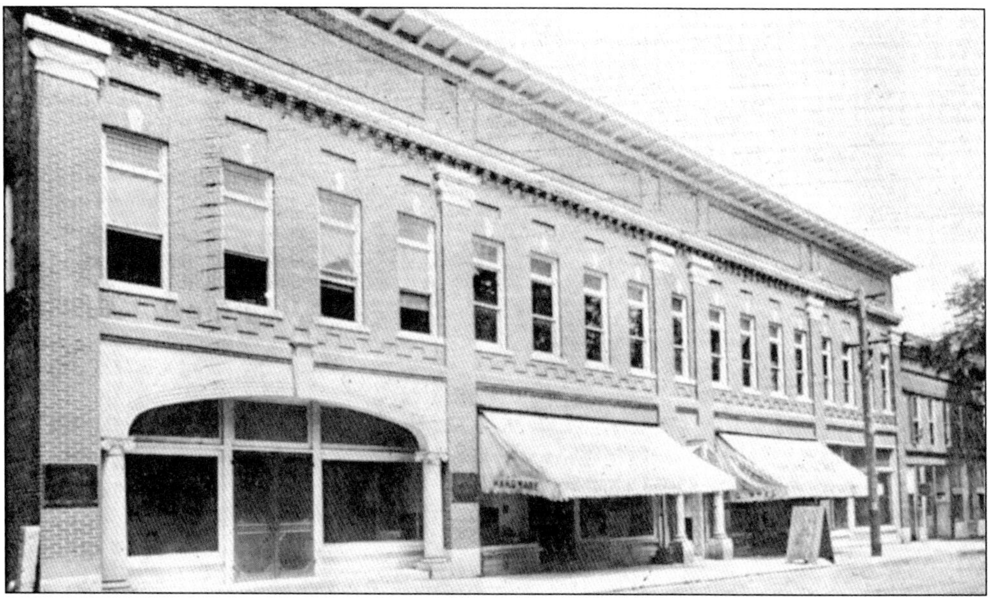

The McNeel Block of buildings on Congress Street housed several businesses in the early 1900s, including the Loan and Savings Bank, the U.S. Post Office, and York Hardware Company. It was owned by Samuel M. McNeel, president of the Loan and Savings Bank and Tavora Cotton Mill. The McNeel Block burned on January 8, 1917.

The Thomson Company, Inc., was located on Congress Street near the intersection with Liberty Street in the first decade of the 1900s. J. F. Thomson was president and manager of the company, which sold a variety of products including dry goods, clothing, and shoes. This postcard photograph was taken during the "fall opening" of October 3–4, 1906.

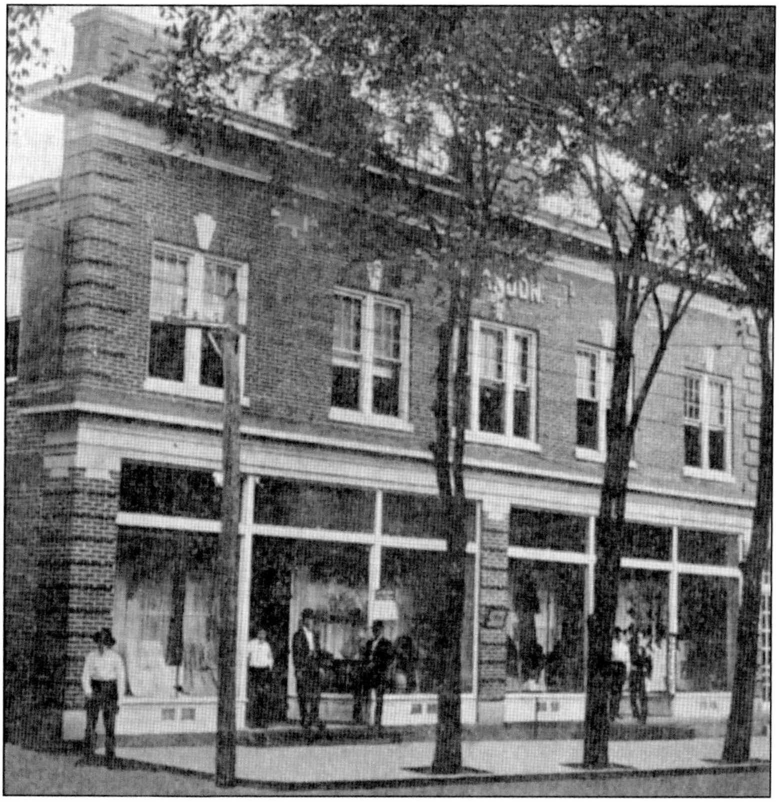

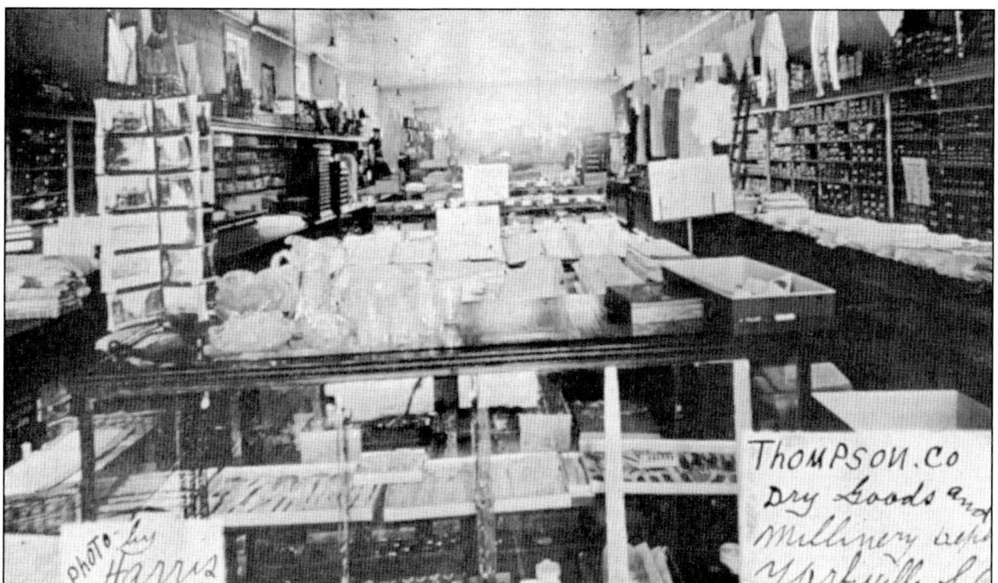

This image shows the interior of the Dry Goods and Millinery Department of the Thomson Company, incorrectly labeled on the postcard as the "Thompson Co."

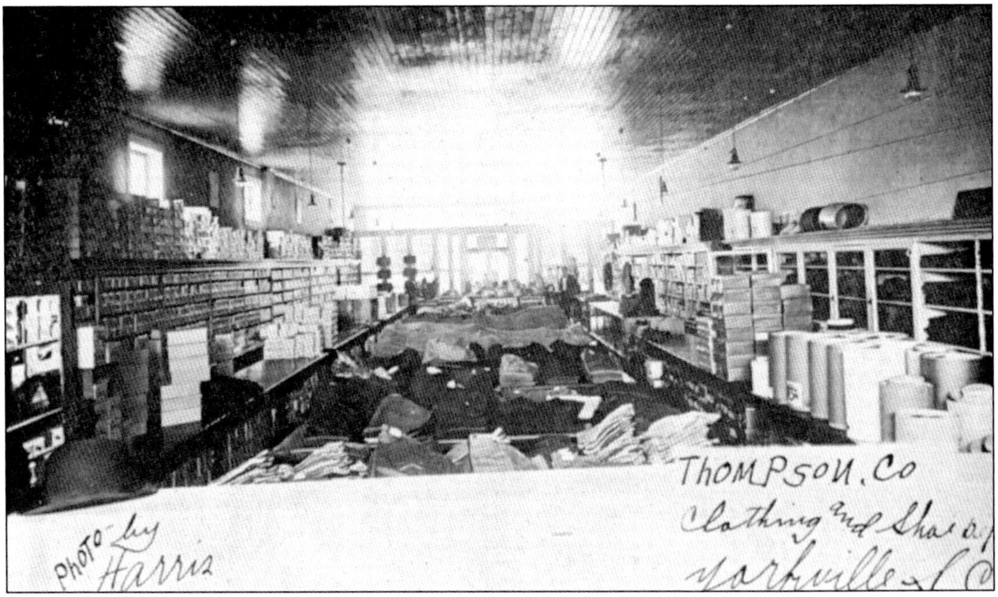

Another view of the interior of the Thomson Company, this time showing the Clothing and Shoe Department, is again incorrectly labeled.

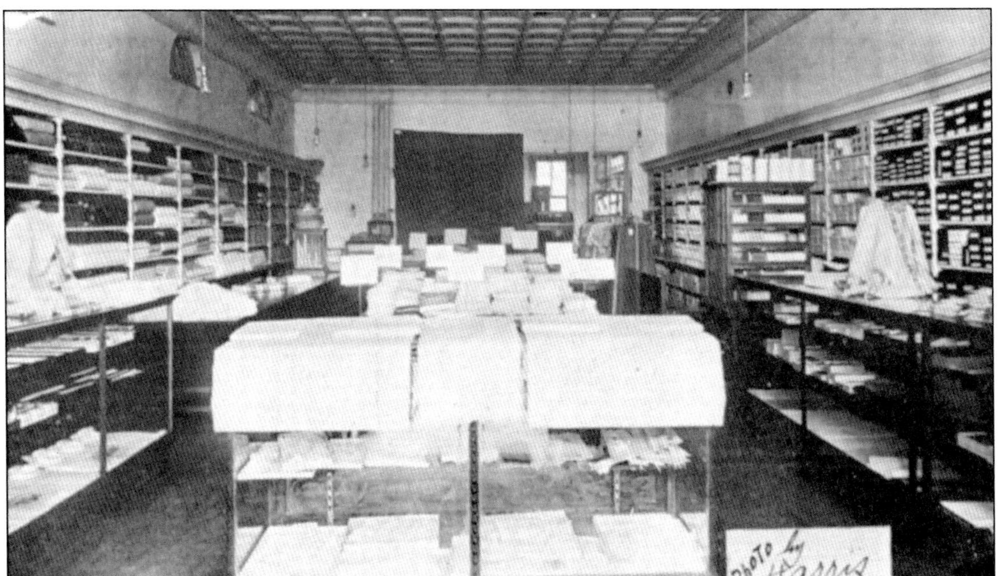

The interior of the Cloud Cash Store *c.* 1905 looked a great deal like the interior of the Thomson Company store. Note the great abundance of textile goods, reflecting the dominance of the textile industry in Yorkville at the time.

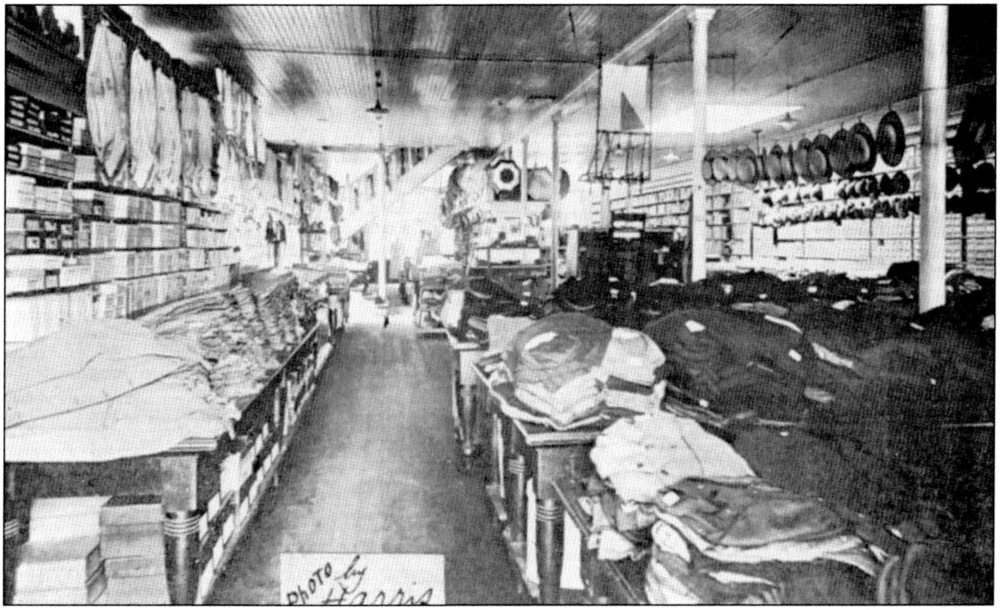

The Kirkpatrick-Belk Company opened in Yorkville in February 1909. This store was a partnership between Belk Brothers Company, a successful family-owned chain of department stores in North Carolina, and J. W. Kirkpatrick, formerly the manager of the Belk Brothers' Gastonia store. The store was located across from the York County Court House and sold dry goods and millinery.

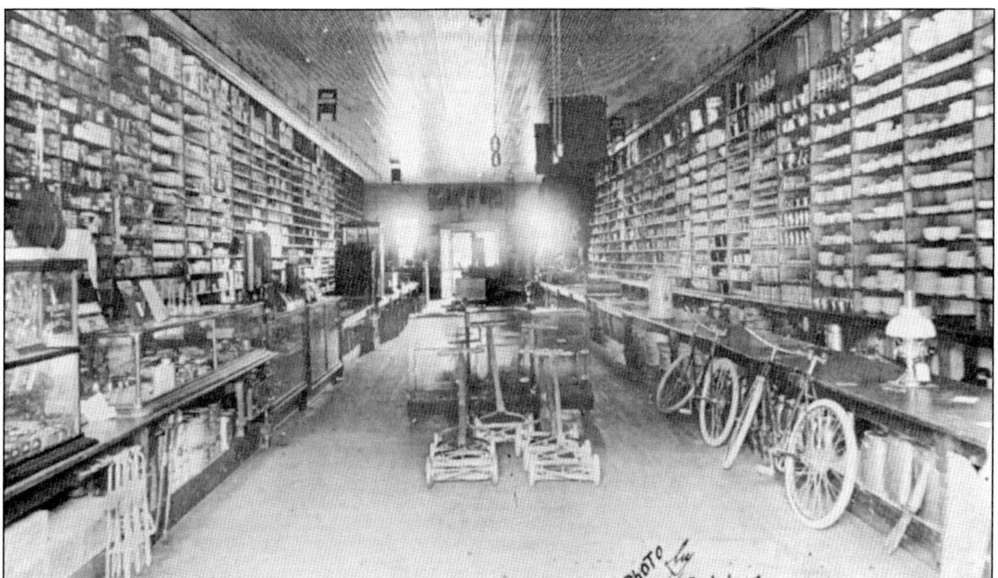

Another important downtown establishment in the early 1900s was the Yorkville Hardware Company. This interior shot demonstrates the variety of items for sale, including bicycles, mechanical lawn mowers, and electric lamps.

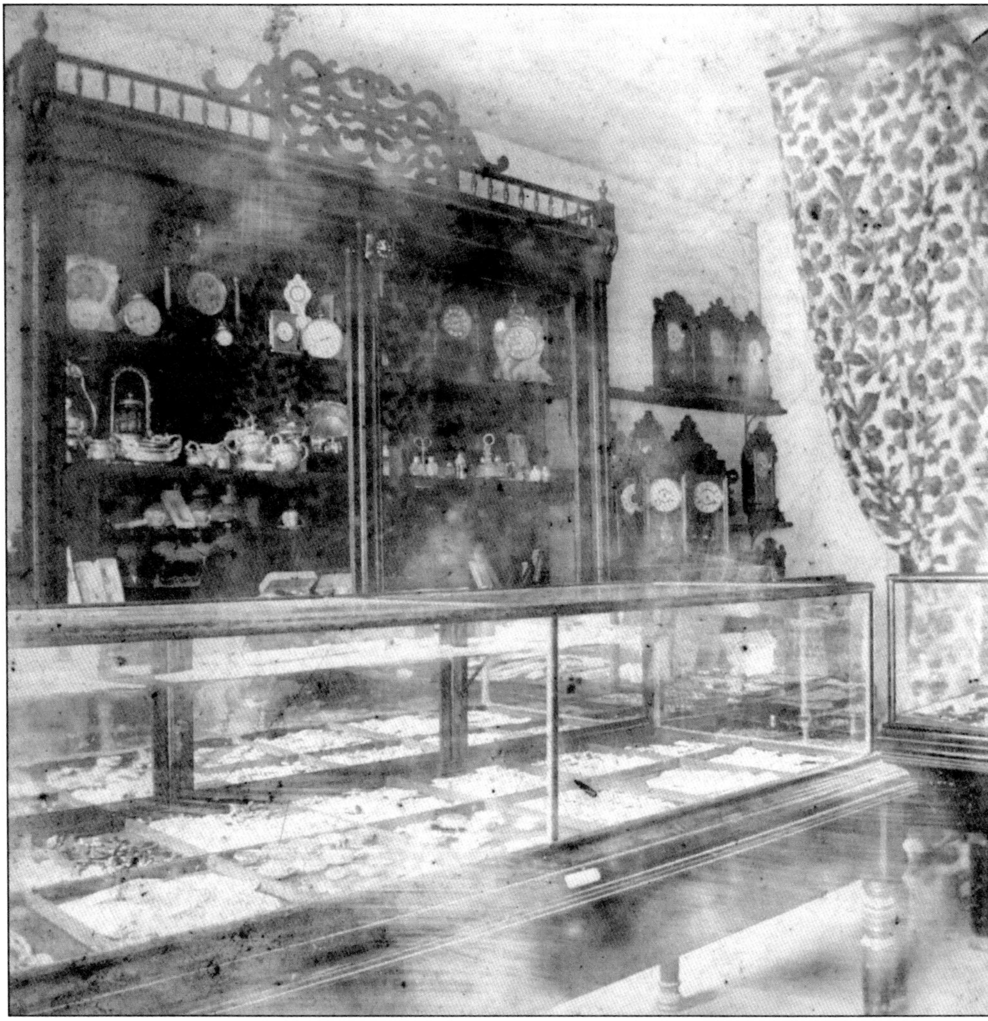

Thomas Withers Speck was a jeweler and optician. In April 1896, he opened Speck Jewelry in the store of J. M. Ferguson on Congress Street, shown in this photograph taken c. 1908. Speck was also trained as a watchmaker, and it was his job to regulate the city clock when it was installed in the remodeled courthouse in 1896.

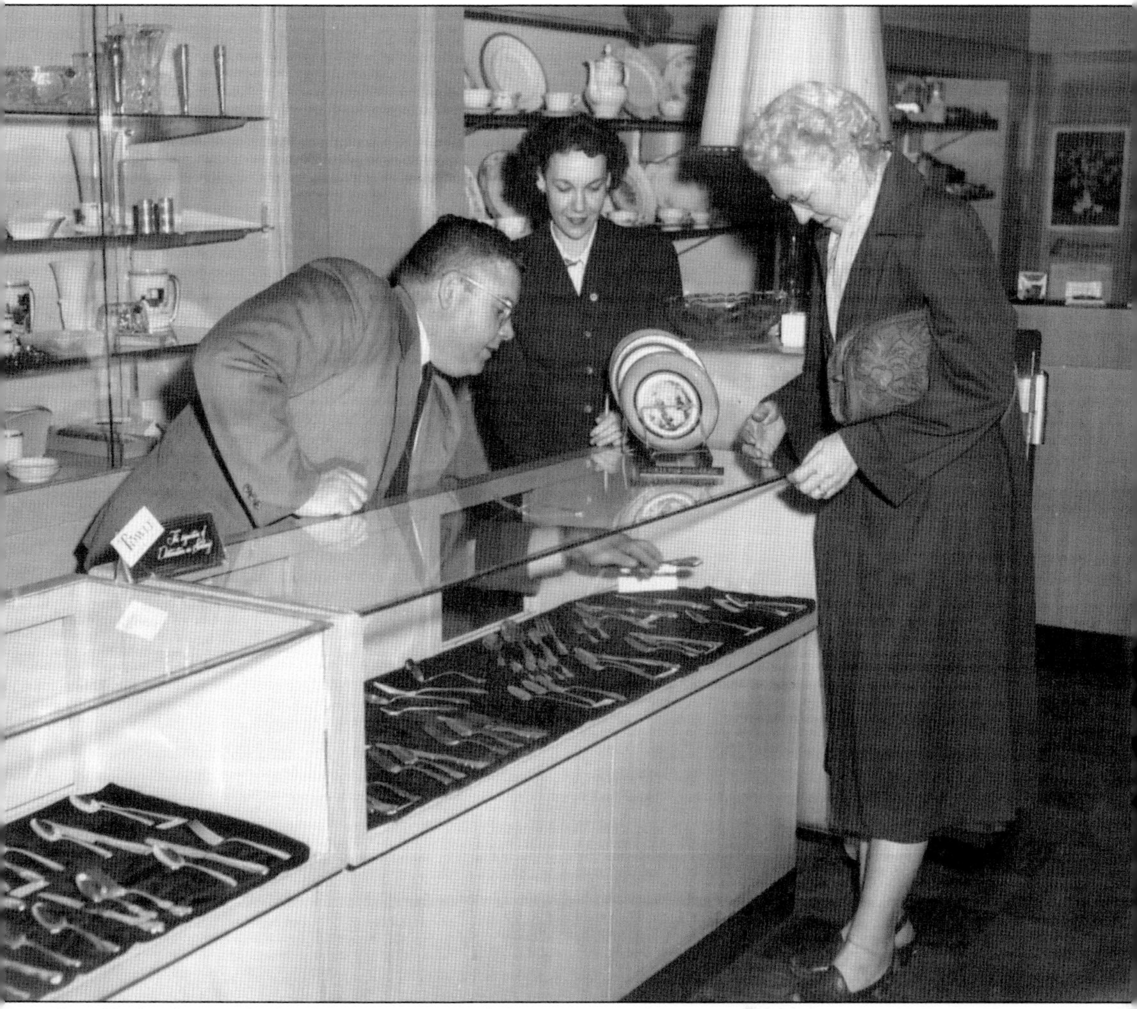

Sheriff Charles A. ("Charlie") Moss owned the Moss Jewelry Store located on Congress Street. Sheriff Moss's son, Lewis Moss, and his wife, Blanche Hancock Moss, ran the business. Lewis and Blanche are seen here waiting on a customer in a photograph from the 1950s. (Courtesy Pat Guerry Hodnett.)

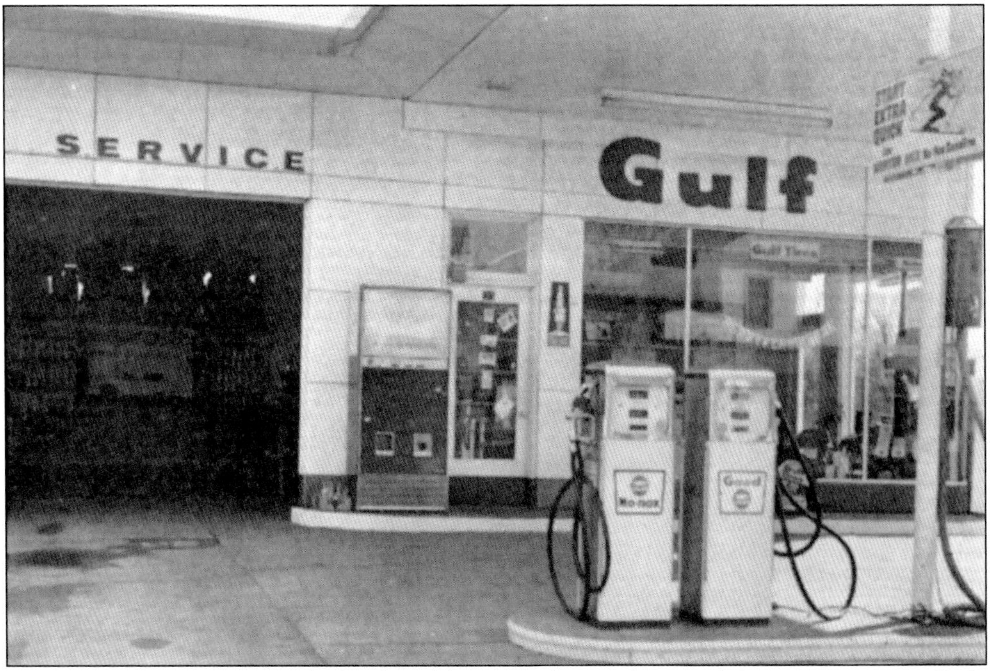

The period of 1945–1975 was the heyday of the privately owned automobile service station in York. These stations offered "full service," which included pumping gas for the customer; checking the oil, water, and tires; and washing windshields. One such station was Miller's Gulf Service, owned by Ernest "Ernie" Miller. Located at 35 South Congress Street, it is shown here as it appeared in 1969. The building is now a NAPA automotive parts store.

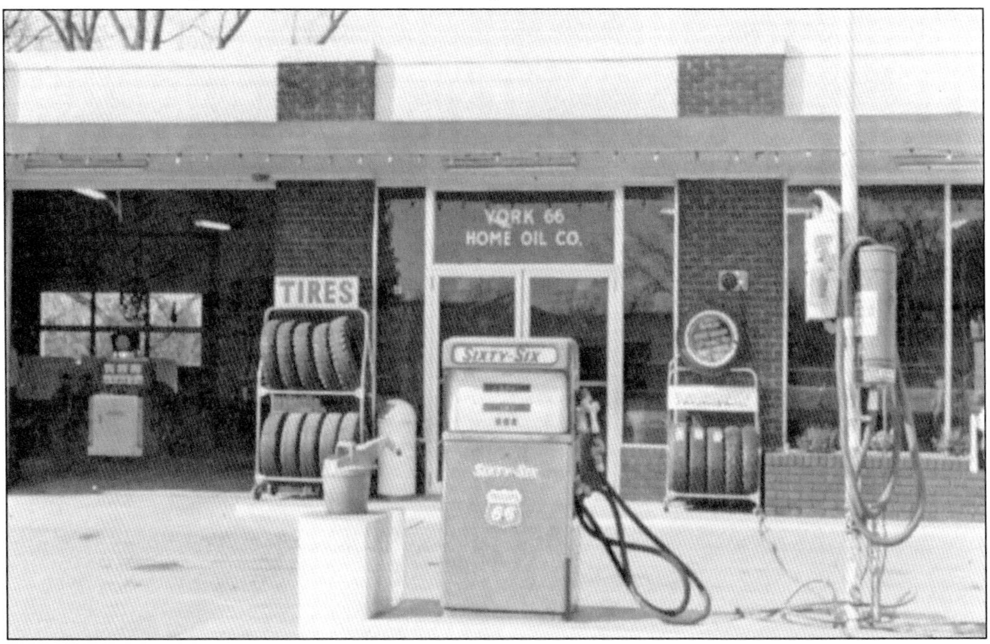

The York 66 Home Oil Company was a Phillips 66 distributor located on 28 South Congress Street, between the Rose Hotel and Latta House. Michael J. Smith was proprietor at the time this photograph was taken *c.* 1969. The building still exists, but it is no longer a service station.

Dover Pure Oil Service Station, owned by Roy M. Dover, was located at the corner of East Liberty and Roosevelt Streets during the 1960s and 1970s. This photograph was taken *c.* 1969.

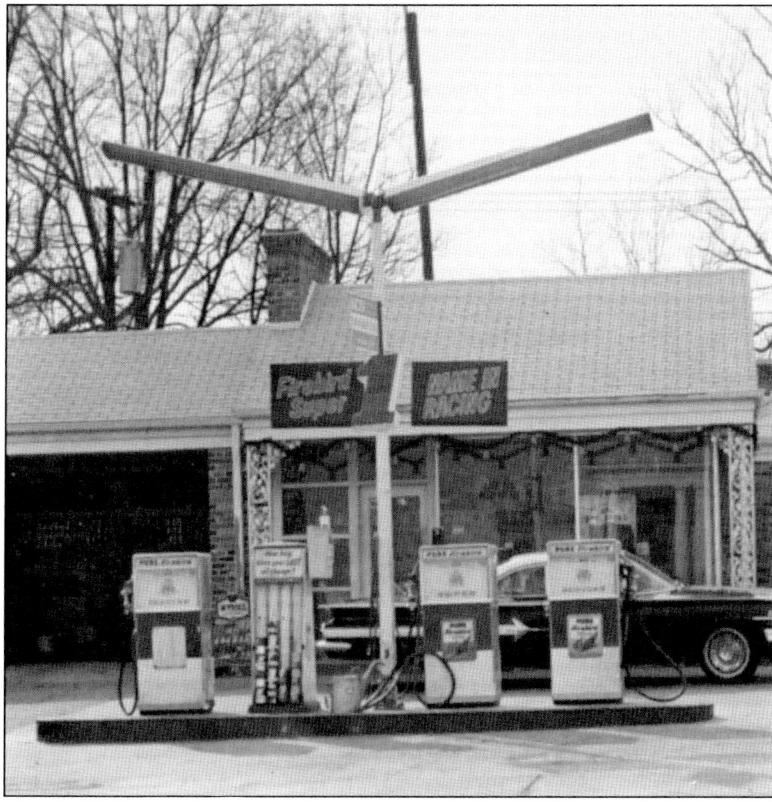

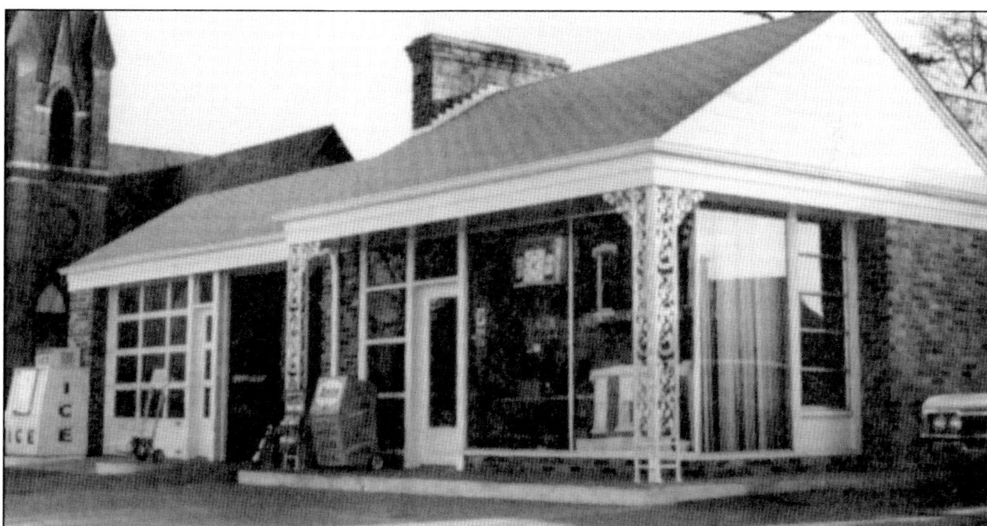

By 1972, Dover Pure Oil had become the Dover Union 76 station. As is evident in this photograph, Dover 76 was adjacent to Trinity Methodist Church, and in the 1980s, the station was torn down and replaced with a new parking lot for the church.

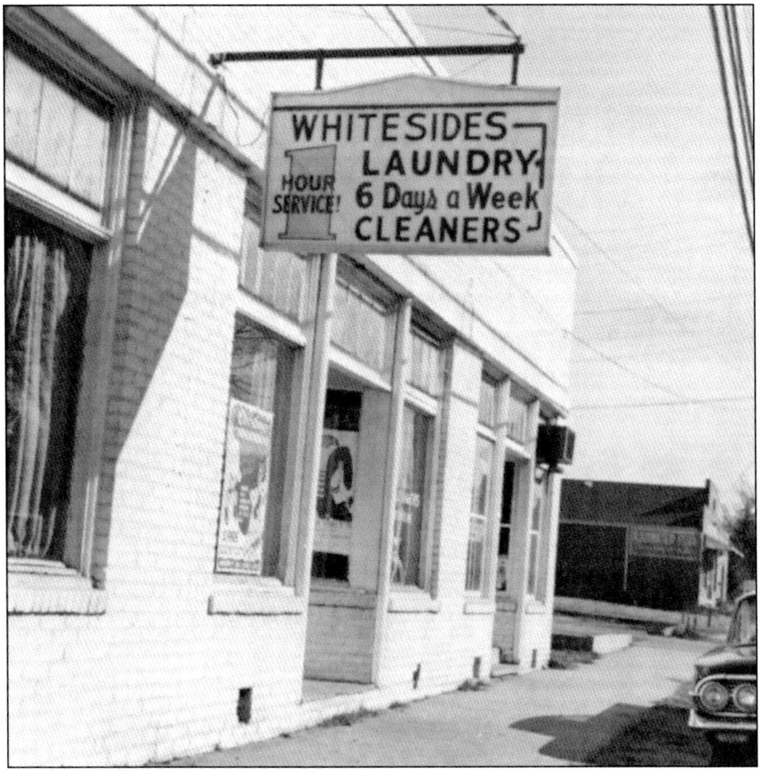

Whitesides Laundry and Cleaners, located at 5 East Madison Street, has been a fixture in downtown York since 1959. Founded by Marshall D. Whitesides, the business is still owned and operated by his son, Marshall D. Whitesides Jr.

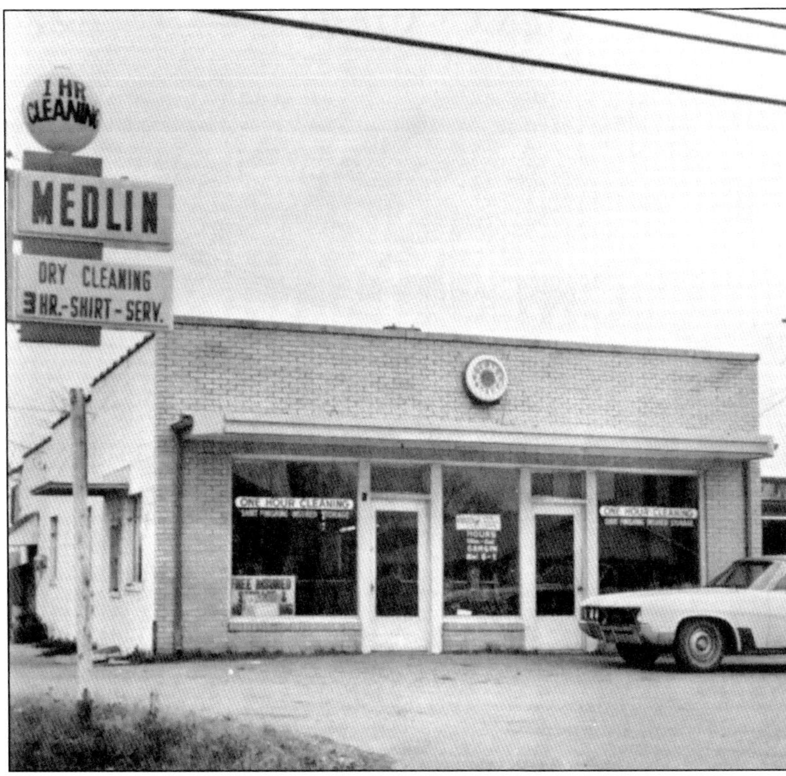

Medlin One Hour Cleaners was located at the corner of Madison and Roosevelt Streets, as shown in this photograph from 1970. The owner was Edward K. Medlin.

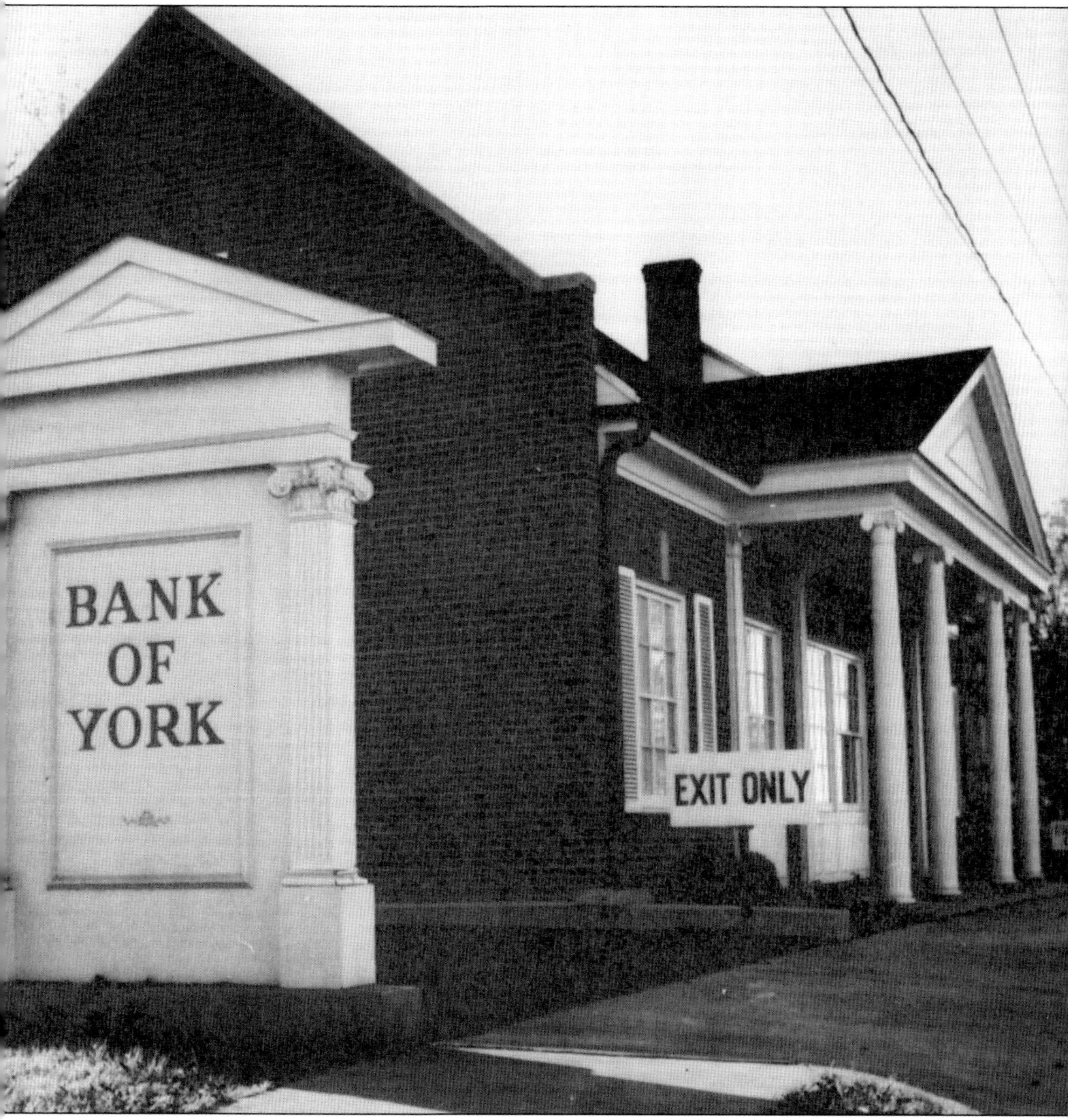

The Bank of York was established in 1935 on South Congress Street in the former First National Bank building as a typical post-Depression-era small-town banking service. This new building at 13 West Liberty Street, located just behind the courthouse, was completed not long before this photograph was taken in 1971.

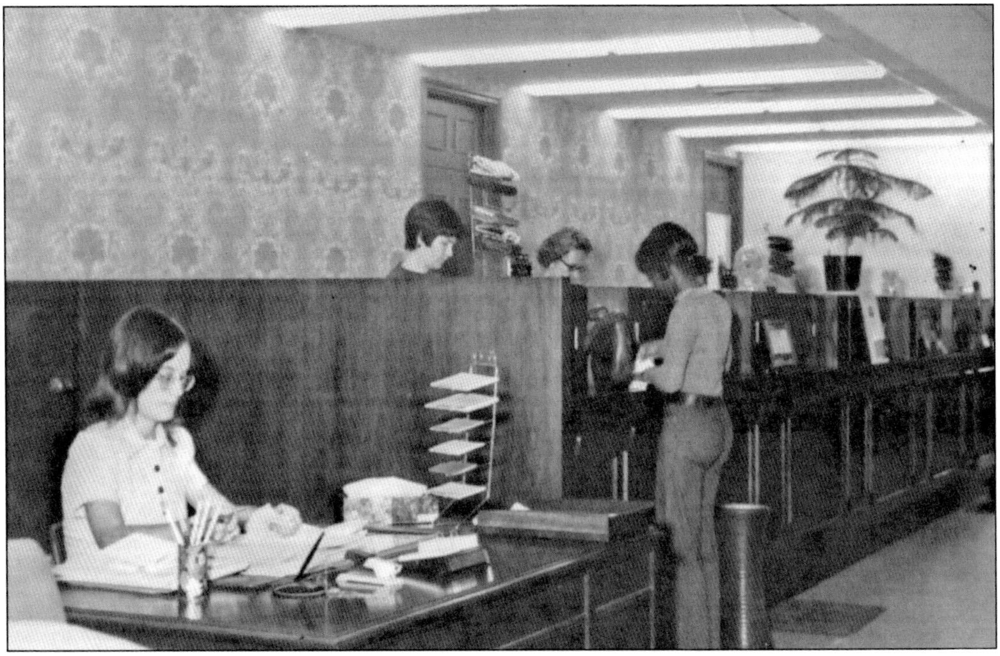

This photograph was taken inside the new Bank of York building on West Liberty Street in 1973. Today the Bank of York system includes the main office on West Liberty and a branch on East Liberty, both in York, as well as a branch in Rock Hill and a branch at Lake Wylie.

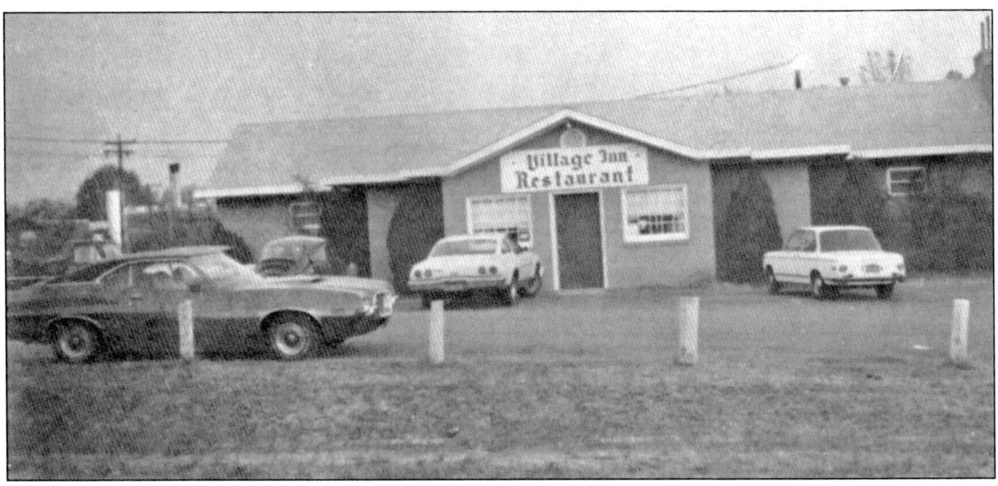

The Village Inn Restaurant on the 321 Bypass was a popular steak house and short-order restaurant for much of the 1960s and 1970s. Myron J. Andrews was the proprietor when this photograph was taken *c.* 1973. In the late 1970s, a stage and dance hall were added, and the building became a "George Jones' Possum Holler" nightclub featuring live country music acts from across the nation. The establishment is now known as the Hollow Lounge.

Three

Industry and Agriculture

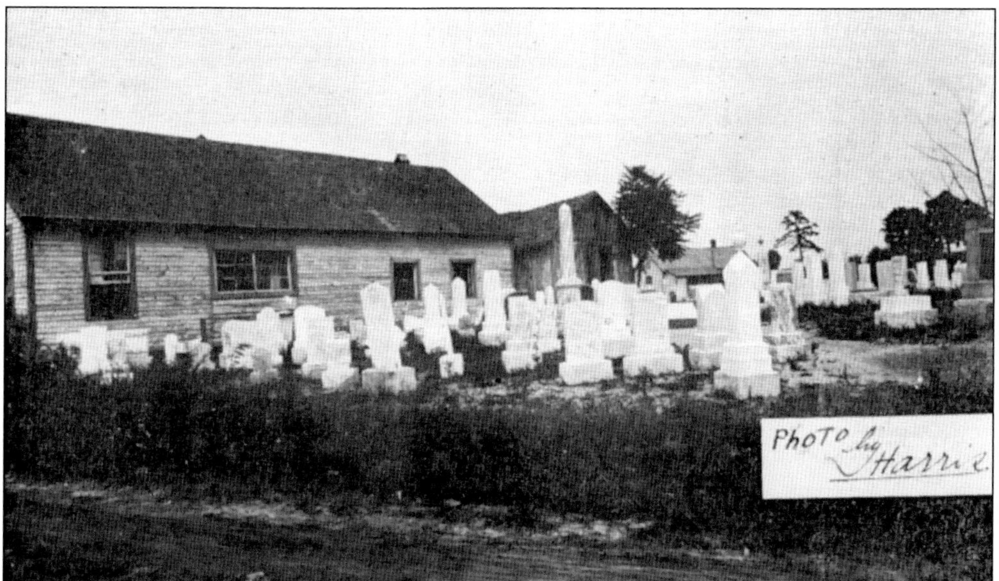

The Palmetto Monument Works on Cemetery Street is shown in this early postcard dated before 1912. It manufactured marble and granite tombstones and grave markers.

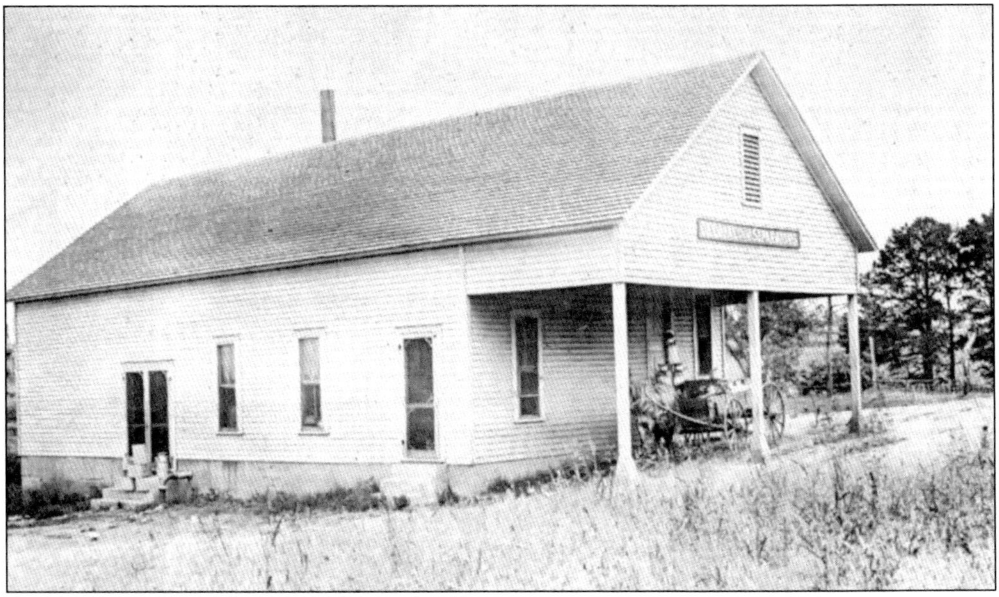

The York Creamery Association had its plant on East Liberty Street for many years. The creamery produced dairy products like butter and ice cream. This photograph dates to before 1912.

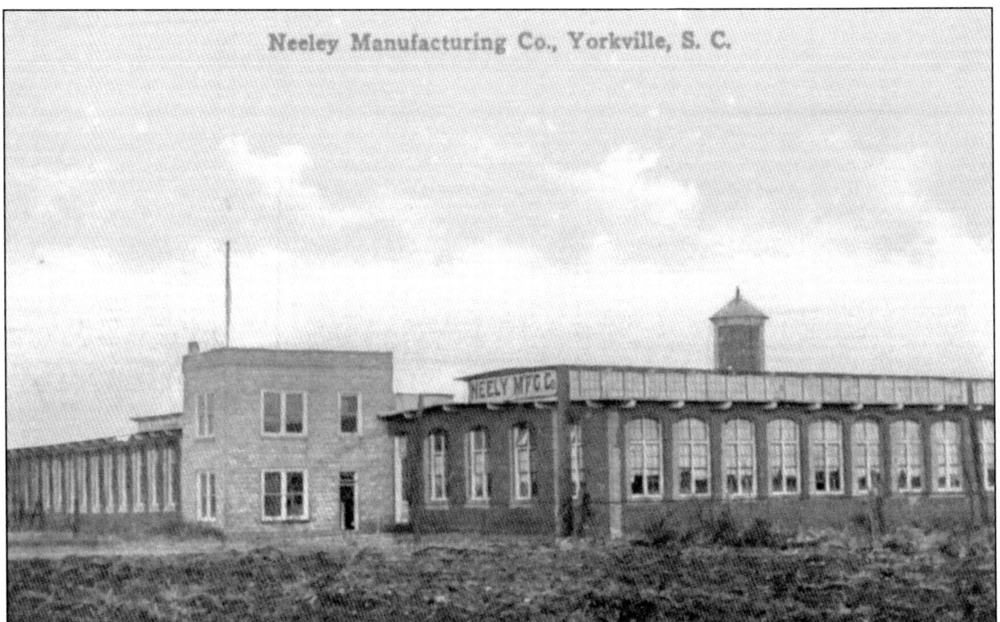

The Neely Manufacturing Company was once one of York's preeminent industries. Located on East Blackburn Street and the Carolina and Northwestern Railway, the company manufactured coarse yarn. This postcard (with the name spelled incorrectly) dates from the early 20th century and was sold by the Thomson Company of Yorkville.

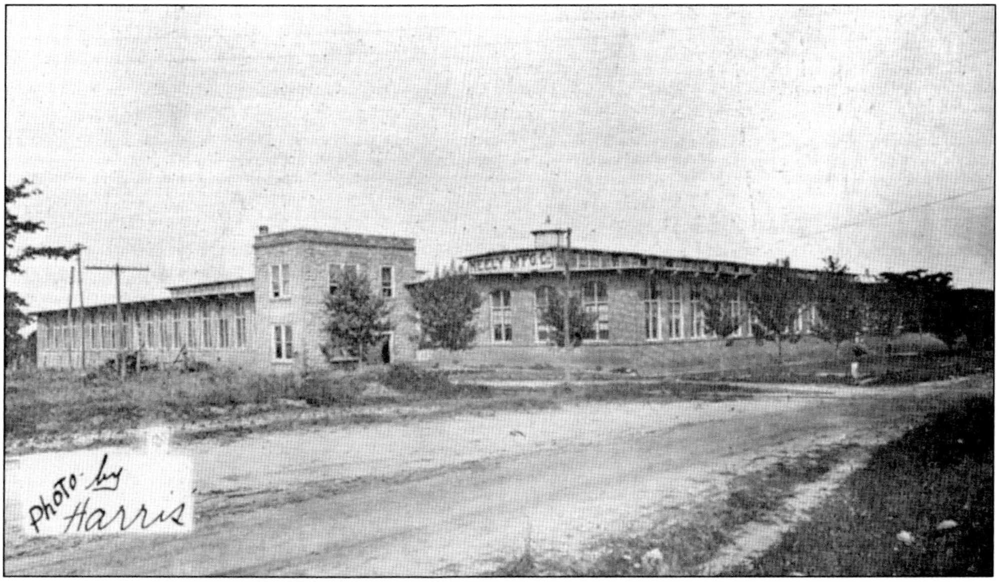

This photograph gives another view of the Neely Manufacturing Company in the early 20th century. In 1910, the president was W. B. Moore and the plant employed 90 people.

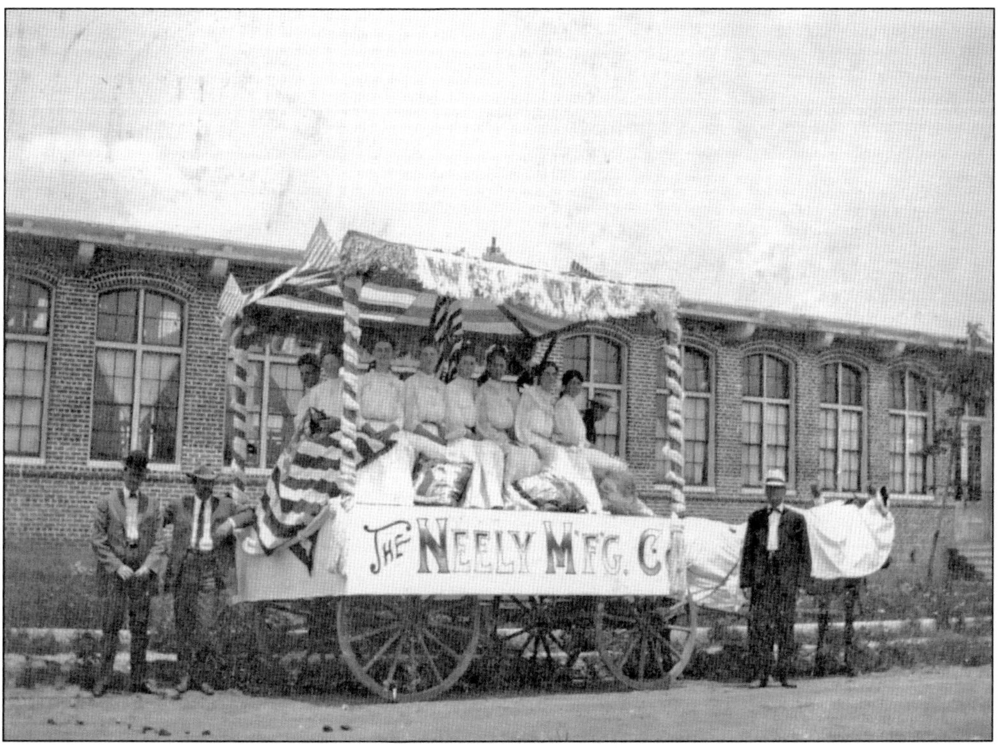

Horse-drawn floats were a popular item in Yorkville parades in the early 1900s. This photograph shows Neely Manufacturing Company's entry in what was possibly a Fourth of July parade.

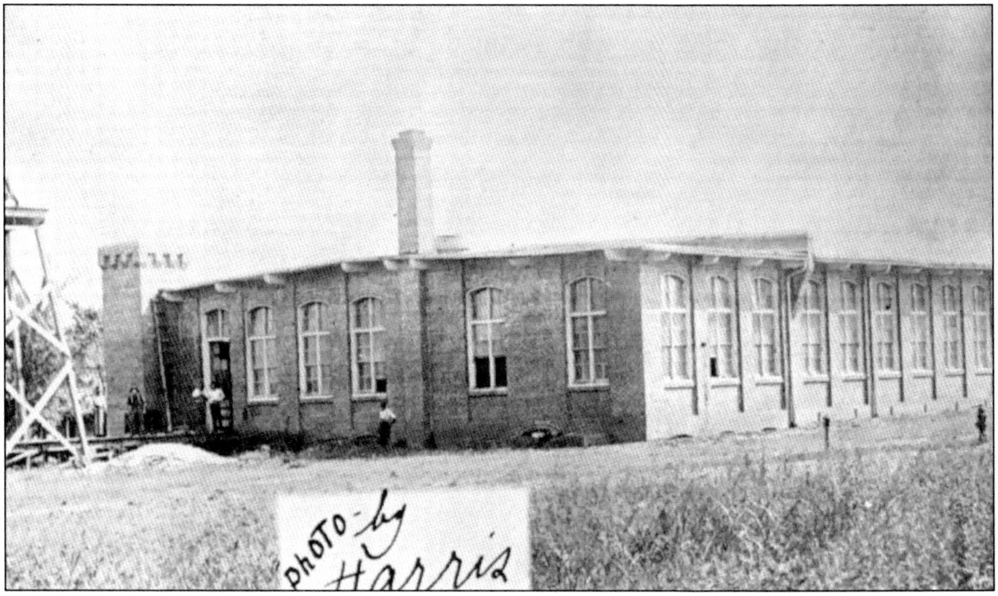

The Lockmore Cotton Mill was established in 1908 on the Southern Railway at the intersection of Blackburn and Madison Streets, on the northeast side of York. Thomas P. Moore was the president and secretary-treasurer when the plant opened. This photograph of the mill was taken around 1912.

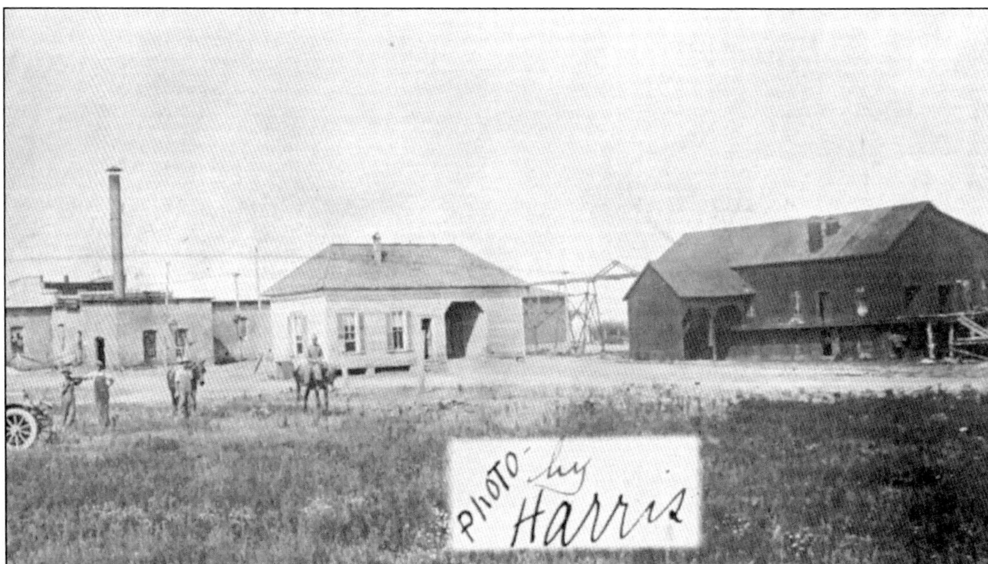

The Victor Cotton Oil Company was located on East Madison Street and the Carolina and Northwestern Railway. The company produced cottonseed oil, and in 1908, when this photograph was taken, the plant manager was William H. Fowler.

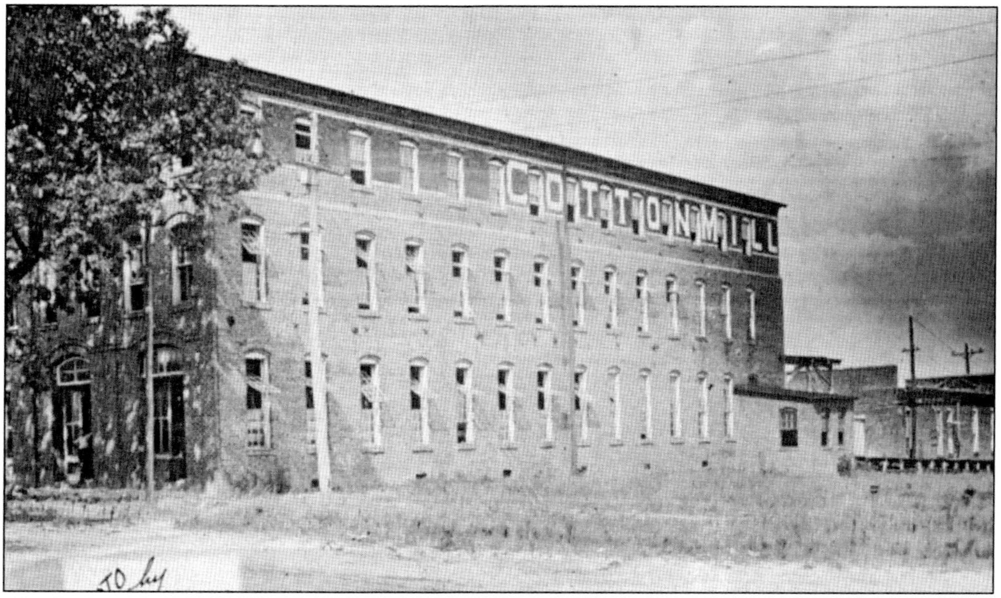

The Tavora Cotton Mills' primary product was yarn. The mill complex was located on South Congress Street along the Carolina and Northwestern Railway, near the intersection with Chester Road. When this photograph was taken c. 1905, the president was Samuel M. McNeel, who also owned the Loan and Savings Bank. The Tavora Mill was demolished in the 1980s, and the site is now occupied by a car wash.

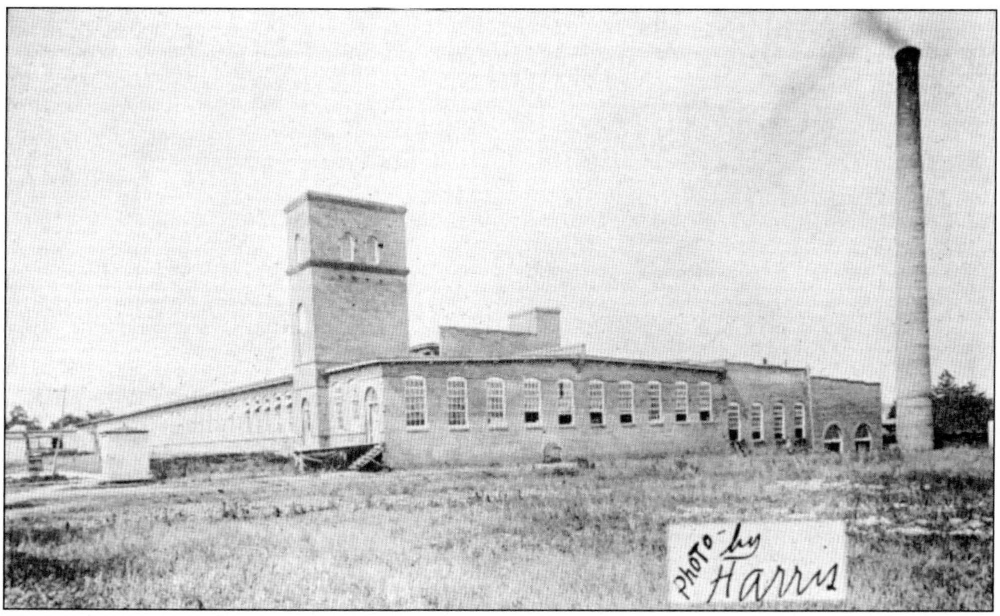

The York Cotton Mill was located on Hunter Street, on the northeastern edge of the city limits. Col. Joseph G. Wardlaw was the president and secretary-treasurer of the mill when this photograph was taken c. 1910.

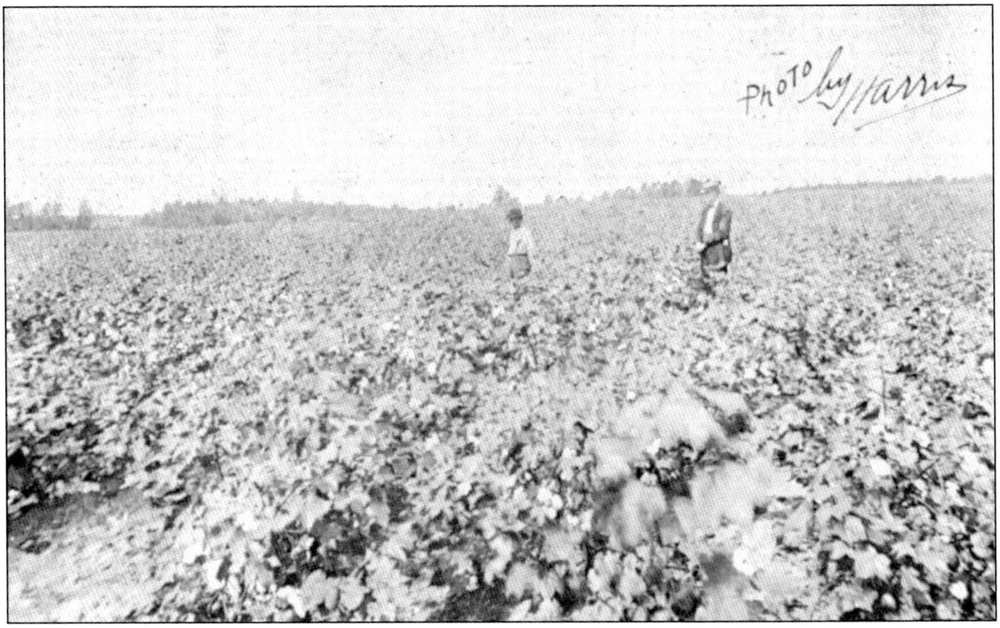

This early photograph of a cotton field near Yorkville was taken before 1912. Cotton was the preeminent cash crop for York County and much of the surrounding area throughout the 19th and much of the 20th century, and thousands of acres of cotton are still grown in York County each year. Harvested cotton was transported to York for processing and textile manufacturing or loaded onto railroad cars for shipment elsewhere in the United States and the world.

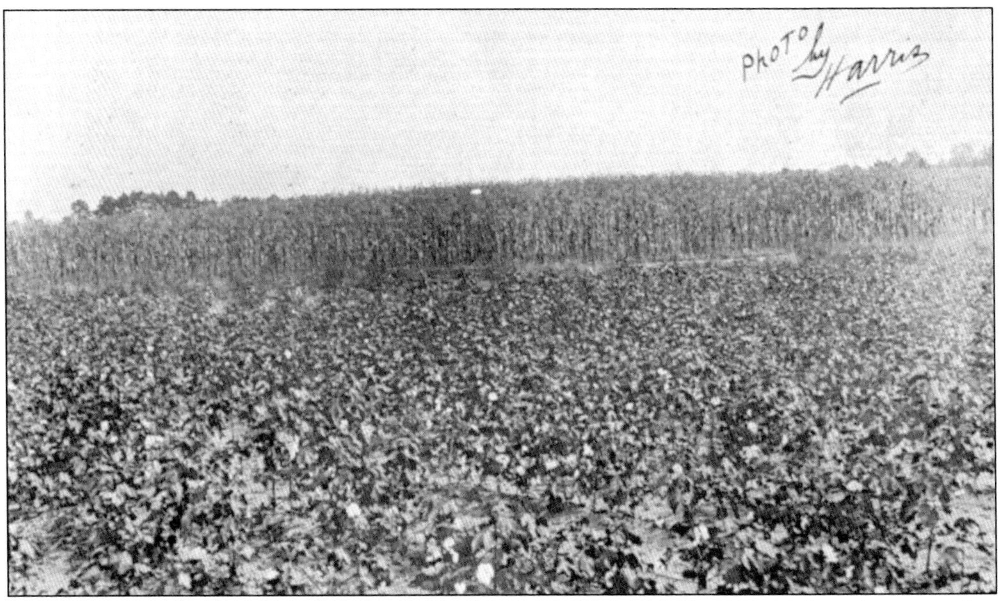

A field of cotton planted alongside a field of corn, visible in the background, is shown in this photograph, also taken prior to 1912. After cotton, corn was the most widely grown and harvested crop in York County during the 19th and 20th centuries, and it is still widely cultivated today.

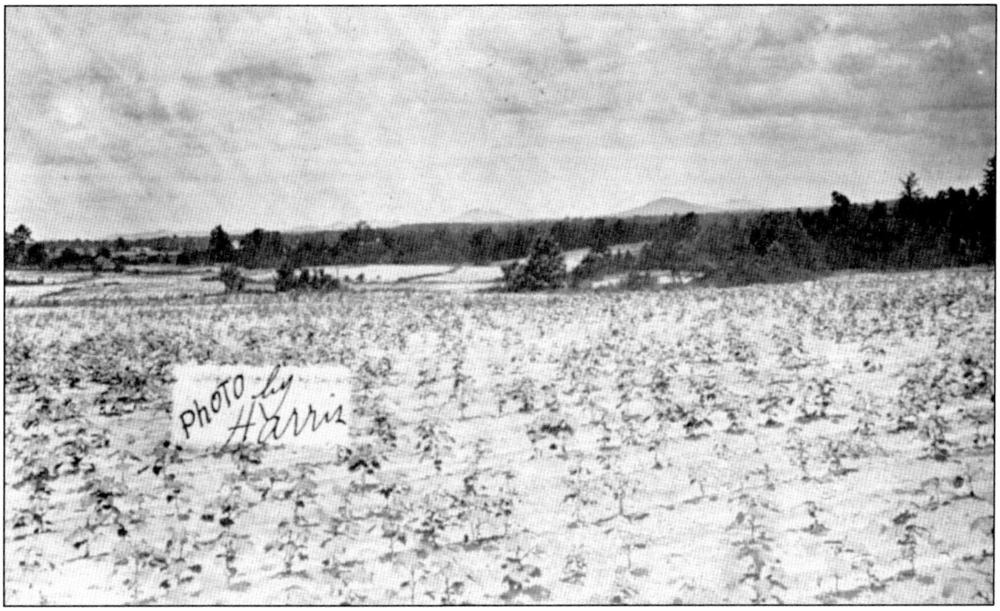

This photograph dates to about 1910 and shows a cotton field located just north of Yorkville. Visible to the north is Kings Mountain, the famous Revolutionary War battle site located in York County just south of the North Carolina border.

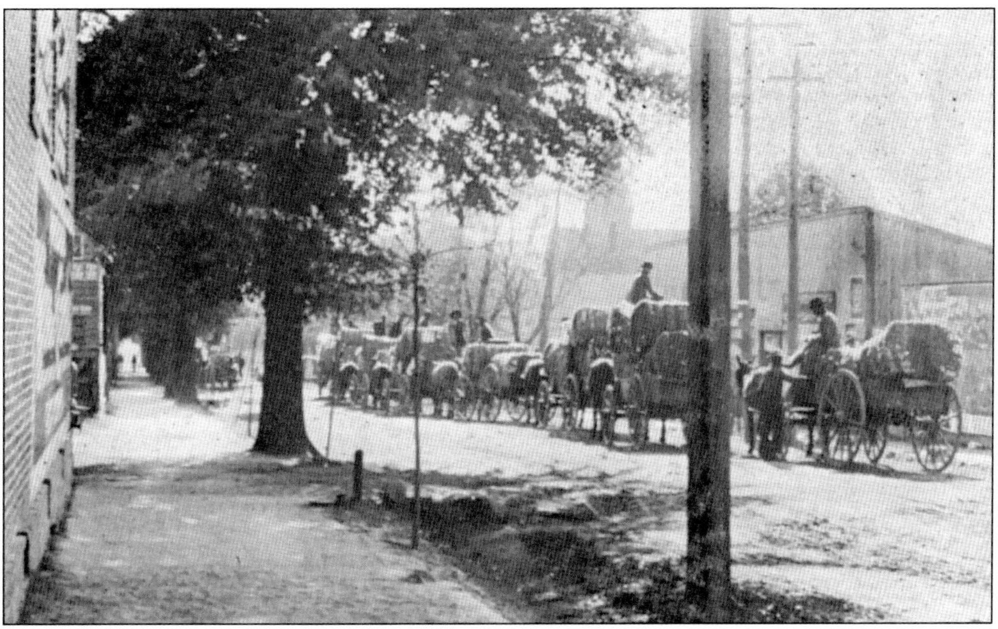

Once harvested, bails of cotton were transported to Yorkville from all over the county by horse-drawn or mule-drawn wagons. Here the cotton would be unloaded for further processing or to be shipped elsewhere. Sites like this were common in Yorkville throughout the late 19th and early 20th centuries. This photograph also dates to around 1910.

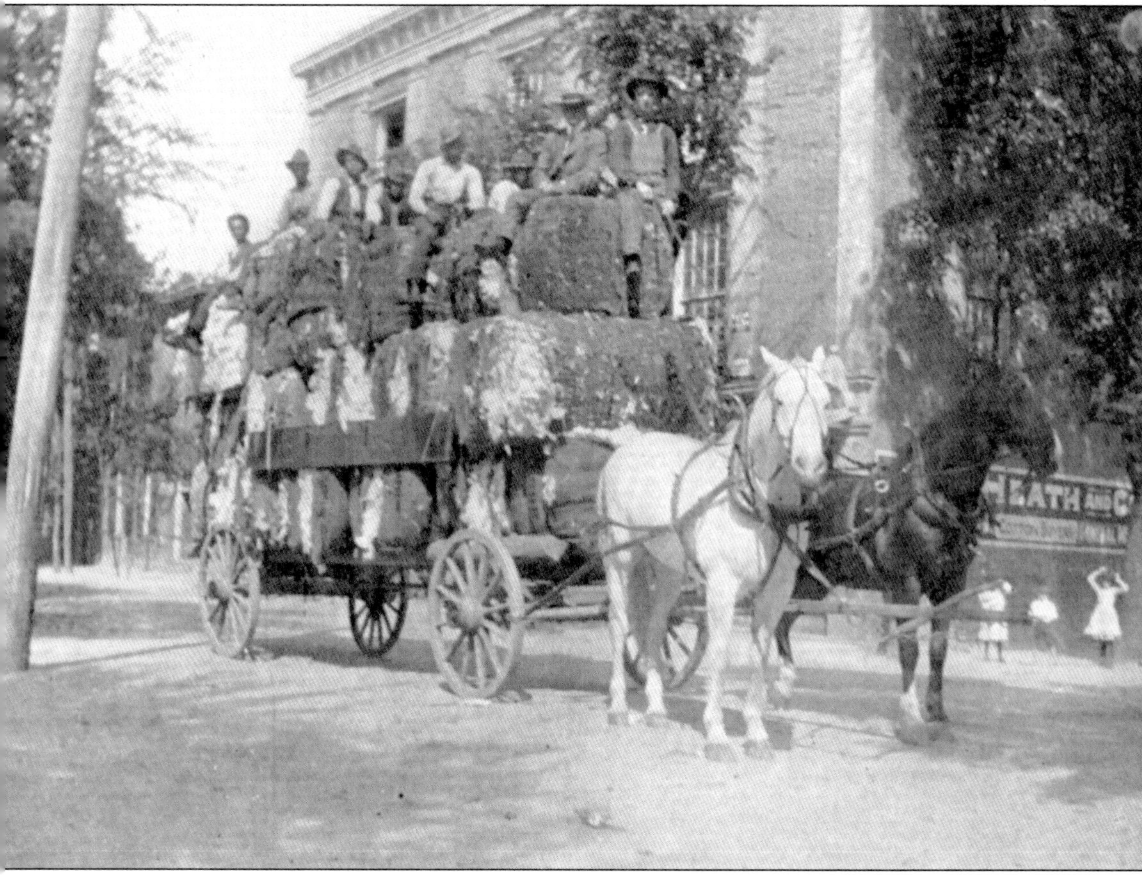

This heavily loaded wagon and its crew were photographed at the intersection of Congress and Liberty Streets *c.* 1910. The cotton was being transported to the Carolina and Northwestern Railway station located just down the street on East Liberty, where it would be loaded onboard freight cars and transported to its final destination.

Four

Transportation

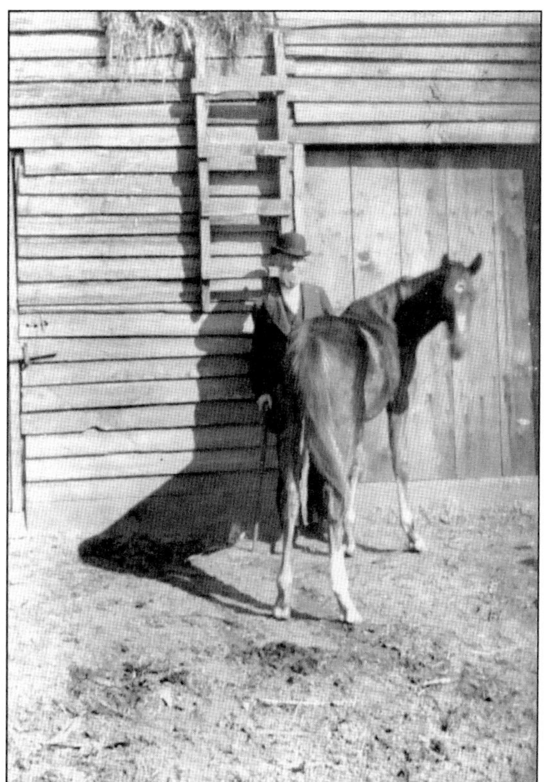

From the time Yorkville was founded in 1786 until well into the 20th century, horses were a common mode of transportation to and from the city. This photograph, made into a postcard by S. W. Watson, shows T. Morrison Whitaker, who raised racehorses near Yorkville in the early 1900s.

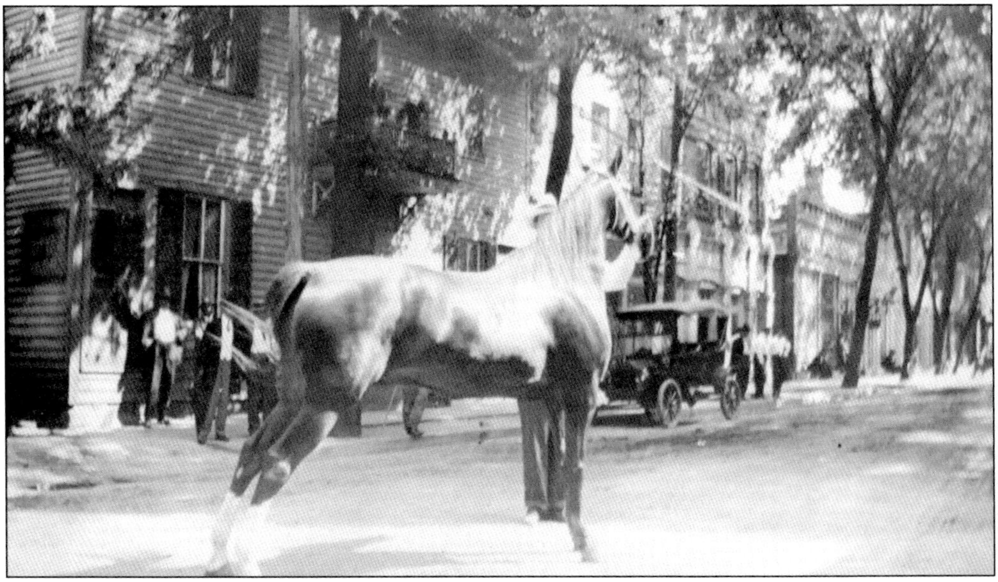

Horses and automobiles were both common sites on the streets of old Yorkville in the early decades of the 20th century, as demonstrated in this early photograph taken c. 1915.

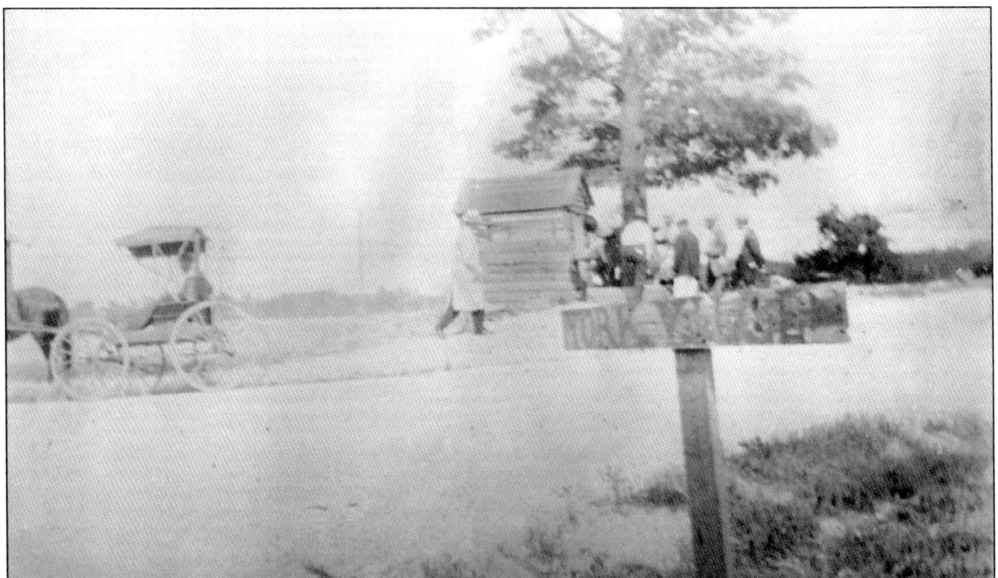

Another early photograph, taken just outside the city around 1915, shows a horse-drawn buggy on a dirt road with a "Yorkville" sign in the foreground.

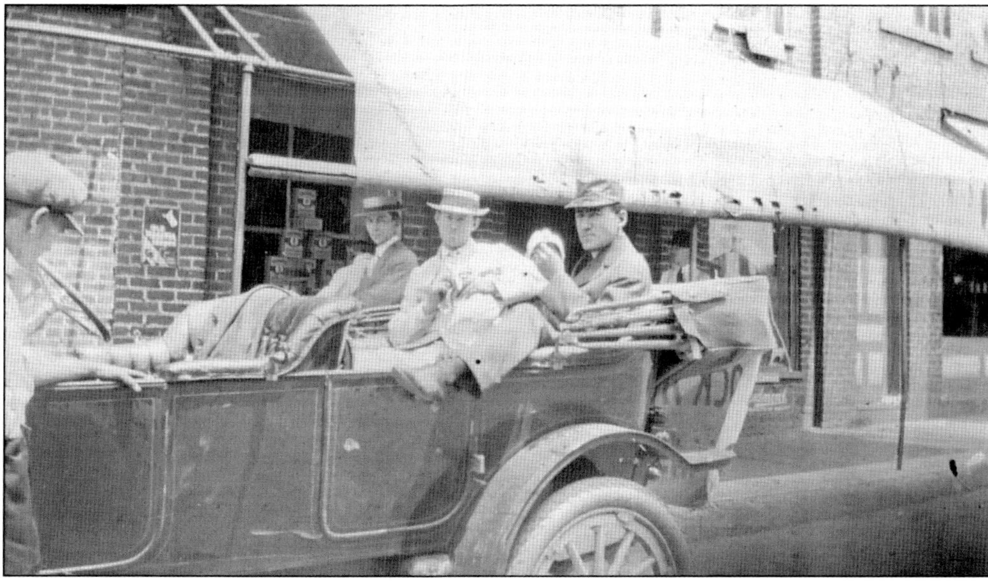

Taken around 1915, this photograph shows a group of men in downtown Yorkville seated in a 1913 Ford Model T touring car.

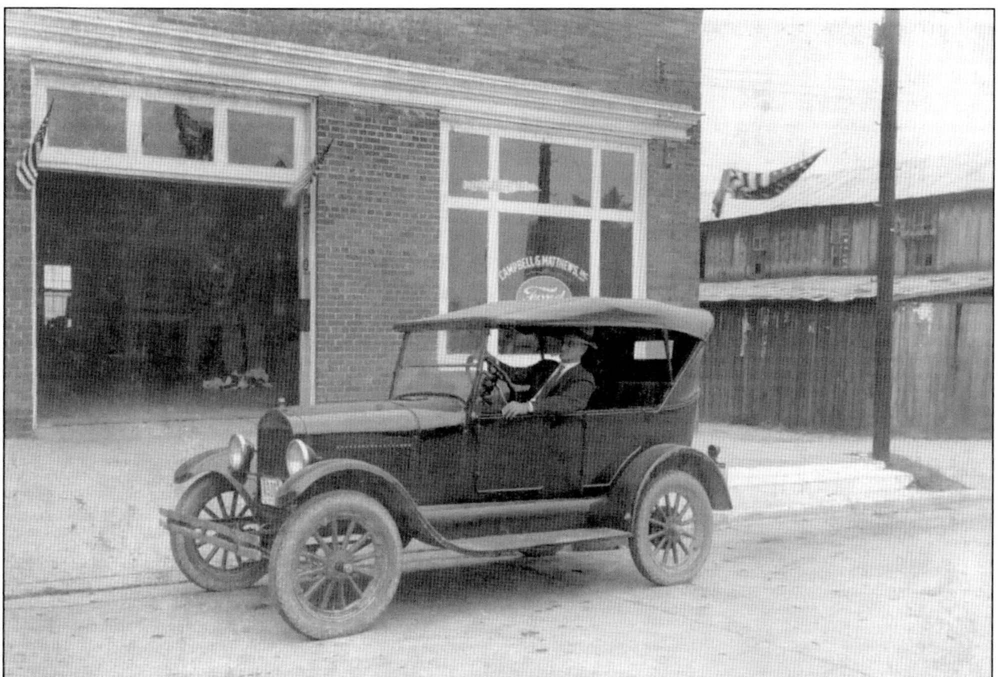

Campbell and Matthews, Inc., was the Ford dealership on North Congress Street in York in the 1920s.

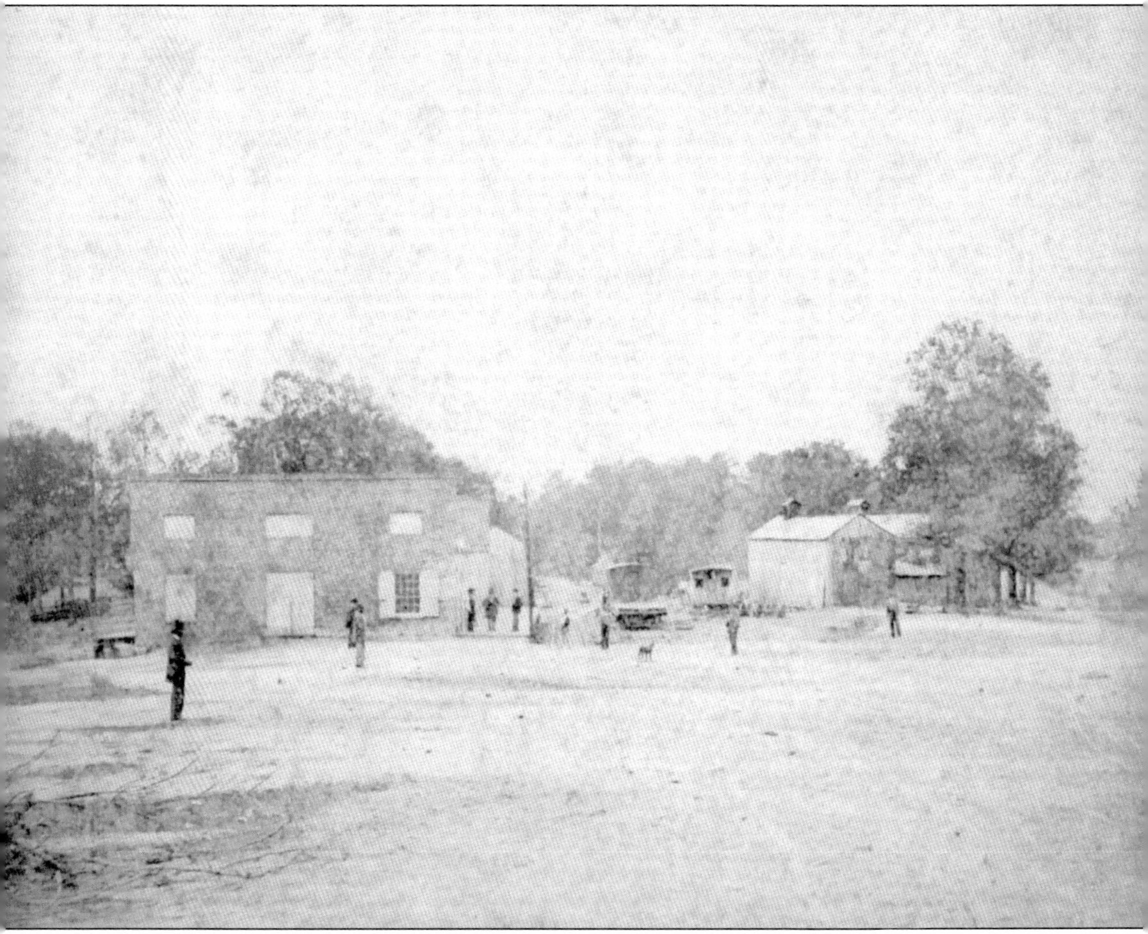

York County's first railroad was laid from Chesterville to Yorkville in 1852. Called the Kings Mountain Railroad (KMR), the original plans called for the line to extend into North Carolina, but a shortage of funds halted construction until after the Civil War. The KMR was incorporated into the newly formed Chester and Lenoir Narrow Gauge Railroad Company in 1873, and by 1875, the new narrow-gauge track had been installed from Chesterville to Yorkville. The track then proceeded due north into North Carolina, finally reaching Lenoir in May 1884. This early photograph shows the Chester and Lenoir Railroad depot in Yorkville sometime before 1897.

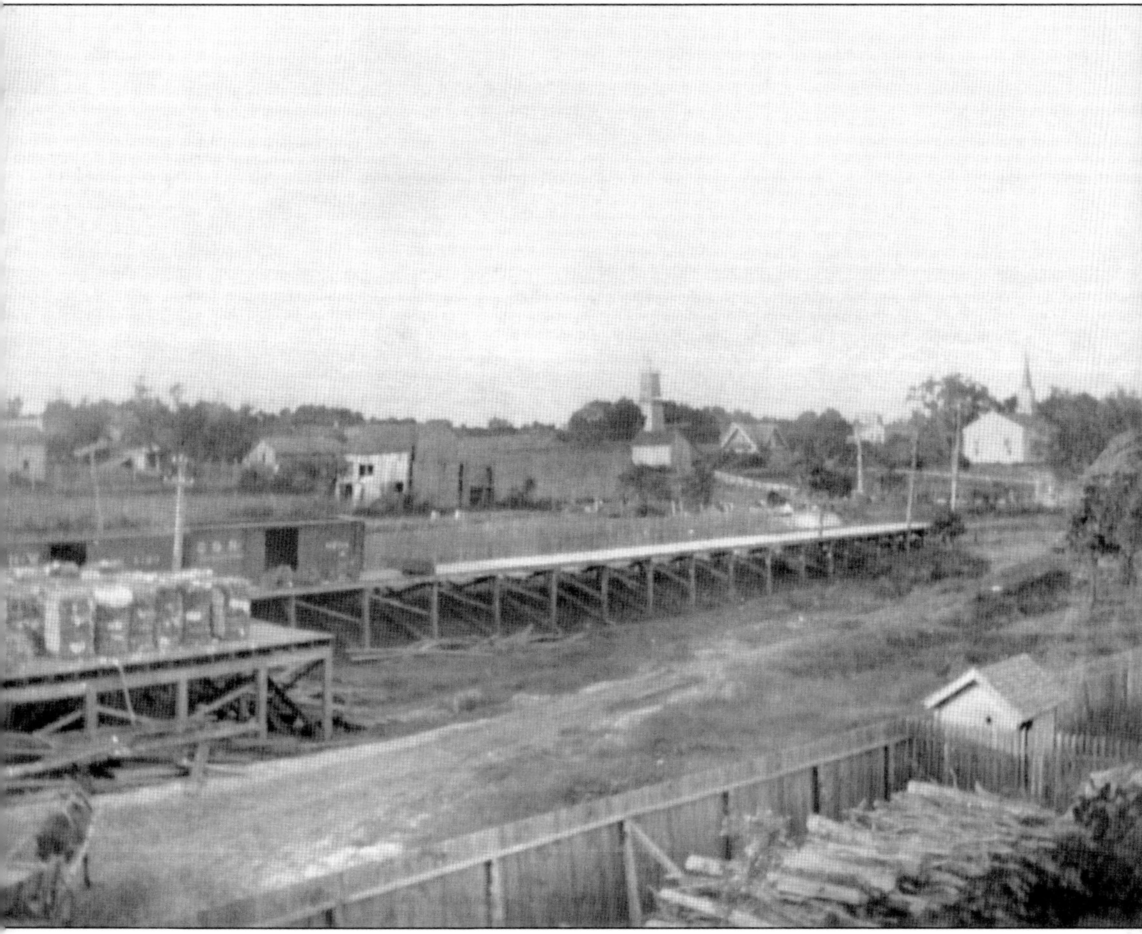

In 1897, the Chester and Lenoir Railroad was reorganized as the Carolina and Northwestern Railway Company, or C&NW. The C&NW converted the track from Chesterville through Yorkville to Lenoir back to standard-gauge track in 1902, making it possible for larger, heavier trains to use the line. This photograph, dated September 1899, shows the cotton platform at the old C&NW passenger and freight depot, located off East Liberty Street.

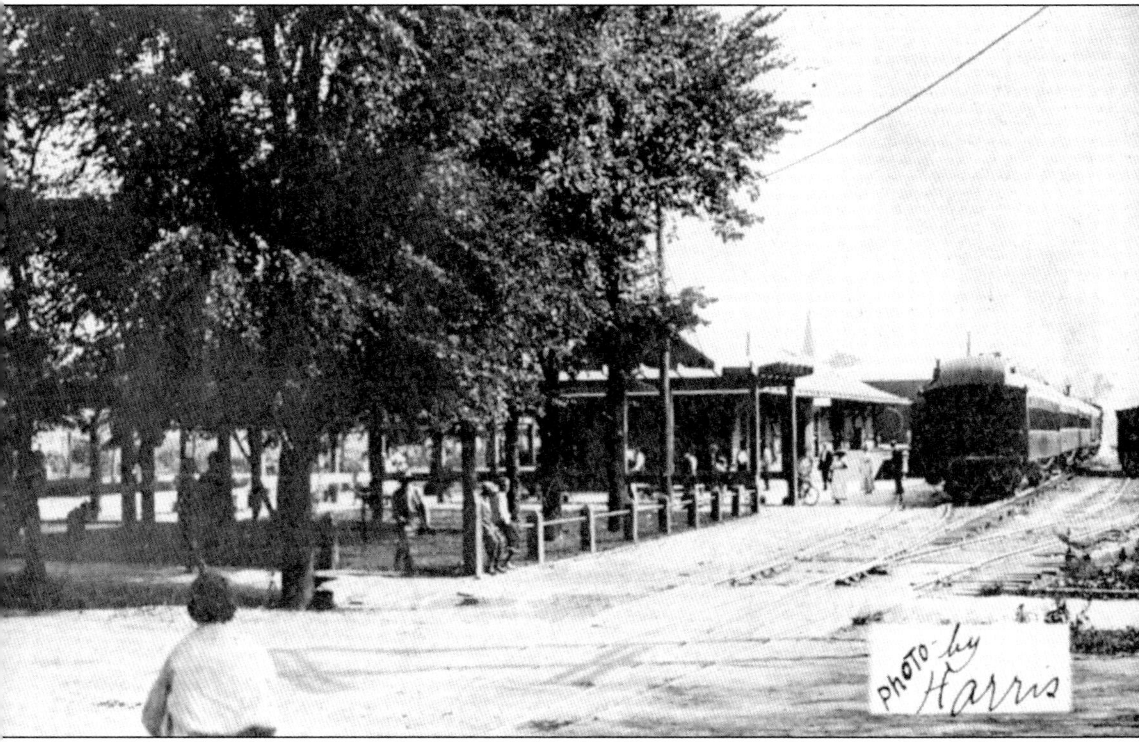

About the year 1908, the Carolina and Northwestern Railway Company constructed this new passenger and freight depot off East Liberty Street. This depot remained in service until the railroad ceased operations in the early 1970s. The building is now the home for the York Chamber of Commerce.

Five

CHURCHES AND CEMETERIES

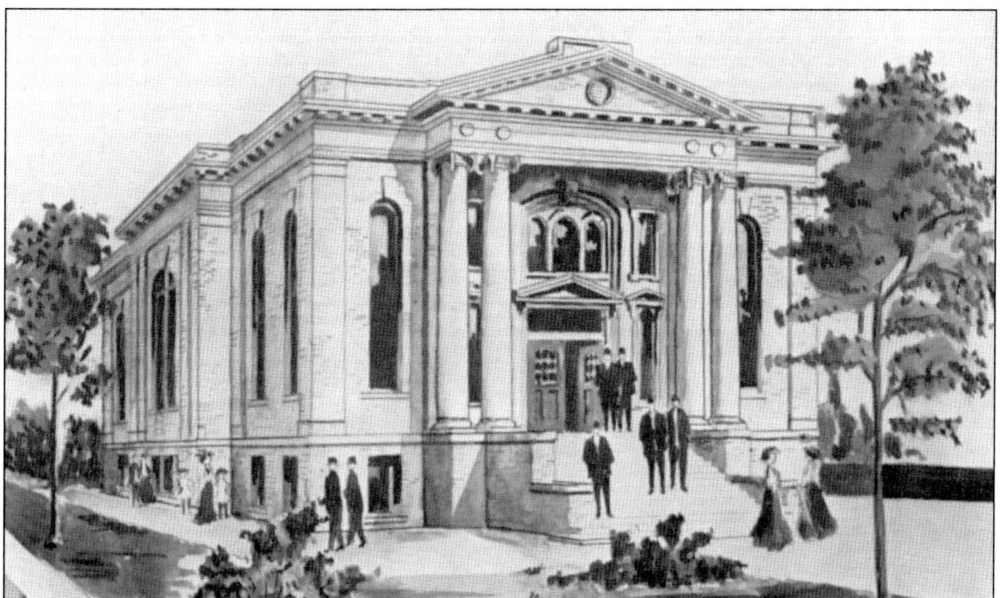

York Associate Reformed Presbyterian (ARP) Church, located at the intersection of North Congress and East Madison Streets, was founded in 1853 and originally met in a large wooden building on an adjacent lot. The present church building was constructed in 1913, as shown in this early drawing. Rev. William C. Ewart was the pastor then.

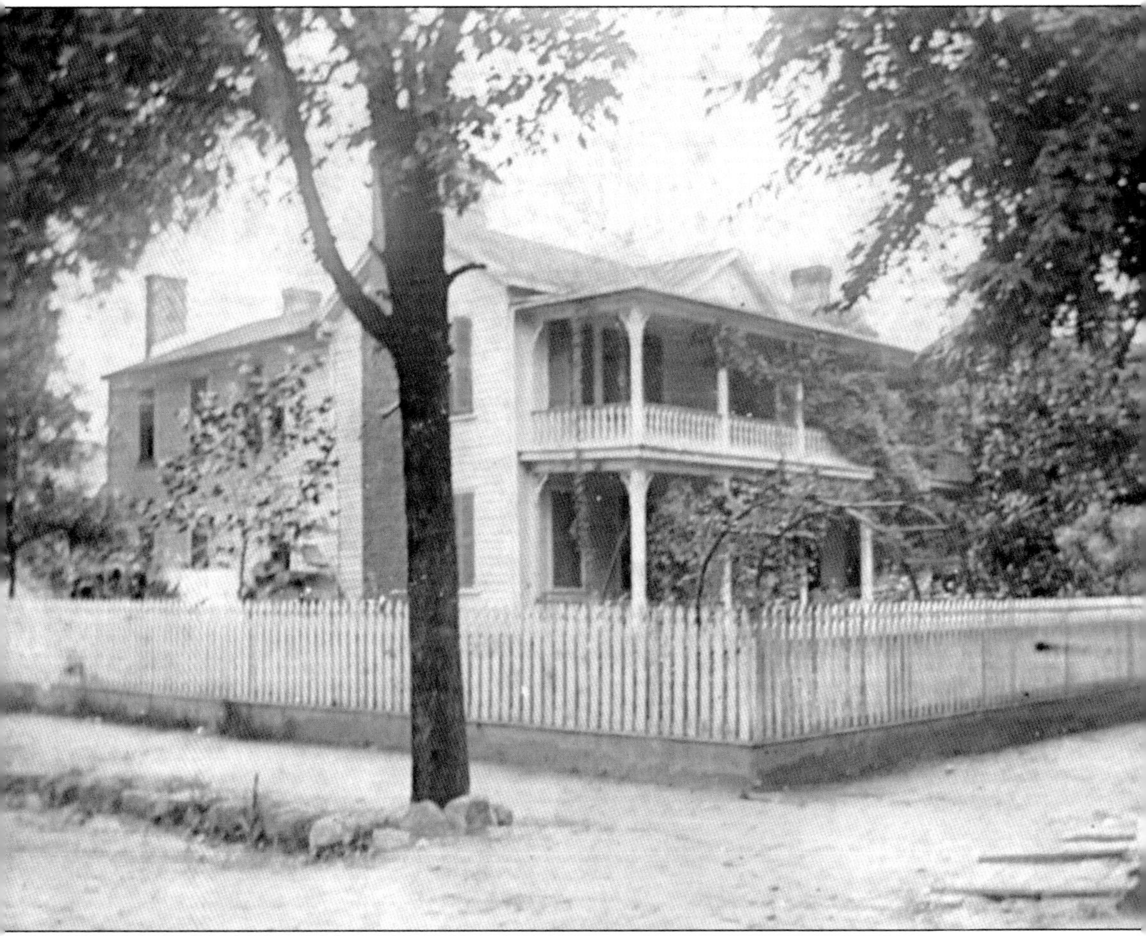

The original manse for the York ARP Church, shown in this early-20th-century photograph, was located at the corner of Madison and Congress Streets.

First Baptist Church, on the corner of South Congress and West Jefferson Streets, was organized in May 1866 as the Yorkville Baptist Church. The present building was constructed in 1891, when Rev. I. Murray was pastor. This photograph shows the church as it appeared c. 1910.

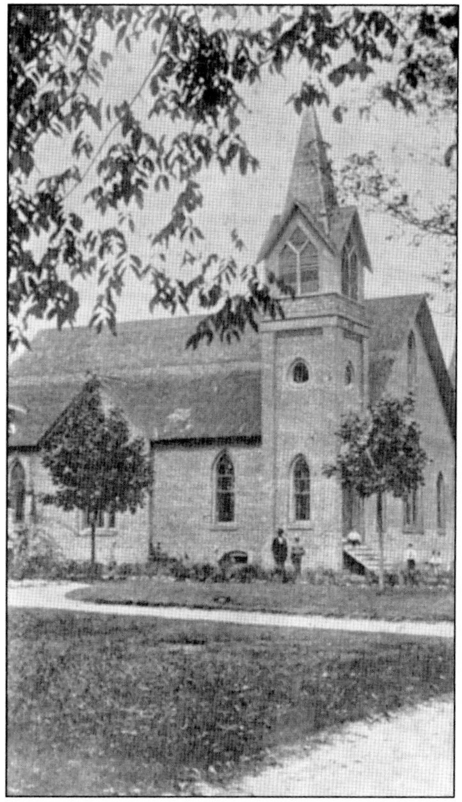

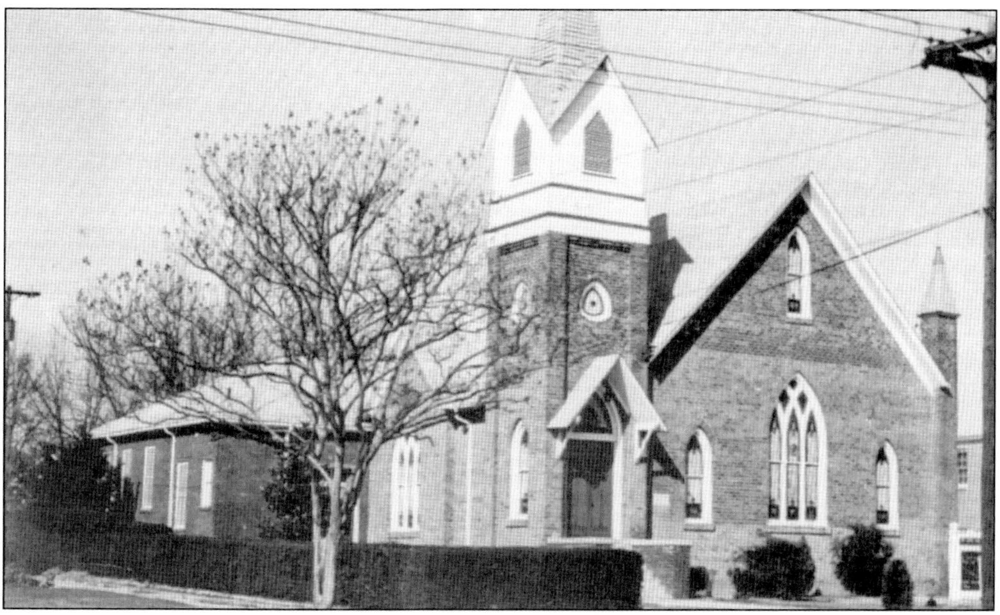

A later postcard shows the First Baptist Church as it appeared in the mid-20th century.

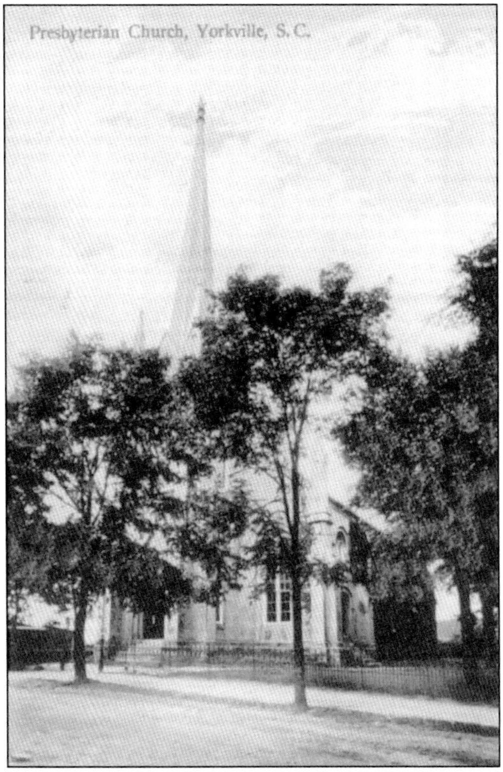

York's First Presbyterian Church was organized in 1842 and initially met in a wooden building located on West Liberty Street, across the street from its present location. Rev. Ernest E. Gillespie was the pastor when this photograph of the second church building was taken *c.* 1908.

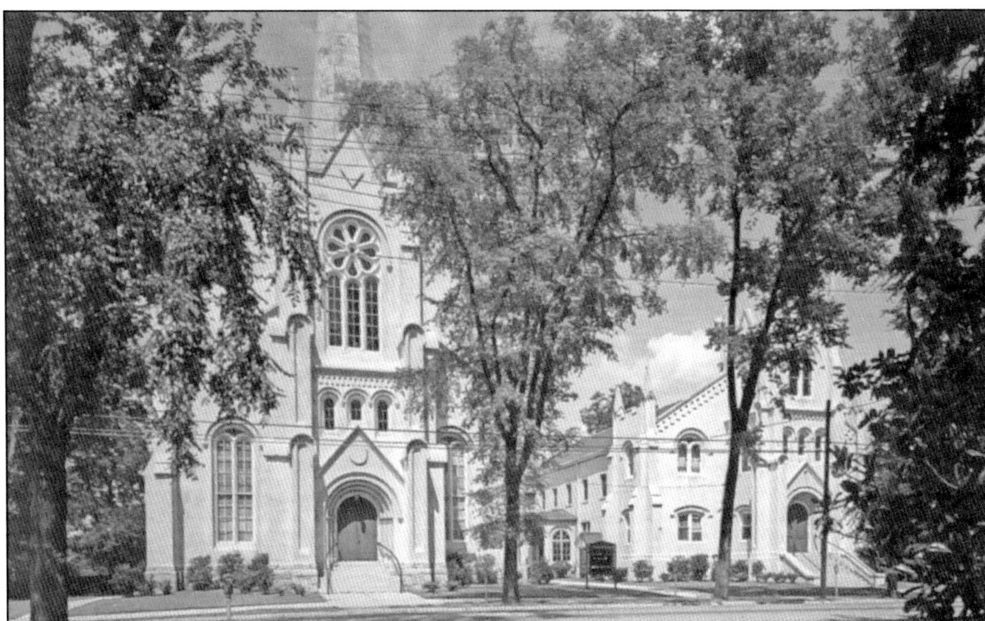

Designed by Charleston architect Robert Walker in 1846, construction of the present First Presbyterian Church building began *c.* 1860 and was not completed until after the end of the Civil War. This later photograph of the First Presbyterian Church comes from a mid-20th-century postcard. The building to the right contains the church offices.

The Church of the Good Shepherd on East Liberty Street was officially established in 1852 and was the first Episcopal church in York County. The plain, Gothic-style sanctuary was constructed in 1855 on a lot donated by Dr. J. M. Lowry. When this photograph was taken *c.* 1908, the rector was Rev. J. O. Babbin (or Bablin).

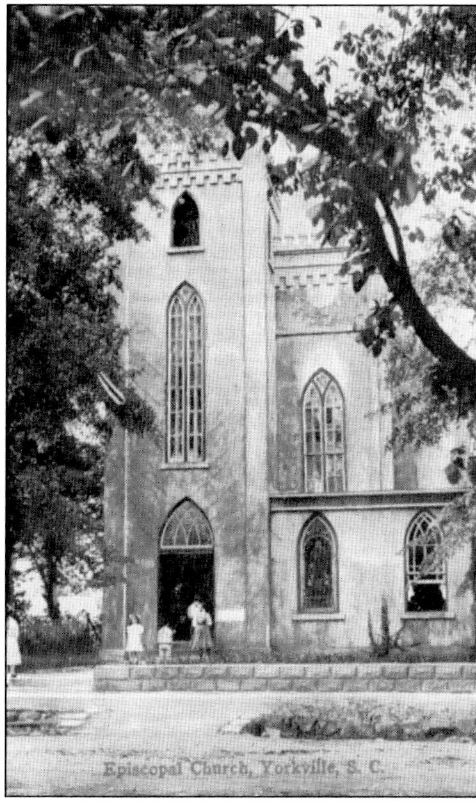

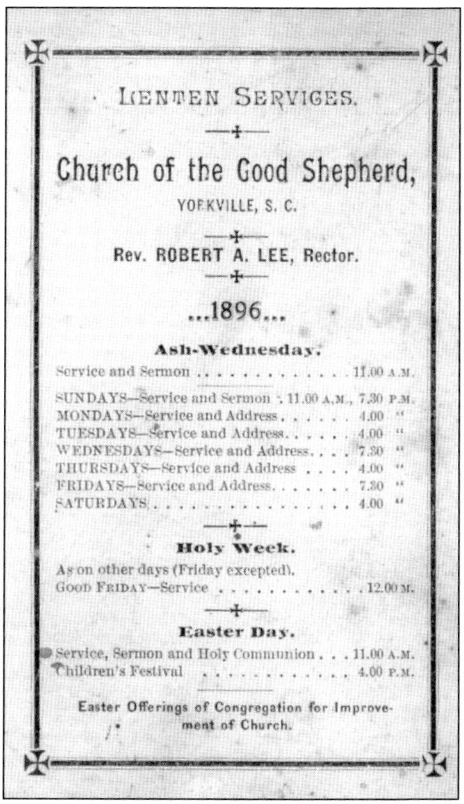

LENTEN SERVICES.

Church of the Good Shepherd,

YORKVILLE, S. C.

Rev. ROBERT A. LEE, Rector.

...1896...

Ash-Wednesday.

Service and Sermon . . . . 11.00 A.M.

SUNDAYS—Service and Sermon . 11.00 A.M., 7.30 P.M.
MONDAYS—Service and Address . . . . . . 4.00 "
TUESDAYS—Service and Address. . . . . . 4.00 "
WEDNESDAYS—Service and Address. . . . 7.30 "
THURSDAYS—Service and Address . . . . 4.00 "
FRIDAYS—Service and Address. . . . . . . 7.30 "
SATURDAYS . . . . 4.00 "

Holy Week.

As on other days (Friday excepted).
GOOD FRIDAY—Service . . . . 12.00 M.

Easter Day.

Service, Sermon and Holy Communion . . . 11.00 A.M.
Children's Festival . . . . 4.00 P.M.

Easter Offerings of Congregation for Improvement of Church.

This Lenten services bulletin for the Episcopal Church of the Good Shepherd dates to the year 1896.

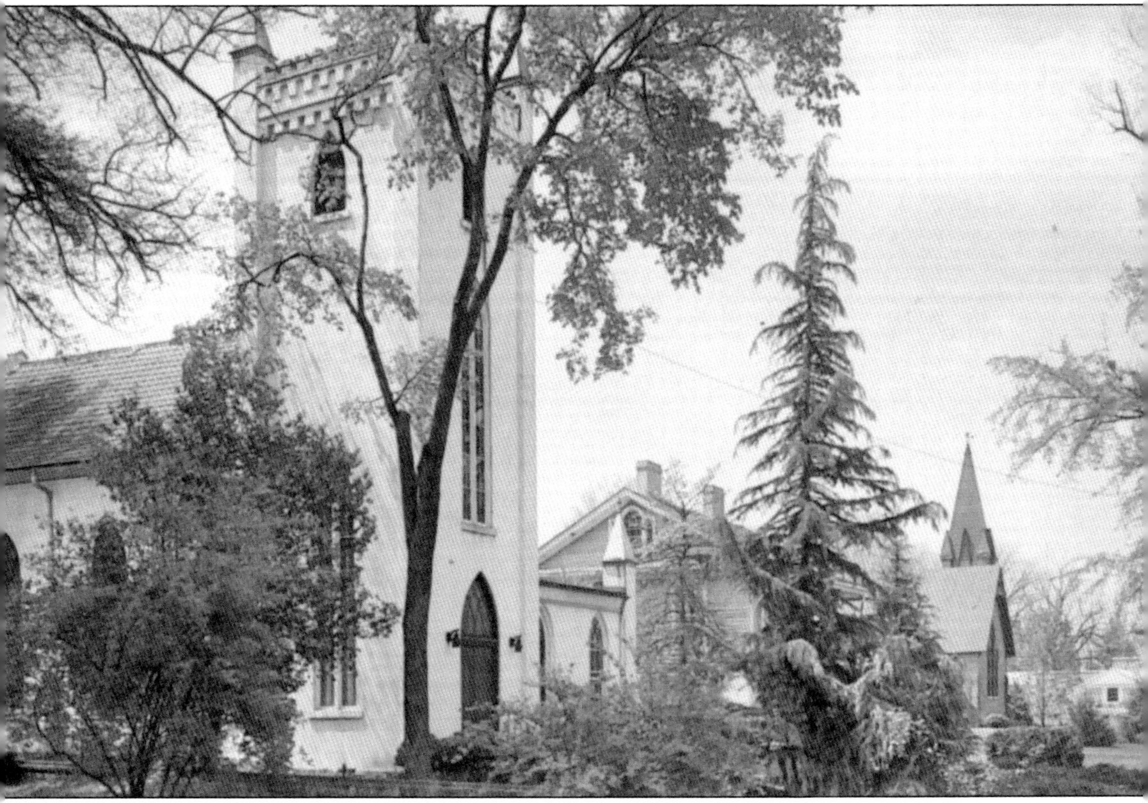

This nice view of the Episcopal Church of the Good Shepherd and Trinity Methodist Church shows the close proximity of the two churches on East Liberty Street, with the Episcopal church parish house located between the two.

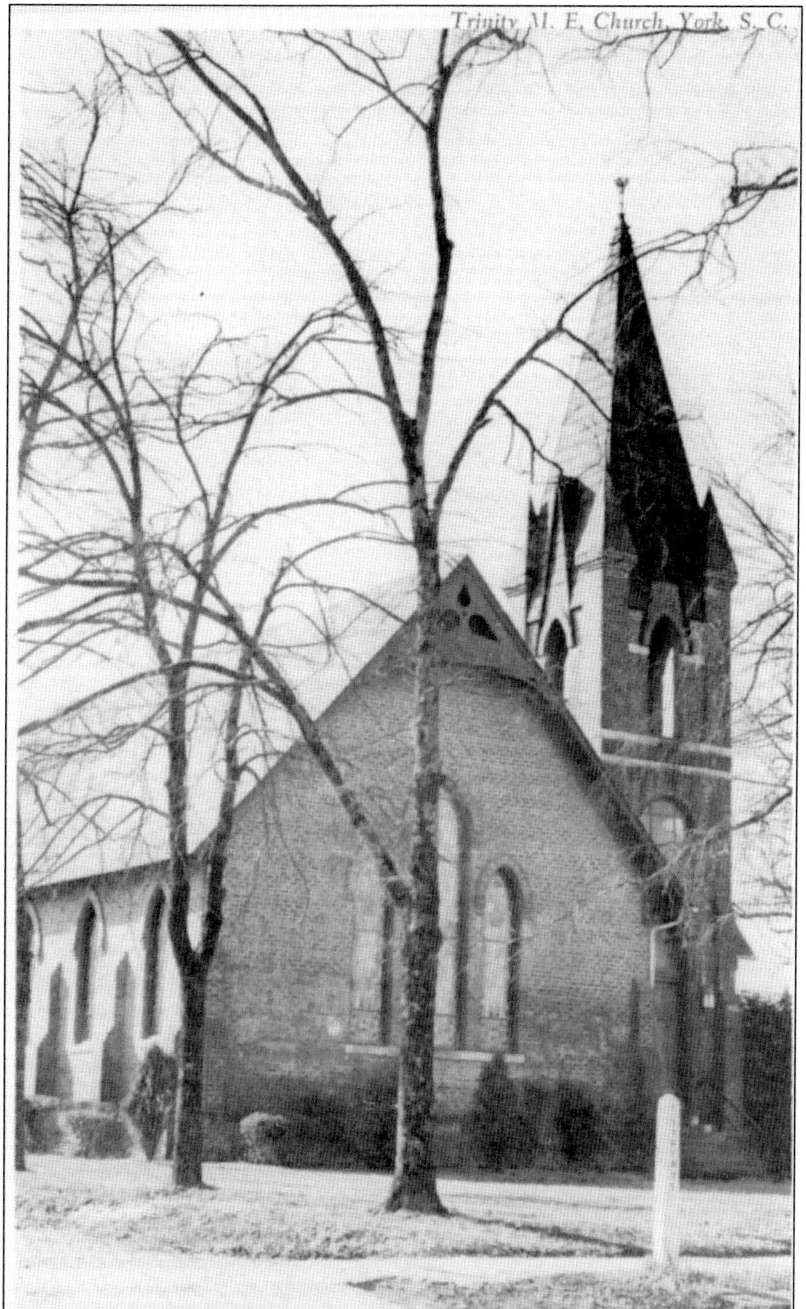

Trinity Methodist Church, originally known as Trinity Methodist Episcopal Church, was organized by Rev. William Gassaway in 1824. The first church building was a wooden structure located on Trinity Street adjacent to the old Trinity Cemetery. In 1882, the congregation moved to the former Independent Presbyterian Church building on East Liberty, where Rose Hill Cemetery is now located. The present Trinity Methodist Church building, located at the corner of Trinity and East Liberty Streets, was constructed in 1890 and is shown in this photograph from the early 1900s.

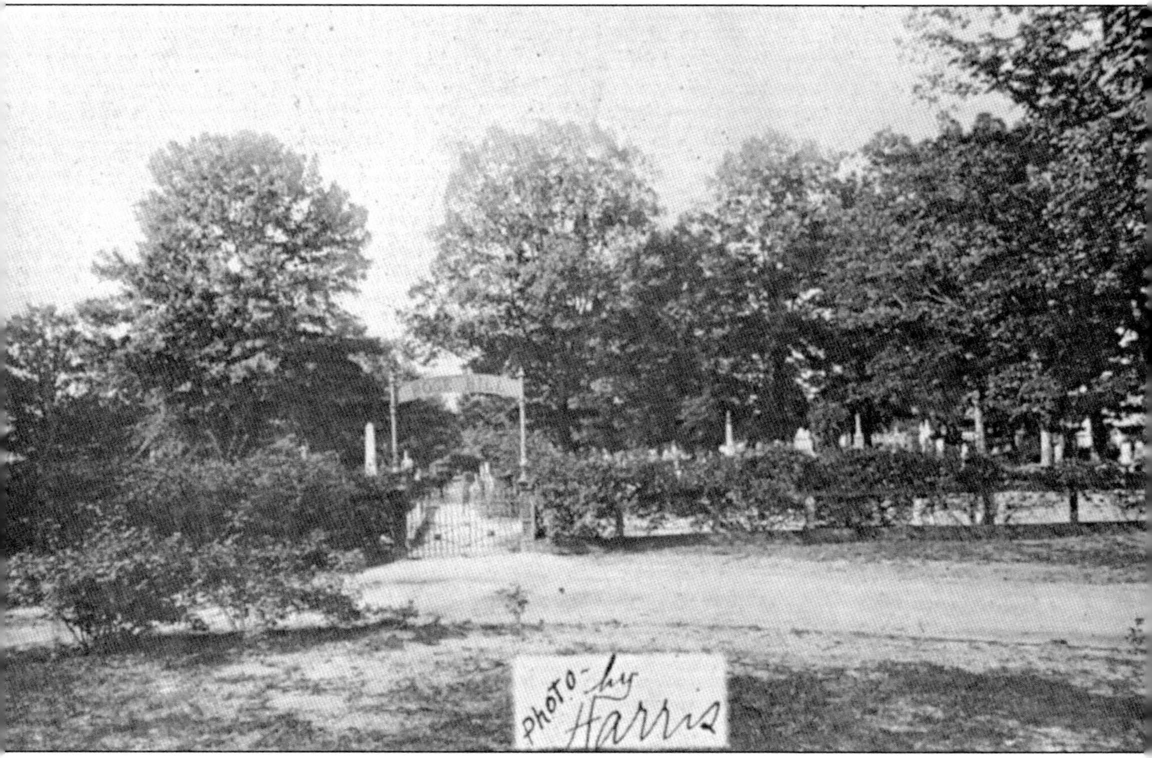

The Rose Hill cemetery was organized in 1829 on the former site of the Independent Presbyterian Church, at the corner of East Liberty and Cemetery Streets. Rose Hill is a privately owned burial ground operated by a self-perpetuating board of directors and includes the graves of many of York's most famous and prominent citizens.

Six

SCHOOLS

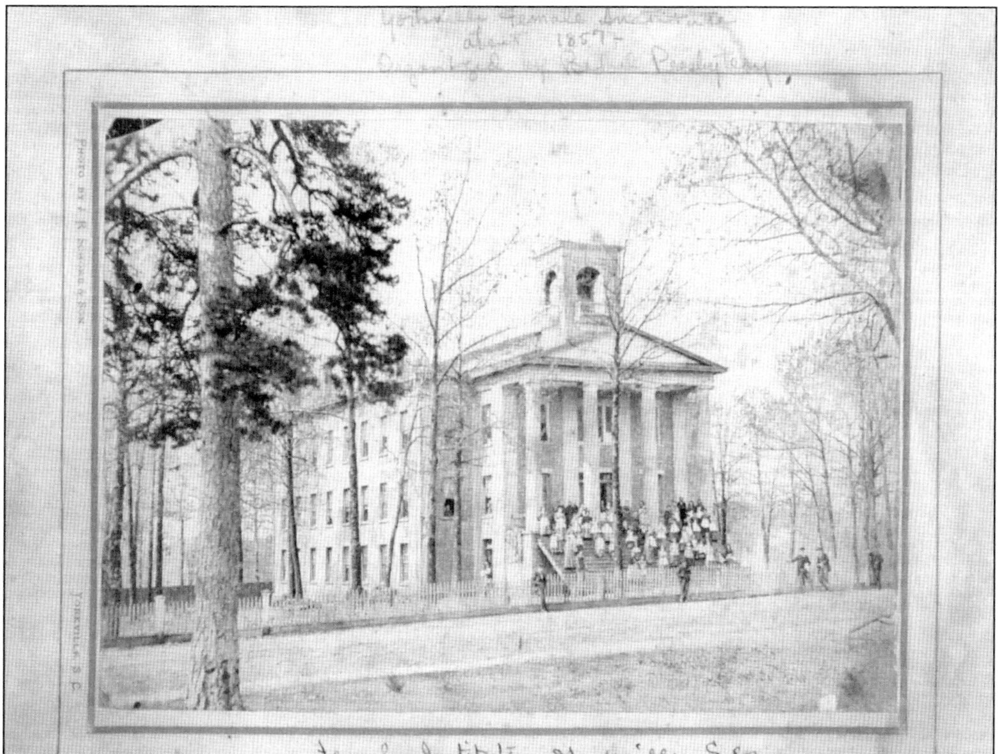

The Yorkville Female Institute was founded by the Bethel Presbytery in 1852 on the site now occupied by the McCelvey Center on Jefferson Street. This photograph of the Yorkville Female Institute was taken *c.* 1857. In the 1860s and 1870s, the school was known variously as the Yorkville Female College, the Yorkville Female Seminary, and the Yorkville Female Institute. Boys were admitted in 1879. In 1888, the school ceased operations as a private facility for girls and boys and went public as the Yorkville Graded School. The building was completely destroyed by fire *c.* 1900.

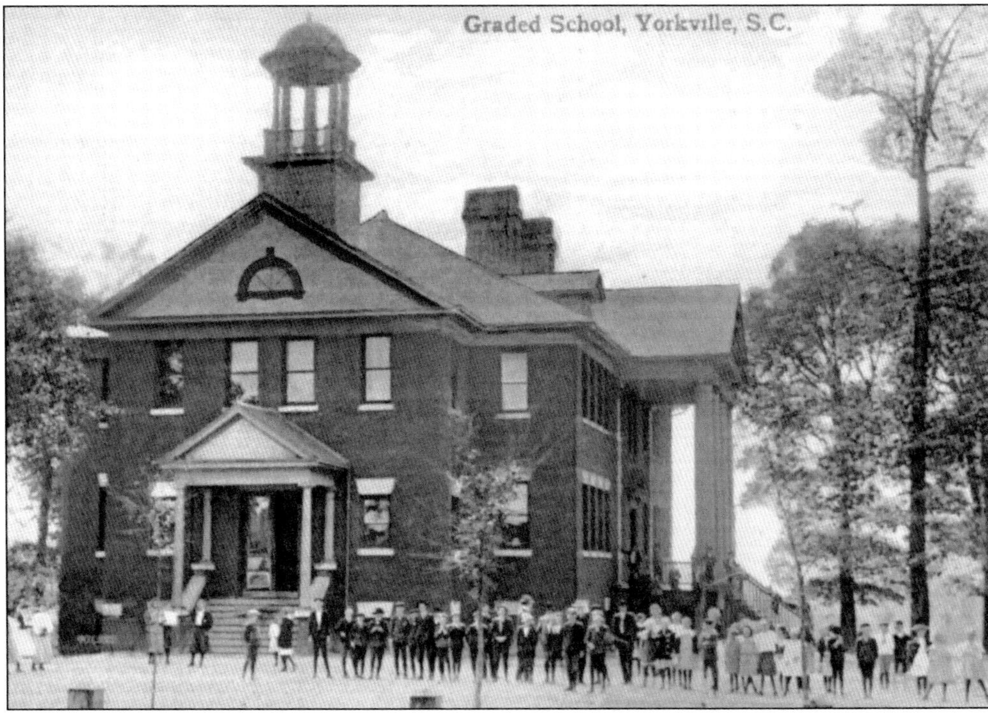

After it burned, the Yorkville Graded School was rebuilt in 1902 and officially opened in April 1903. This photograph shows the building as it appeared c. 1908.

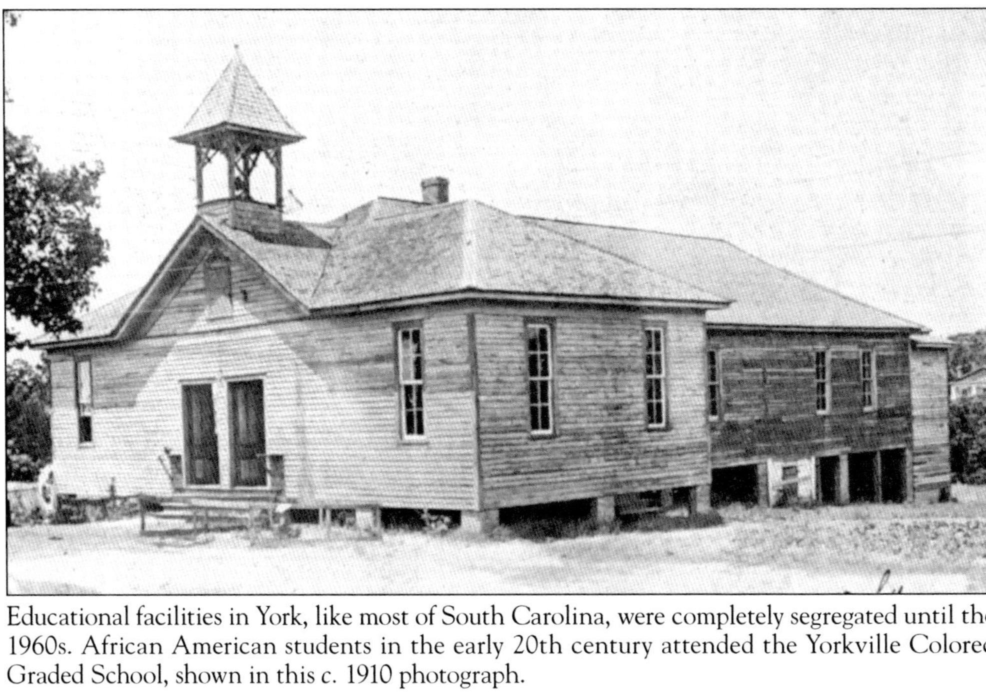

Educational facilities in York, like most of South Carolina, were completely segregated until the 1960s. African American students in the early 20th century attended the Yorkville Colored Graded School, shown in this c. 1910 photograph.

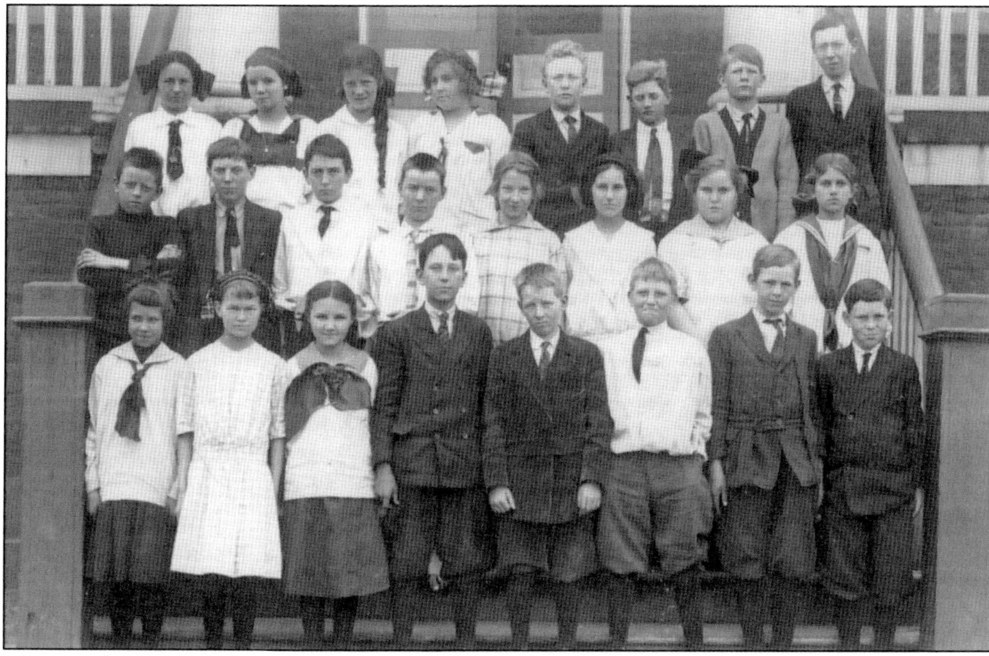

This is a class picture from the Yorkville Graded School *c.* 1915. The students' names are written on the back of the postcard as follows, from left to right: (first row) Dell Alexander, Mattie Mae Brown, Mamie Bratton, Robert Betts, Henry Stafford, Joe Wardlaw, Withers Adickes, and Tommy Speck; (second row) Landon Louthiane, Edison Wallace, Tom Woods, unidentified, Viola Johnson, Miriam Betts, Sue Meek Allison, and Sarah Jones; (third row) Mary Hope, unidentified, Pauline Oates, unidentified, Joe Herndon, J. W. Quinn, Henry Whitener, and Tracy Walsh.

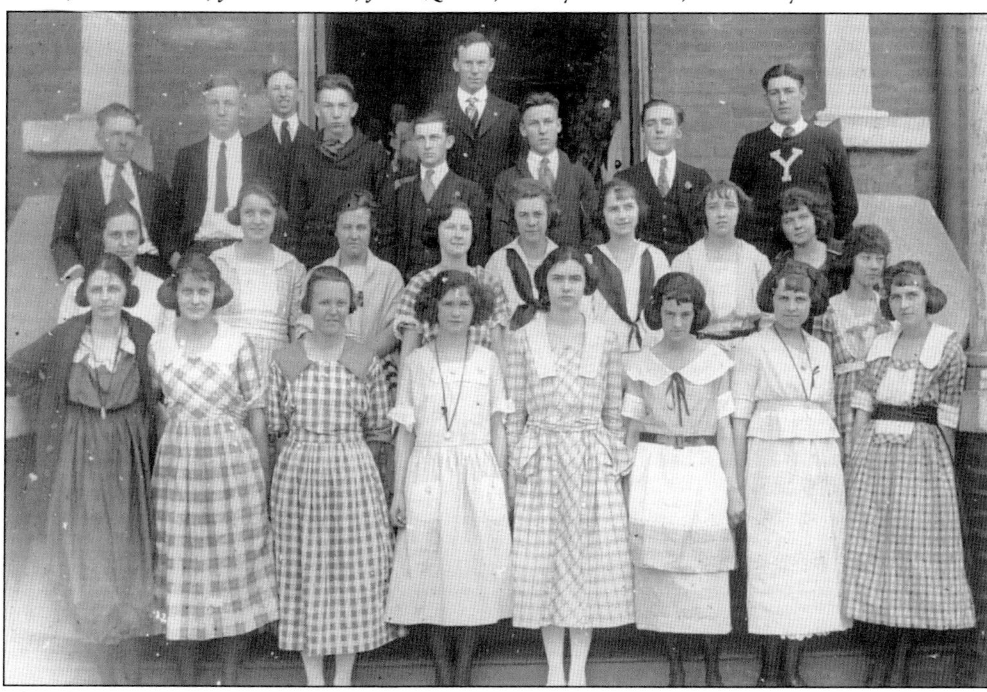

This class picture from Yorkville High School is also dated *c.* 1915.

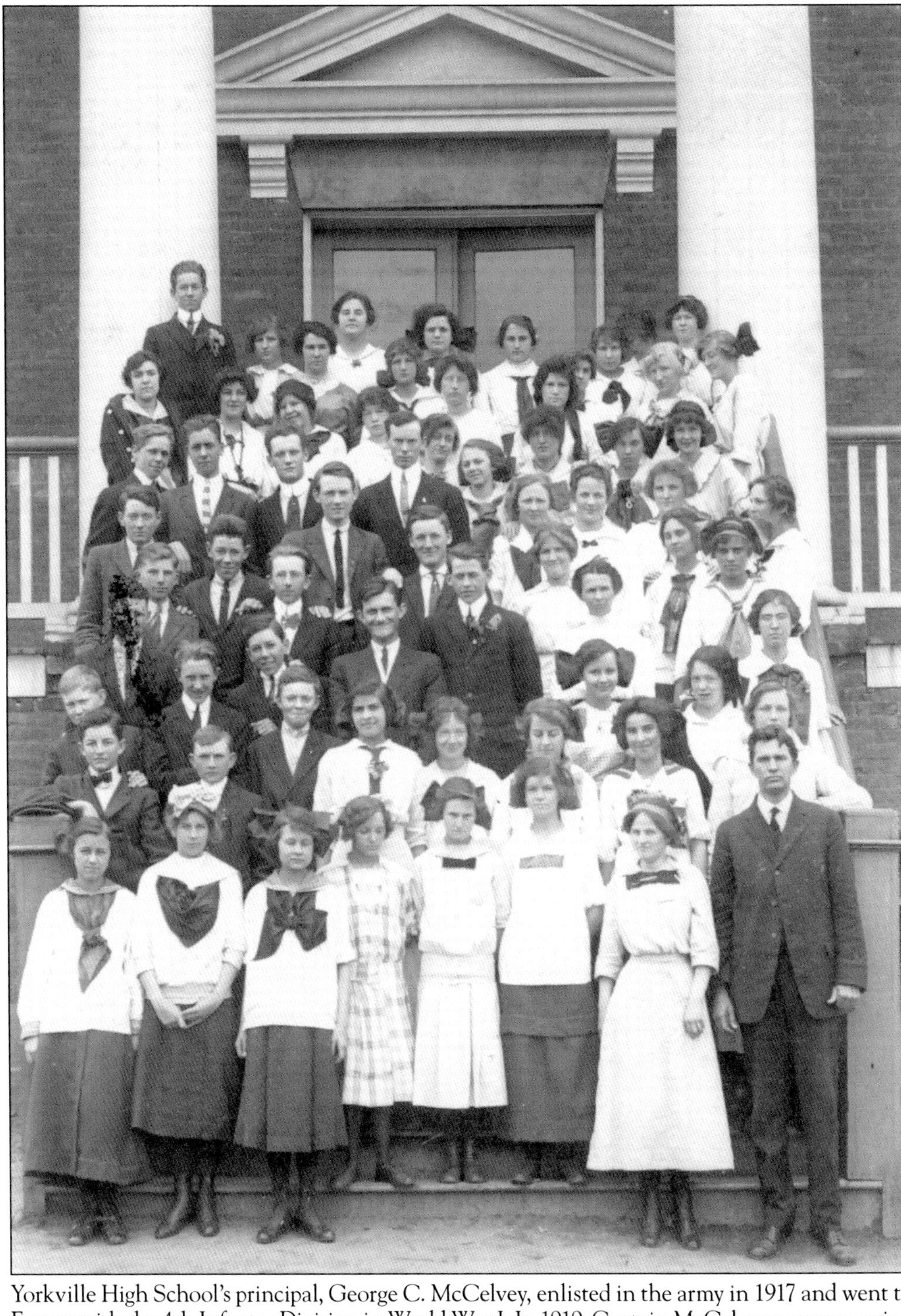

Yorkville High School's principal, George C. McCelvey, enlisted in the army in 1917 and went to France with the 4th Infantry Division in World War I. In 1919, Captain McCelvey was recovering from wounds received in the war when he received this postcard with a picture of his students at Yorkville High School. The following notation was written on the back: "My dear Captain, Much welcome to our over-seas boys, and best wishes for a speedy and complete recovery for 'Mac.' "

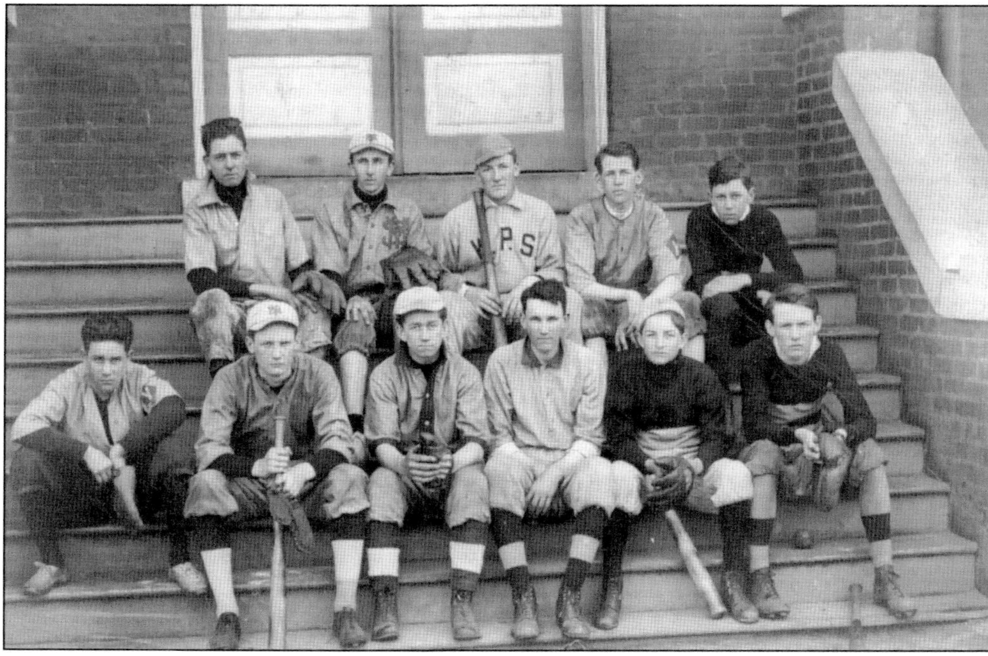

This photograph shows the Yorkville High School baseball team c. 1915 posing at the side-entrance steps to the building.

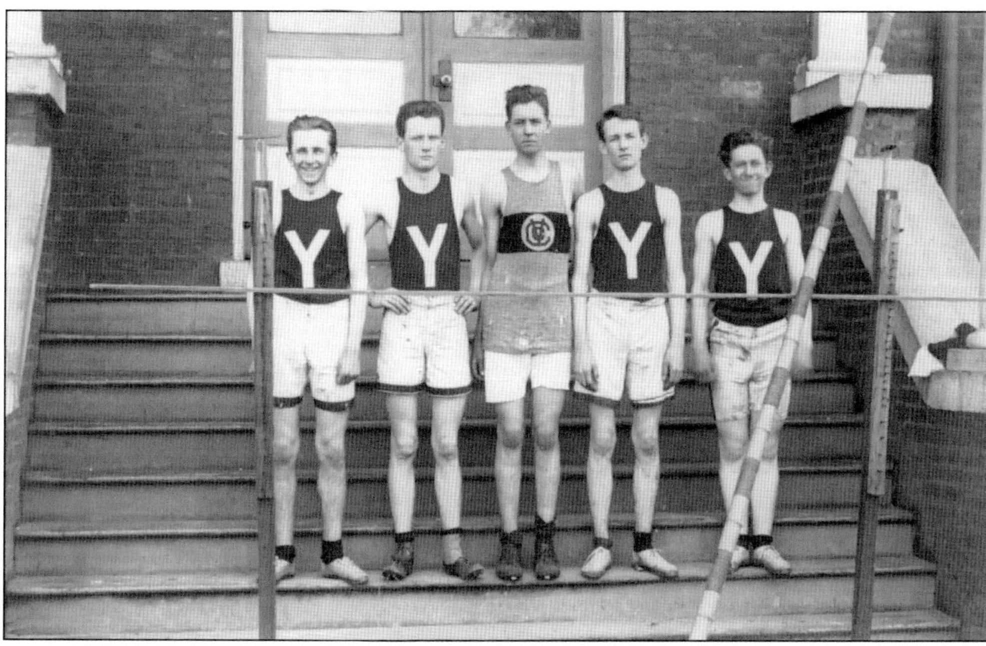

Another athletic program at Yorkville High School was the pole jumping team, shown in this photograph taken c. 1915.

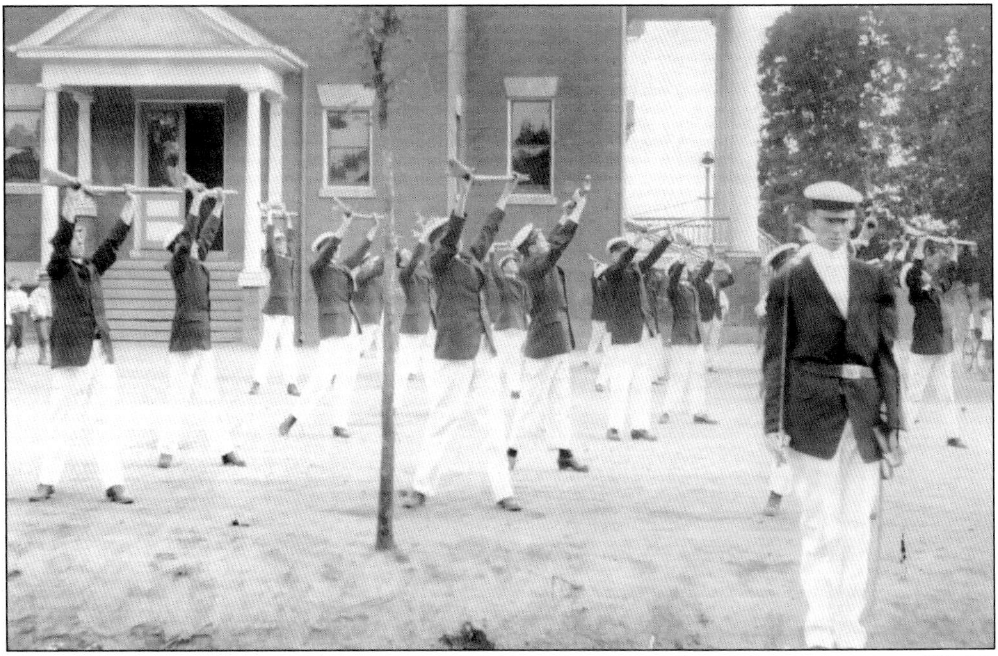

The Yorkville High School military company (shown here *c.* 1915) was the predecessor of York's modern high school ROTC programs.

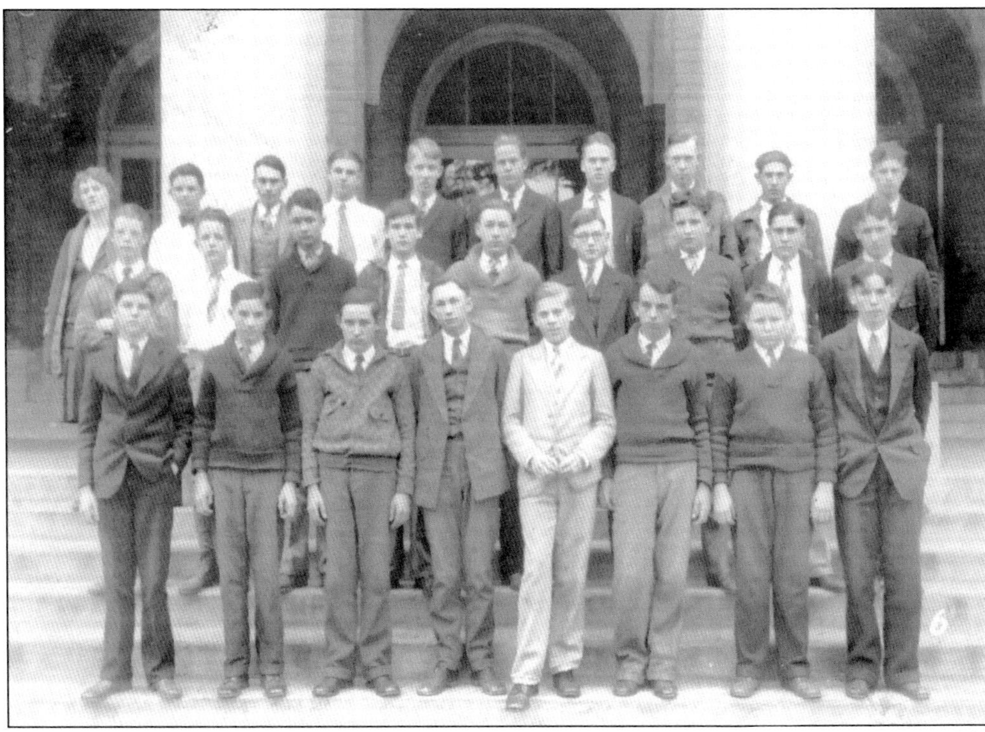

The Yorkville High School ninth-grade class posed for this photograph on the front steps of the school in 1928.

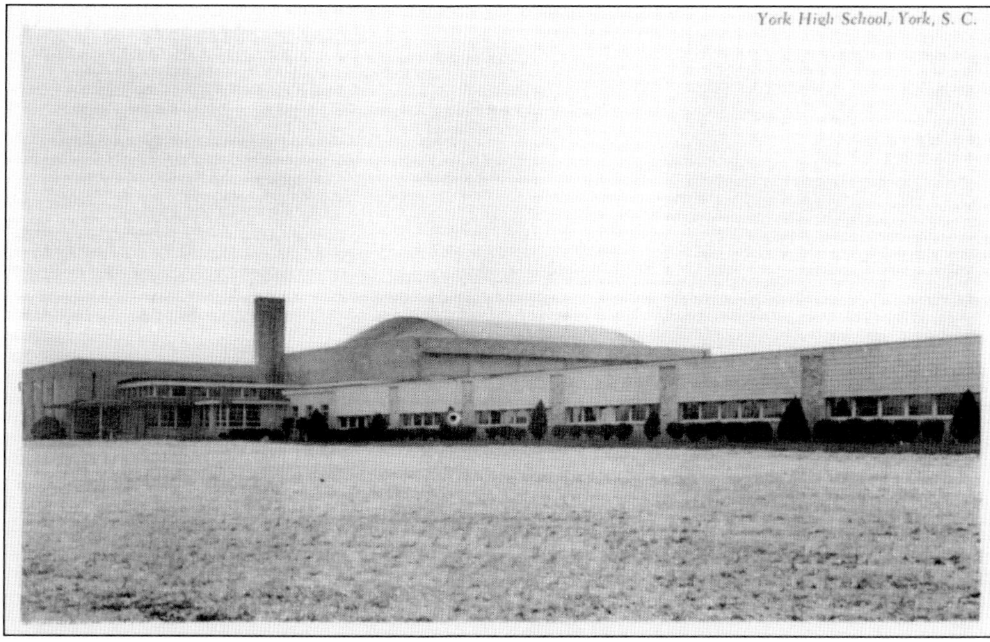

In 1955, this new York High School building was built about one mile east of the York Graded School on Jefferson Street. The old school building then became York Elementary School. This postcard image shows the school as it appeared in the early 1960s. It is now Harold C. Johnson Middle School.

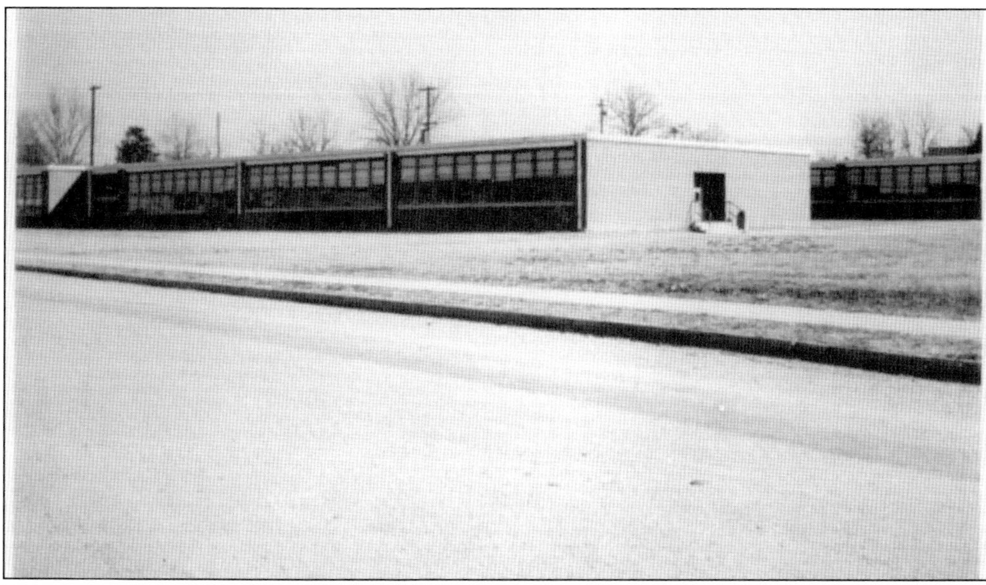

The 1950s saw new school buildings erected and old ones renovated for African American students in York. A new African American elementary school called Jefferson Elementary School, seen in this postcard image from the early 1960s, was constructed in 1955. At the same time, the all-black Jefferson High School received a new classroom wing that included a shop and science laboratory. These schools remained segregated until the 1970–1971 school year, when all of the schools in York were fully integrated. The old Jefferson school buildings now function as school district offices.

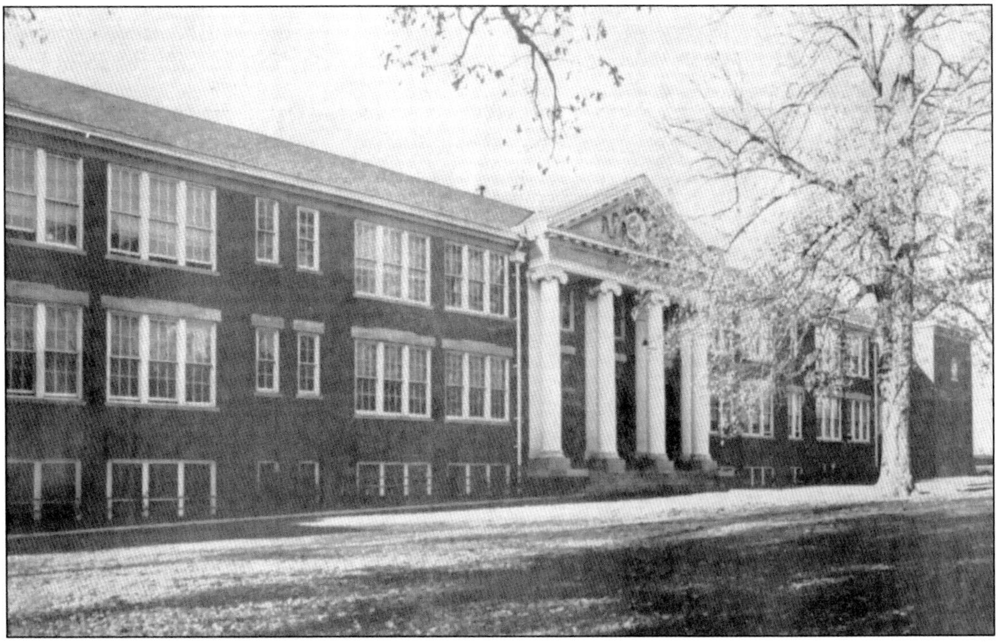

The old Yorkville Graded School building was extensively remodeled in 1922. This photograph shows the front of the school as it appeared in the early 1960s, when it was known as York Elementary School.

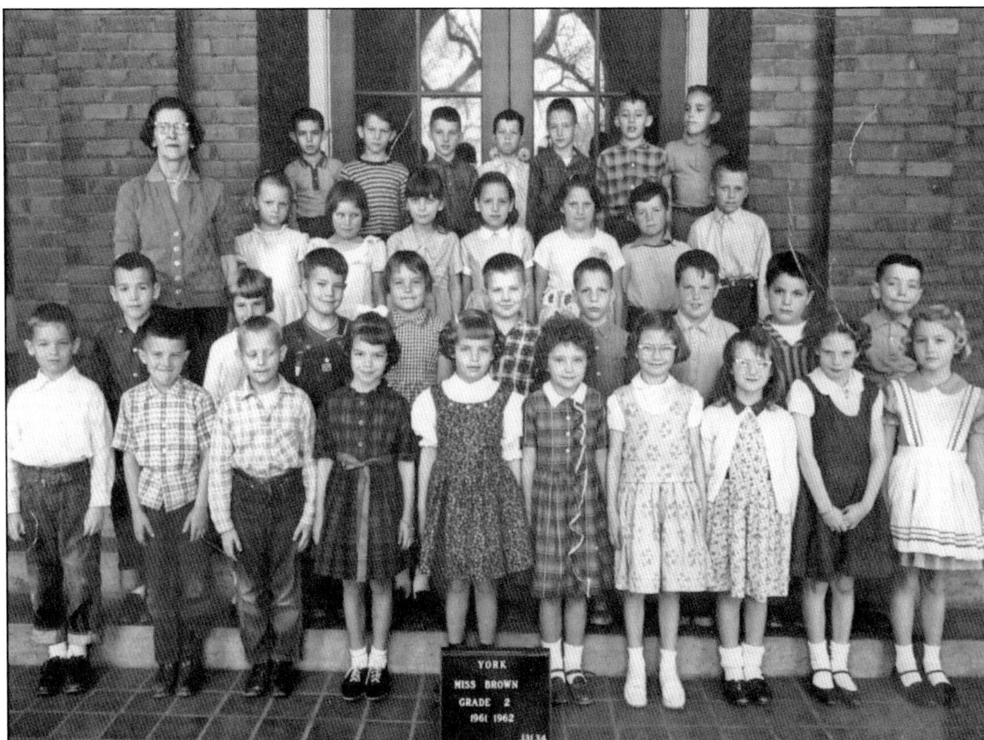

This photograph shows Louise Brown's second-grade class at York Elementary School for the school year 1961–1962.

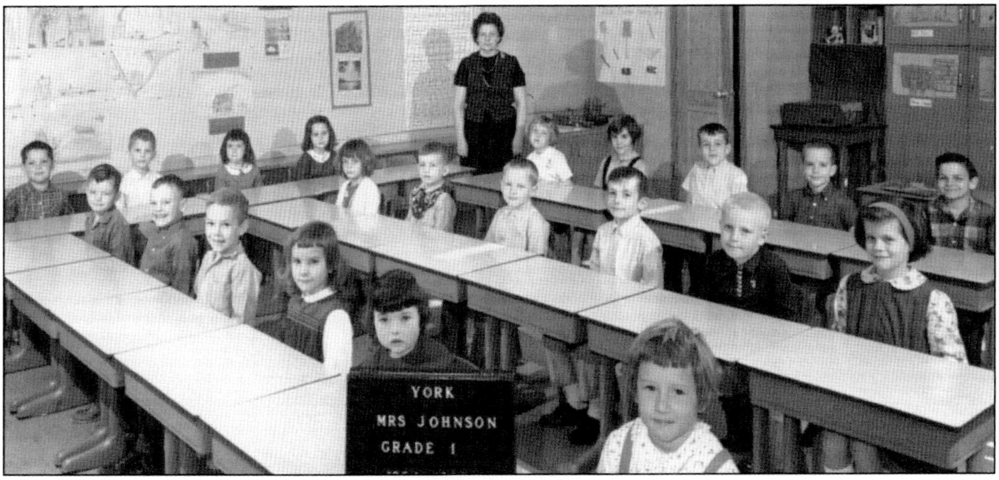

Elizabeth Johnson's first-grade class at York Elementary School for the school year 1964–1965 met in the annex building, a later single-story brick addition built in the 1950s.

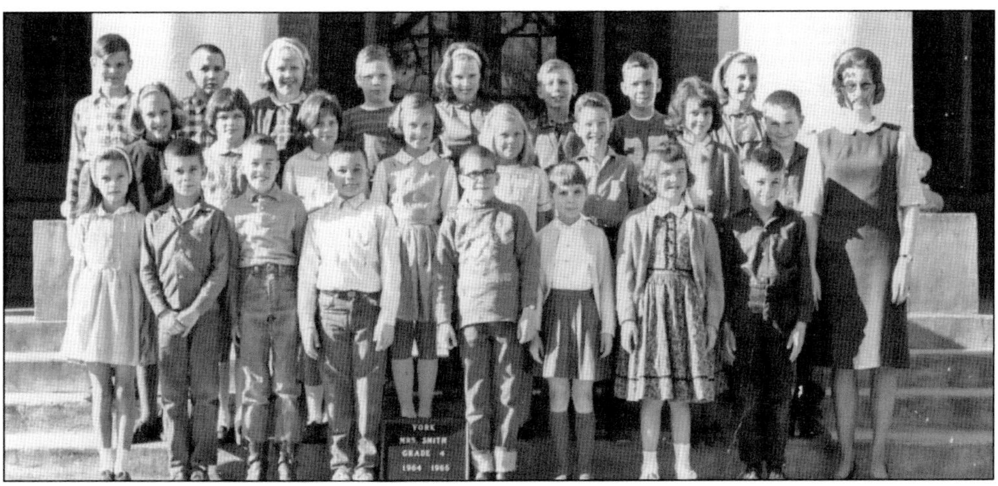
Merwyn Smith's fourth-grade class for the school year 1964–1965 posed for this photograph on the front steps of York Elementary School.

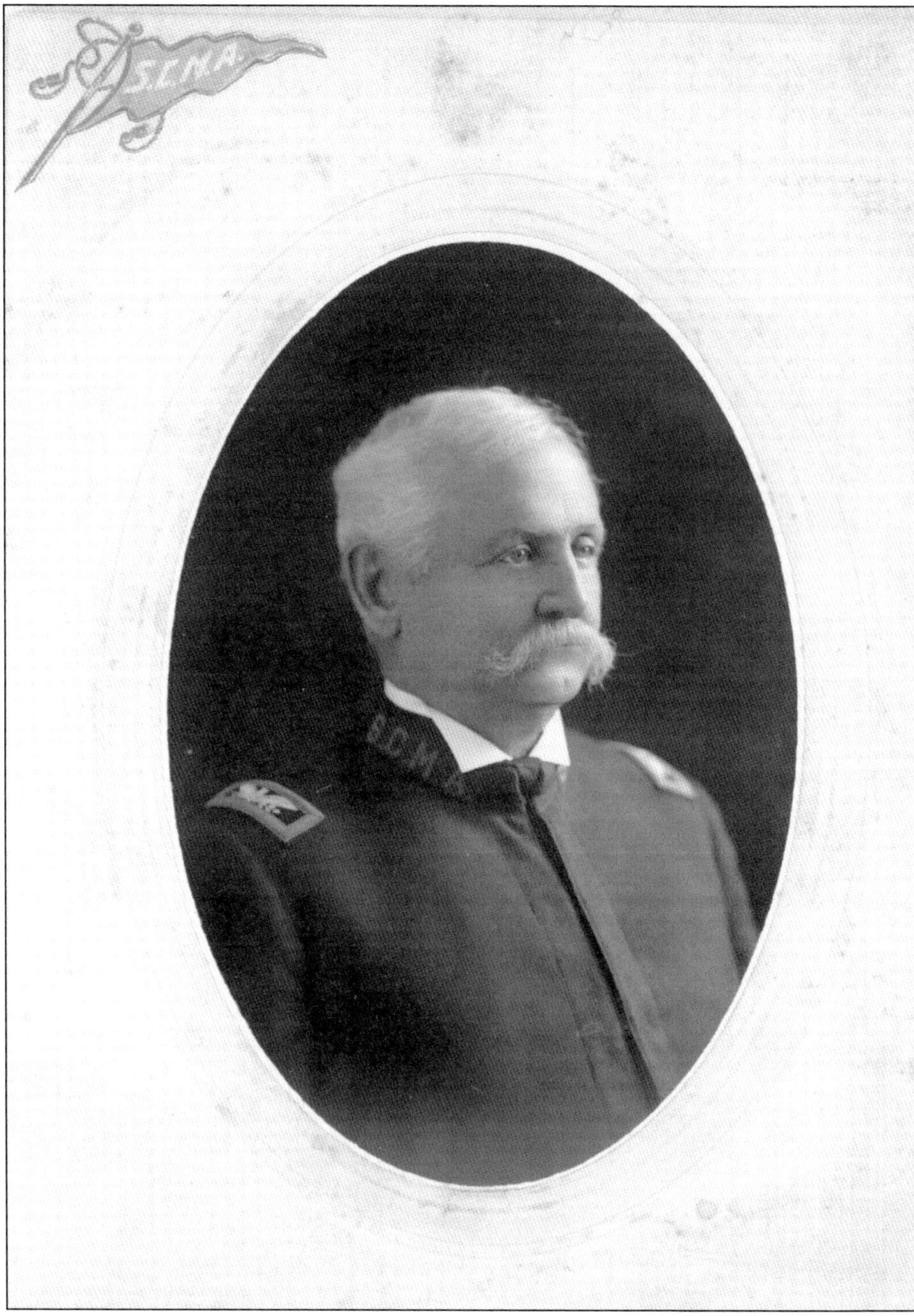

Asbury Coward was a Charleston native and a graduate of the Citadel. In 1855, he and fellow Citadel classmate Micah Jenkins from Edisto Island founded the Kings Mountain Military School on Kings Mountain Street in Yorkville. The school was designed to prepare boys for entrance into either of South Carolina's military academies, the Citadel or the Arsenal Academy in Columbia, and it was very successful. In 1861, the school closed because of the Civil War. Coward served as colonel of the 5th South Carolina Infantry Regiment during the war, and after the war, he reopened the school, which he ran until 1886. Colonel Coward also served as South Carolina's superintendent of education for four years and as director of the Citadel for 18 years.

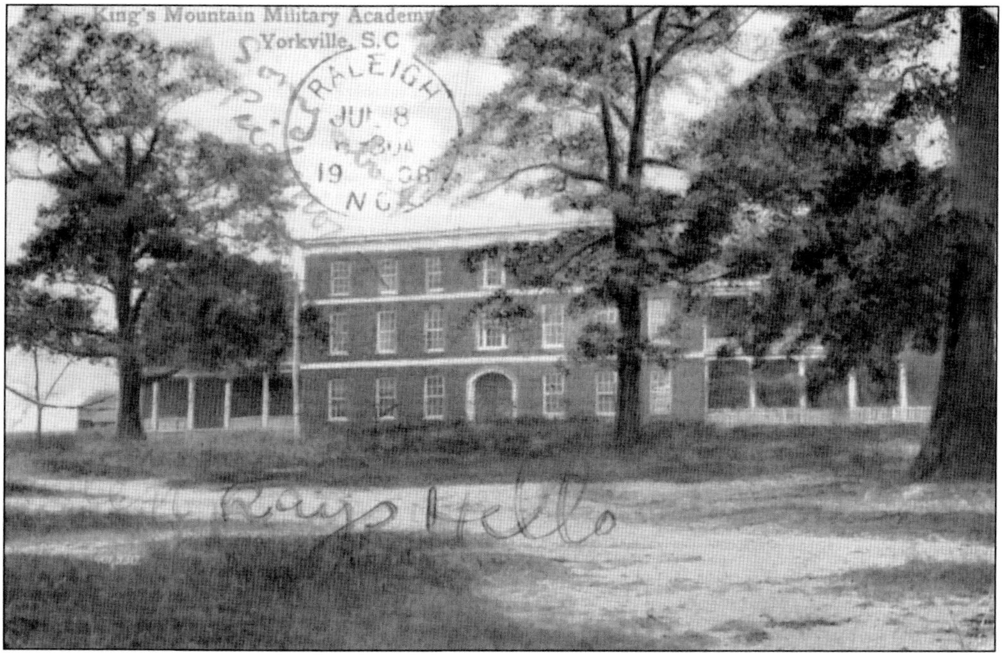

After Asbury Coward closed the Kings Mountain Military School in 1886, there were several unsuccessful attempts to reopen the school. Around 1900, Col. W. G. Stephenson gave the school a new start as the Kings Mountain Military Academy. This view of the academy comes from a postcard dated 1908. The school closed for good a year later.

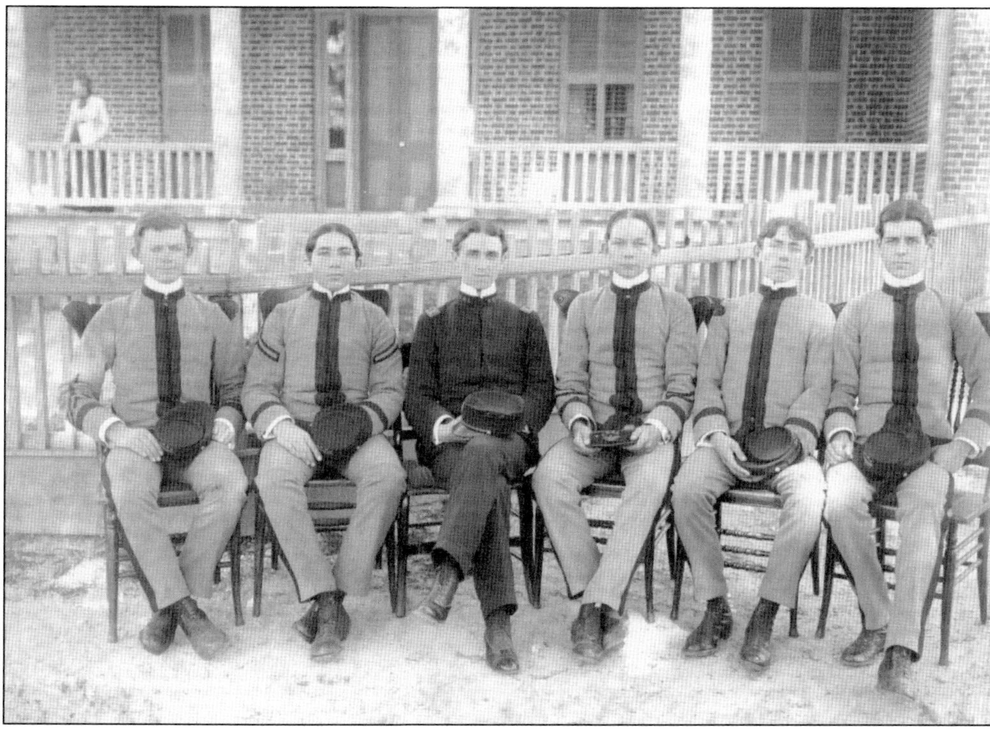

This photograph shows a group of Kings Mountain Military Academy cadets c. 1900.

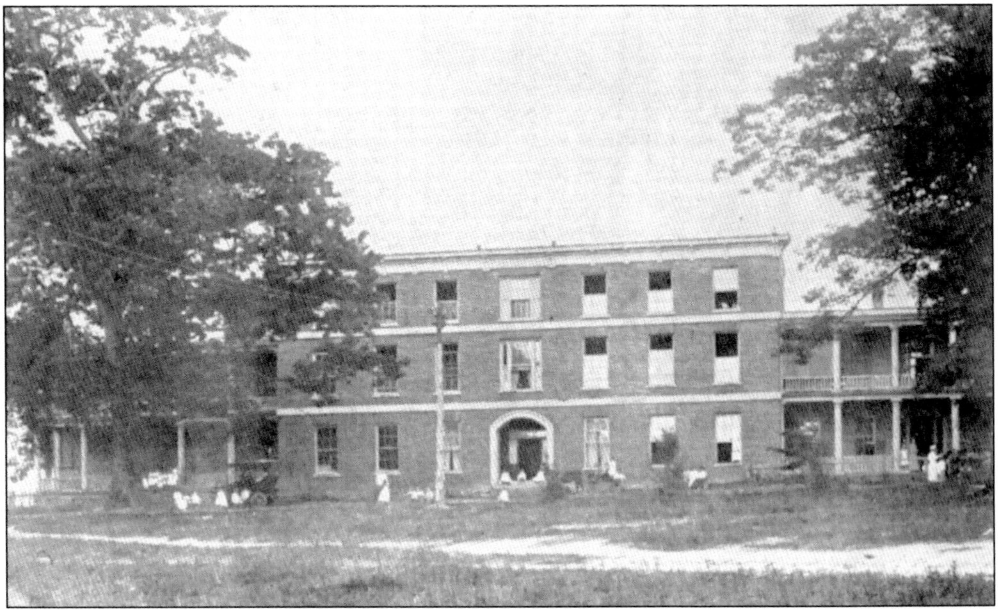

The Episcopal Church Home Orphanage of Charleston purchased the old Kings Mountain Military School site and moved its operations to Yorkville in 1909. This photograph of the orphanage dates to c. 1910, after it had commenced operations at the old military school.

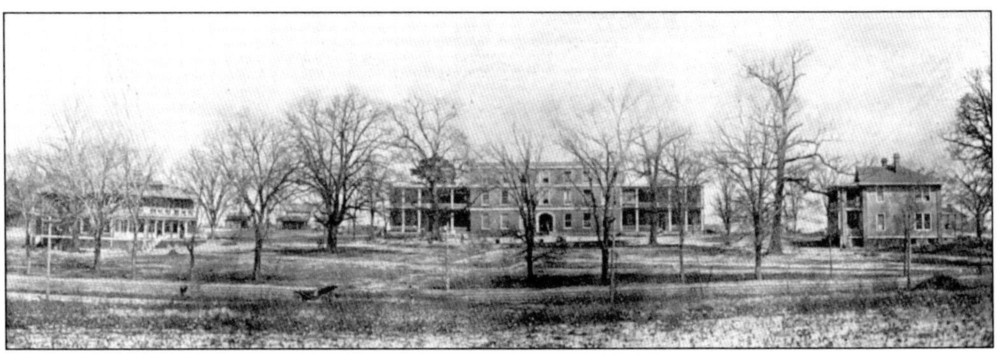

This panorama of the Church Home Orphanage shows the Capers Memorial Building on the left, the main school building in the middle, and the Elizabeth Martin Memorial Cottage on the right. These original buildings were all replaced with modern structures during the 20th century.

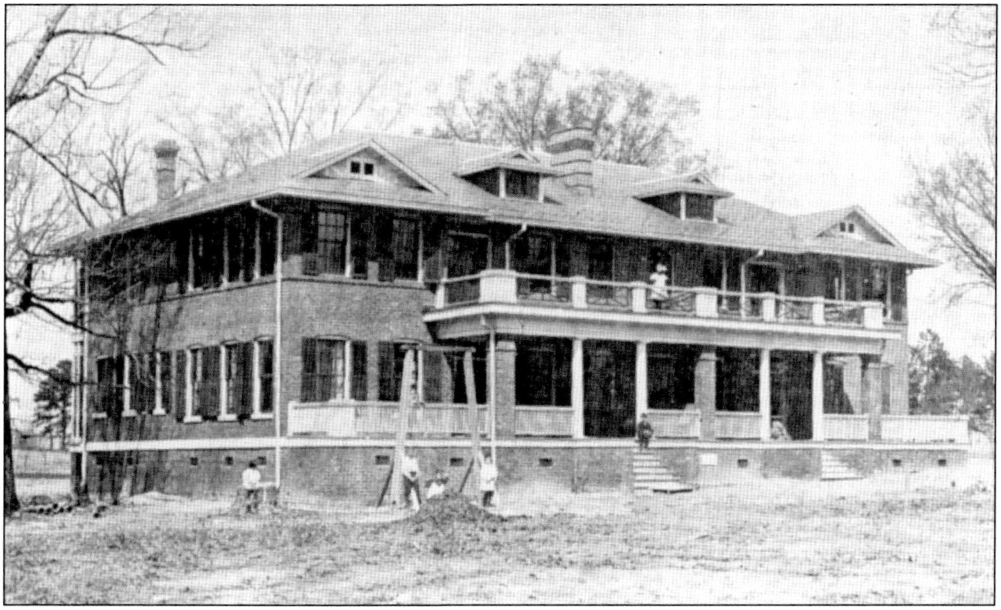

The Capers Memorial Building at the Church Home Orphanage acted as the school's dormitory, as seen in this early-20th-century photograph.

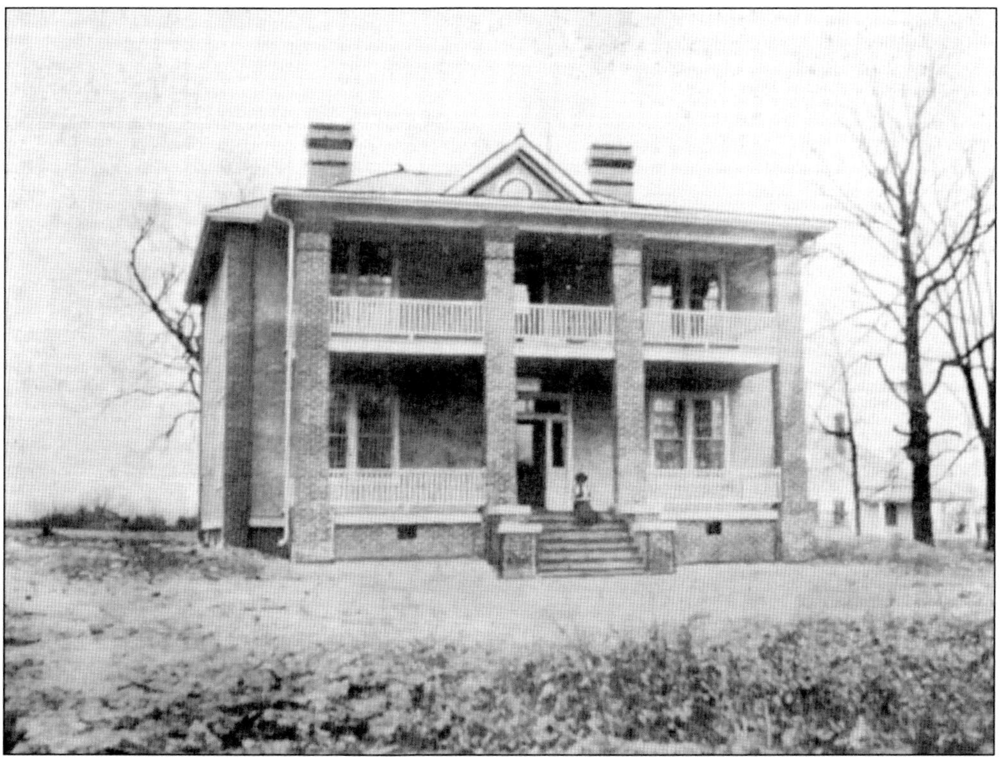

The Elizabeth Martin Memorial Cottage at the Church Home Orphanage was used for administration purposes in the early 20th century.

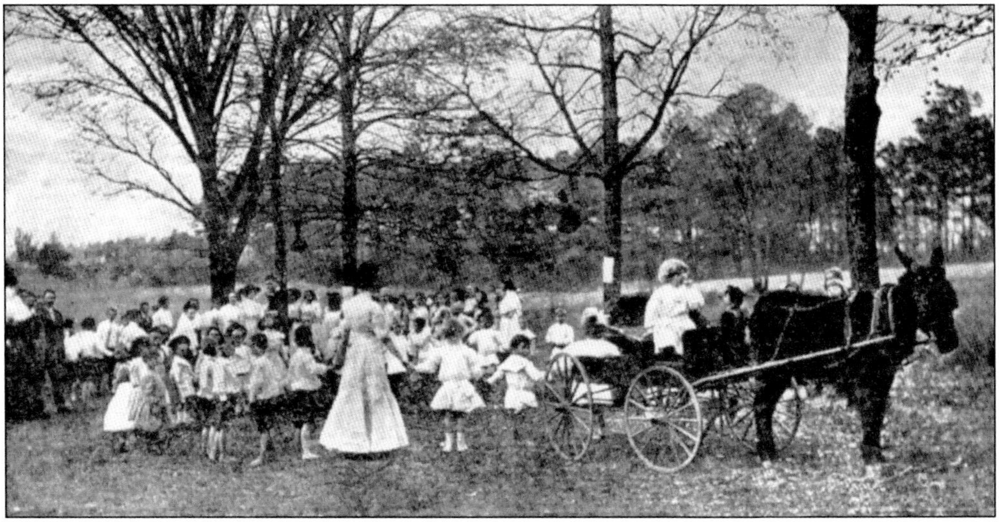

A May Day party at the Church Home Orphanage is documented in this photograph from the early 20th century.

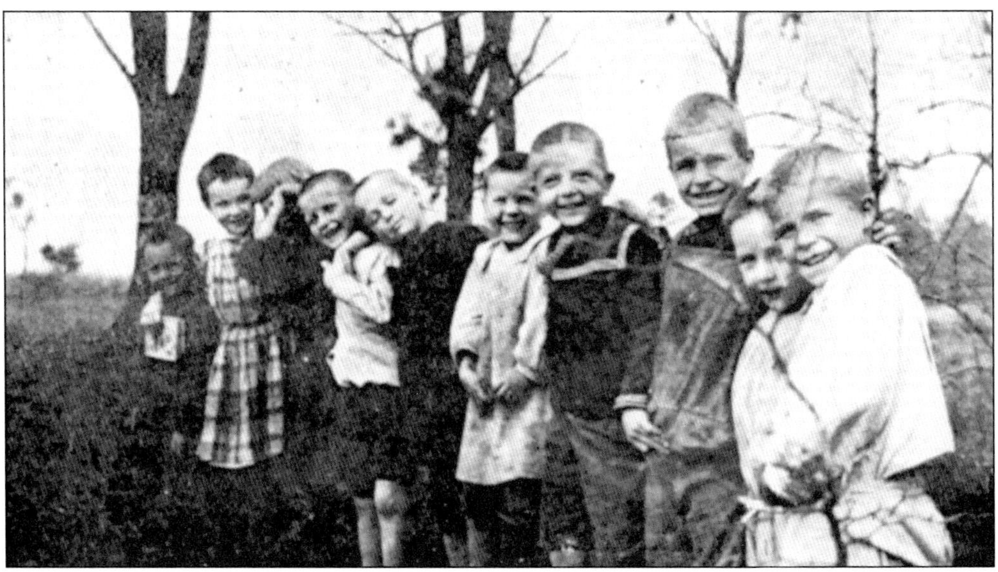

A group of children at the Church Home Orphanage are enjoying playtime in this photograph taken c. 1912.

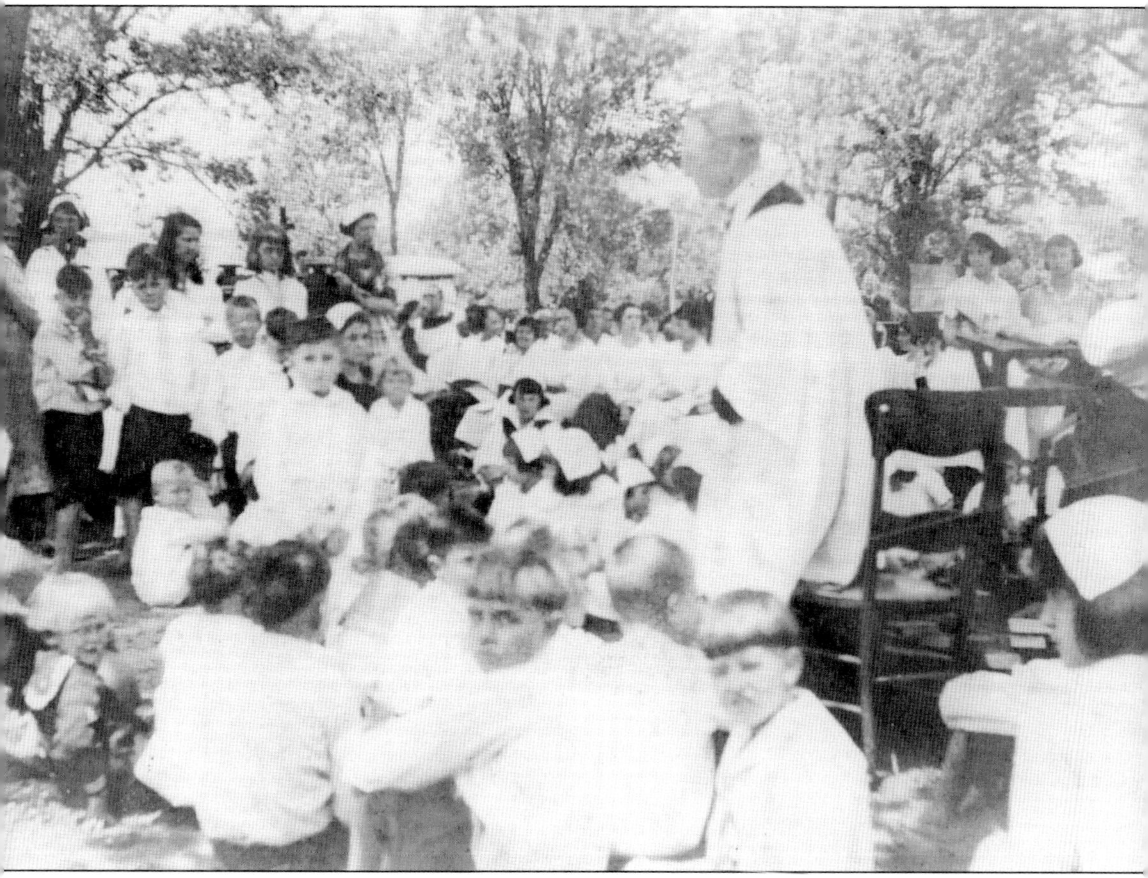

An outdoor Episcopalian church service was captured in this *c.* 1912 photograph taken at the Church Home Orphanage.

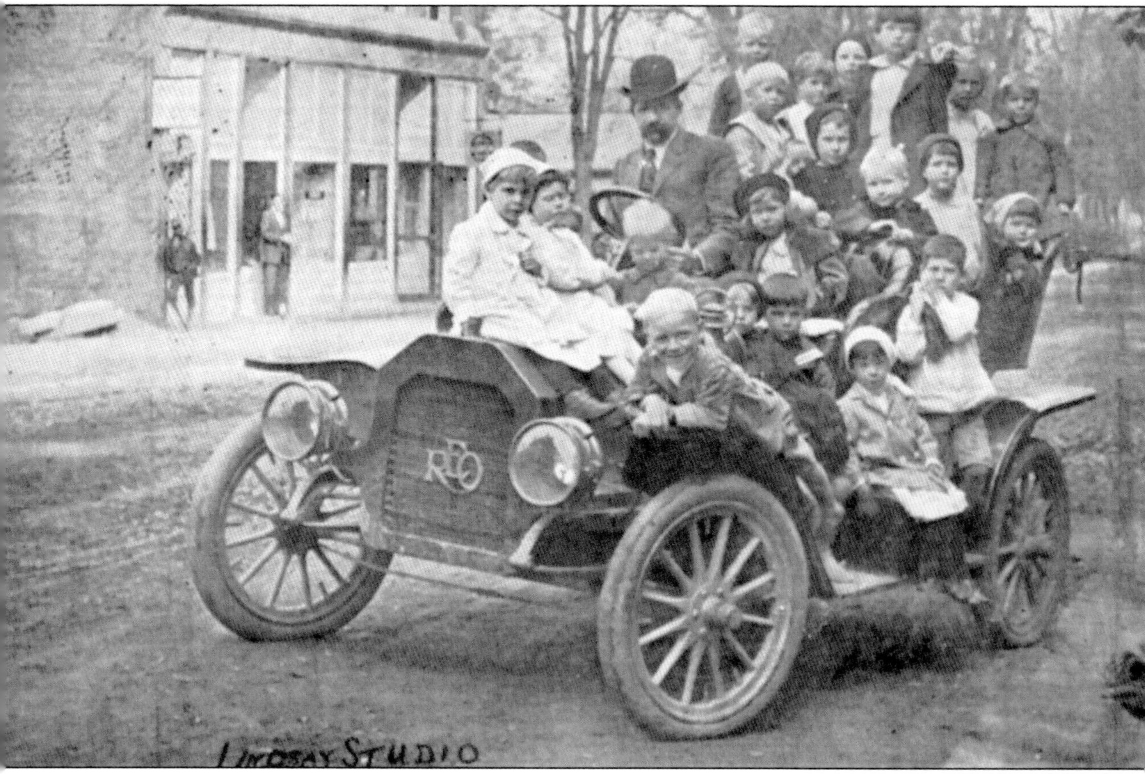

This c. 1912 postcard shows a group of Church Home orphans crowded into the school business manager's car. The automobile is a 1909 or 1910 REO Touring Car.

Seven

MILITARY LIFE

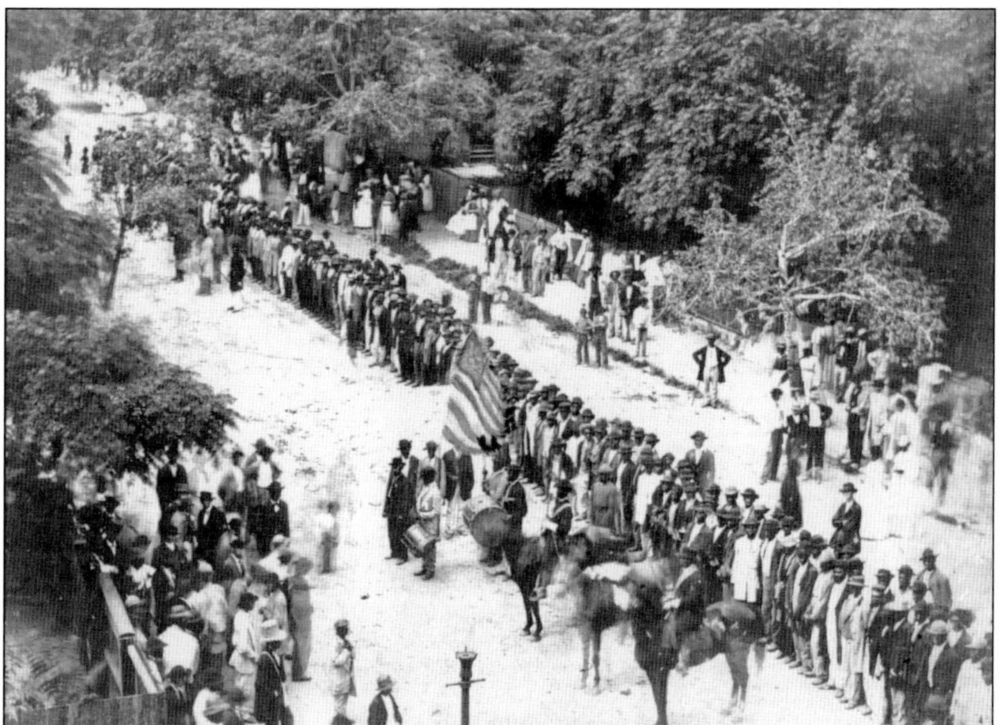

This photograph was taken by Yorkville professional photographer J. R. Schorb, documenting an assembly of York County's African American militia in downtown Yorkville on July 4, 1867. The image of the American flag has been retouched by the photographer.

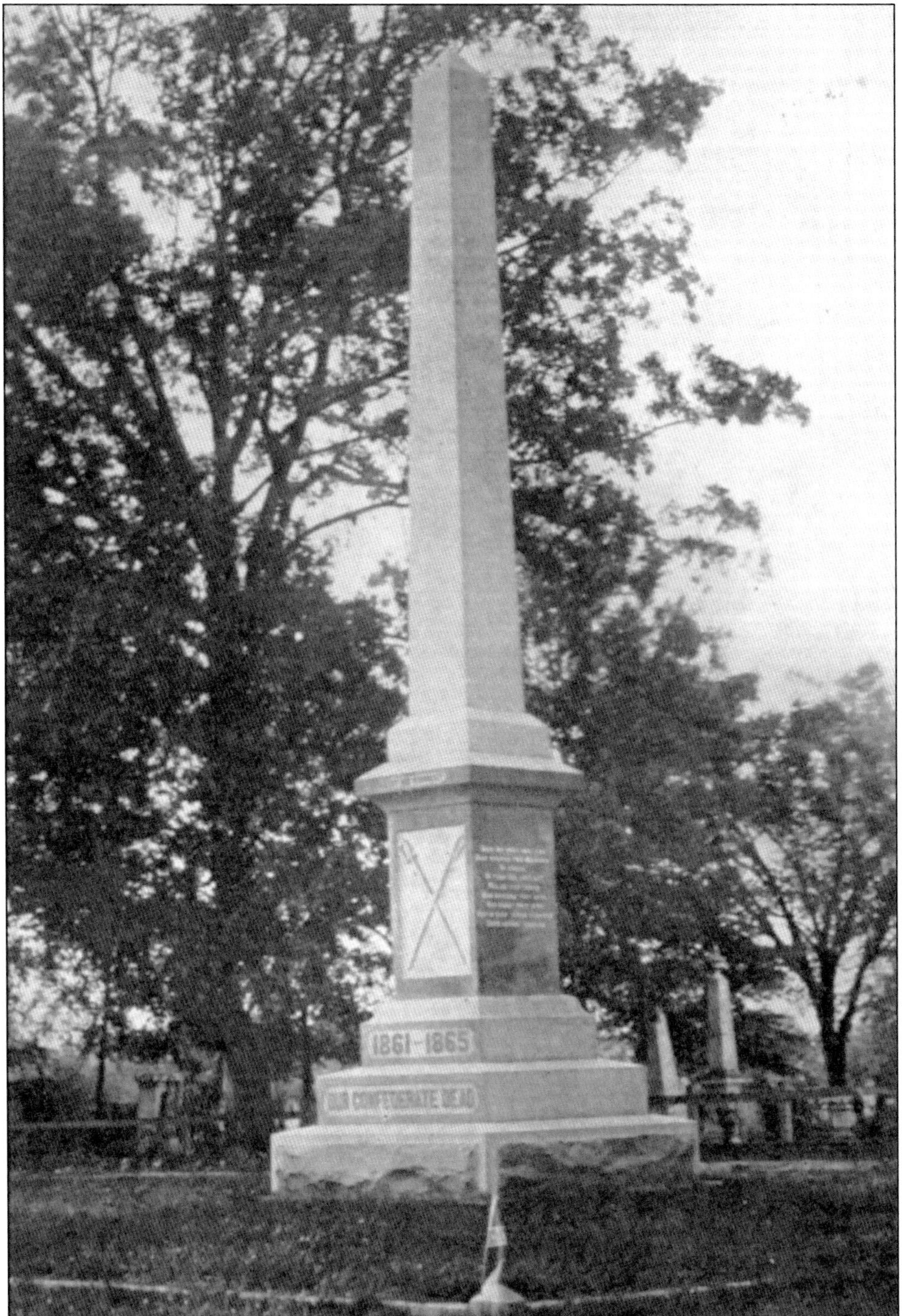

The Confederate Monument at Rose Hill Cemetery on East Liberty Street honors the sacrifices made by York County during the War Between the States. During the War Between the States, more Confederate soldiers died in military service from York County than any other county in South Carolina. This monument was erected under the auspices of the Winnie Davis Chapter of the United Daughters of the Confederacy (UDC). The image is from a postcard dated 1907.

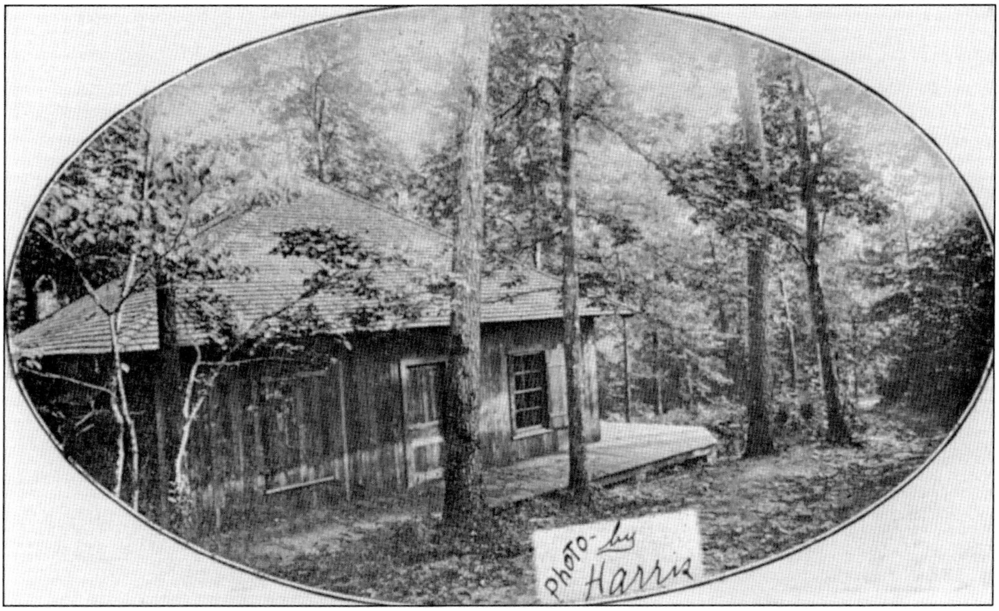

The South Carolina National Guard maintained a presence in York throughout the 20th century. The earliest permanent establishment was this shooting range camp just north of York, utilized by Company L of the 1st Infantry Regiment, National Guard of South Carolina. This photograph dates to *c.* 1910.

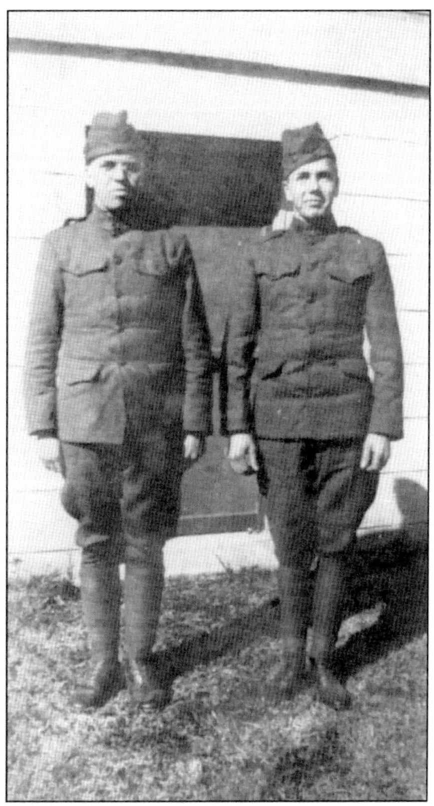

The Glenn brothers, Lamar (left) and William Darby Jr. (right), both served in the U.S. Army during World War I. This 1918 photograph shows the two brothers in their army uniforms.

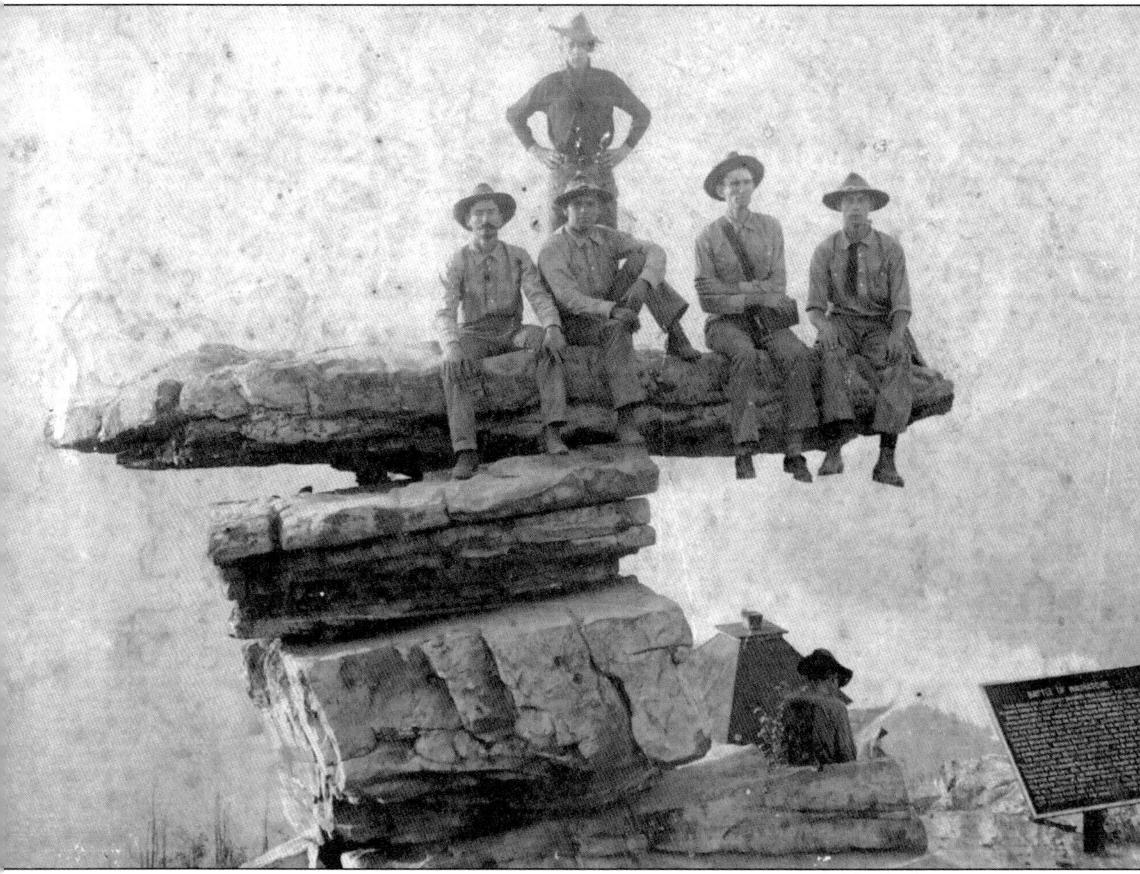

This photograph from the 1920s shows a group of York National Guardsmen during a training exercise on Lookout Mountain in eastern Tennessee. The historical marker on the right side of the picture commemorates the Battle of Wauhatchie Mountain, a Civil War battle that took place in the area on October 28–29, 1863, during the Chickamauga Campaign. It is likely that some of these York guardsmen's fathers fought in that battle while serving in the Confederate army.

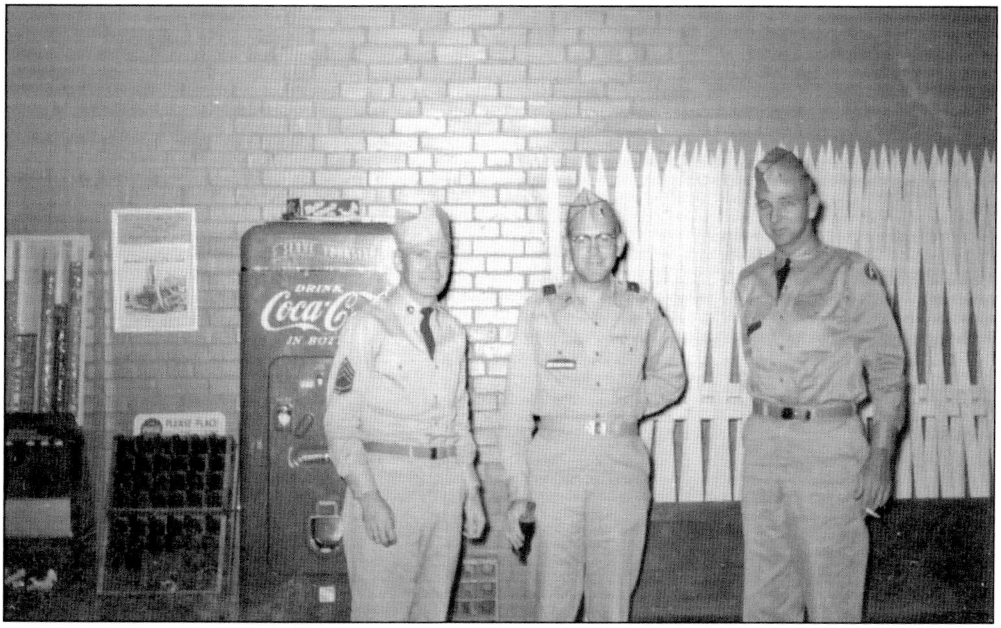

Following the end of World War II, a group of army veterans sought to reestablish a National Guard presence in York. In October 1947, the South Carolina National Guard officially authorized Battery A, 713th Antiaircraft Artillery Gun Battalion, as the York contingent of the National Guard. This photograph shows some of York's early postwar National Guardsmen, still wearing their World War II–style khaki uniforms.

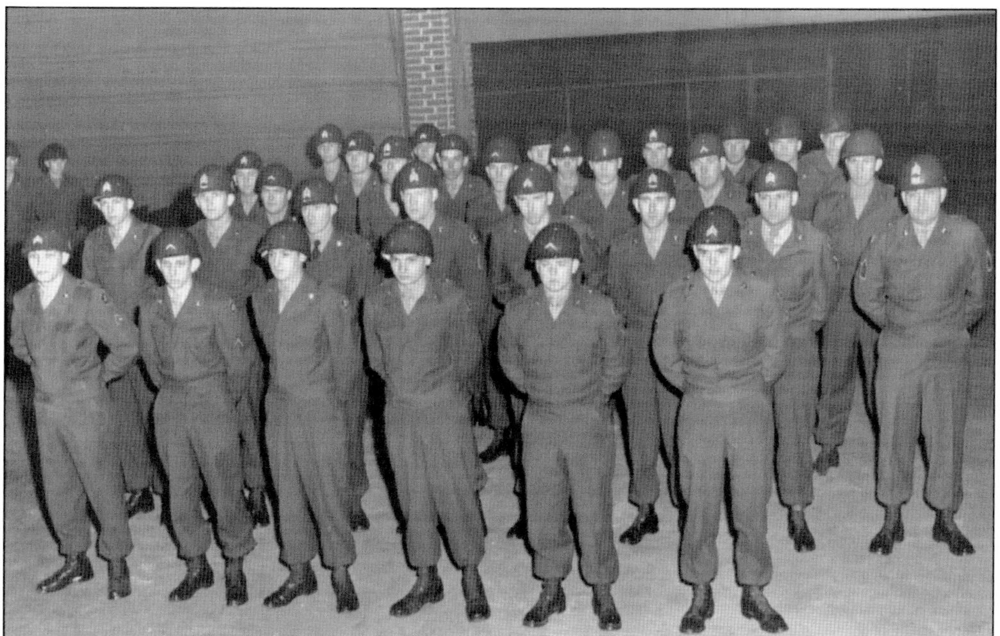

In addition to the antiaircraft battery, during the 1950s, York was also home to the Medical Company of the 218th Infantry Regiment, South Carolina National Guard. Both York National Guard units saw active duty in Korea from 1950 to 1952. In 1958, the two units merged to form Company A, 4th Battalion, 118th Infantry Brigade, South Carolina National Guard.

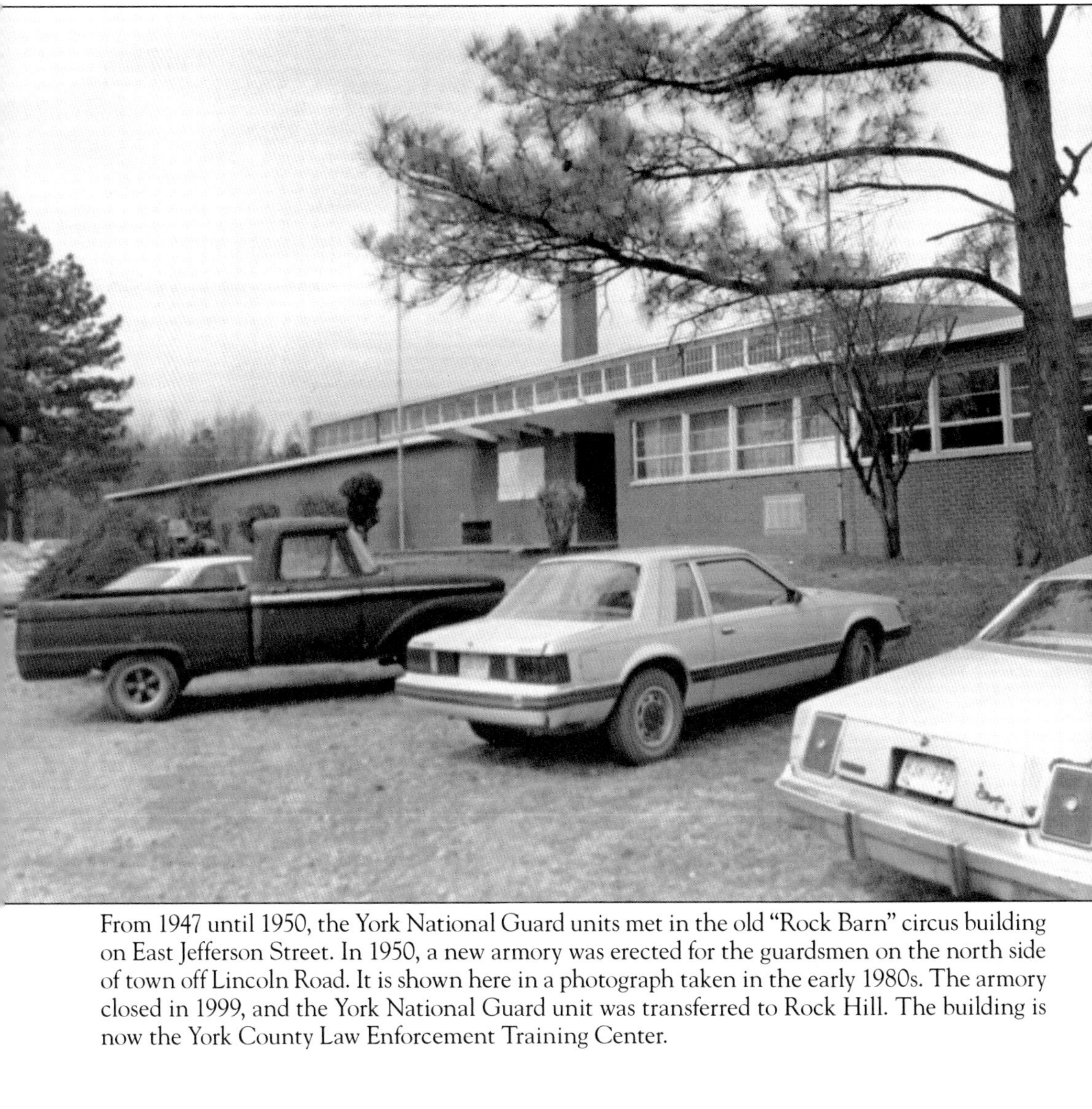

From 1947 until 1950, the York National Guard units met in the old "Rock Barn" circus building on East Jefferson Street. In 1950, a new armory was erected for the guardsmen on the north side of town off Lincoln Road. It is shown here in a photograph taken in the early 1980s. The armory closed in 1999, and the York National Guard unit was transferred to Rock Hill. The building is now the York County Law Enforcement Training Center.

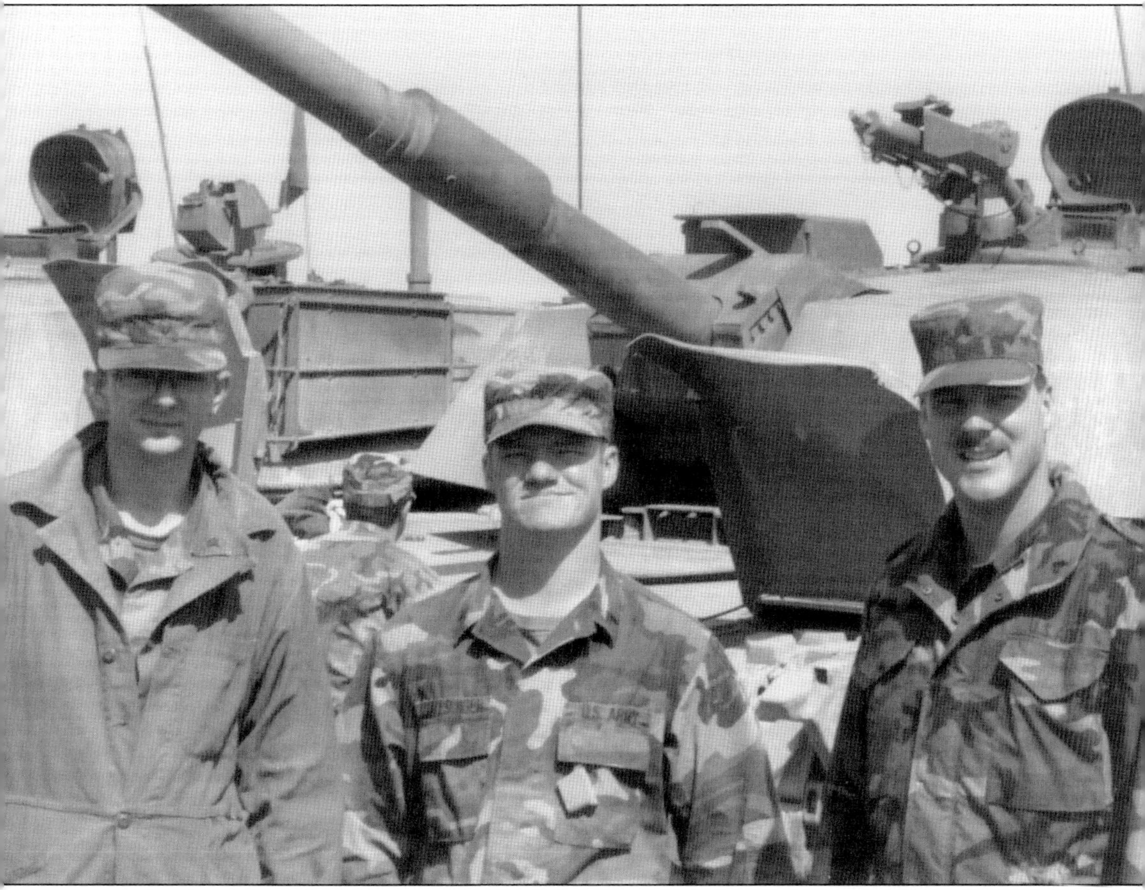

After extensive training as infantry, in 1968, the York National Guard unit converted to mechanized service and became Troop B, 196th Reconnaissance Battalion. In late 1972, the unit transitioned to heavy armored service, becoming the Combat Support Company (CSC), 2nd Battalion, 263rd Armored Regiment, 218th Infantry Brigade. This group of York National Guardsmen poses proudly in front of their M1 Abrams tank during advanced training at Fort Stewart, Georgia, in 1984.

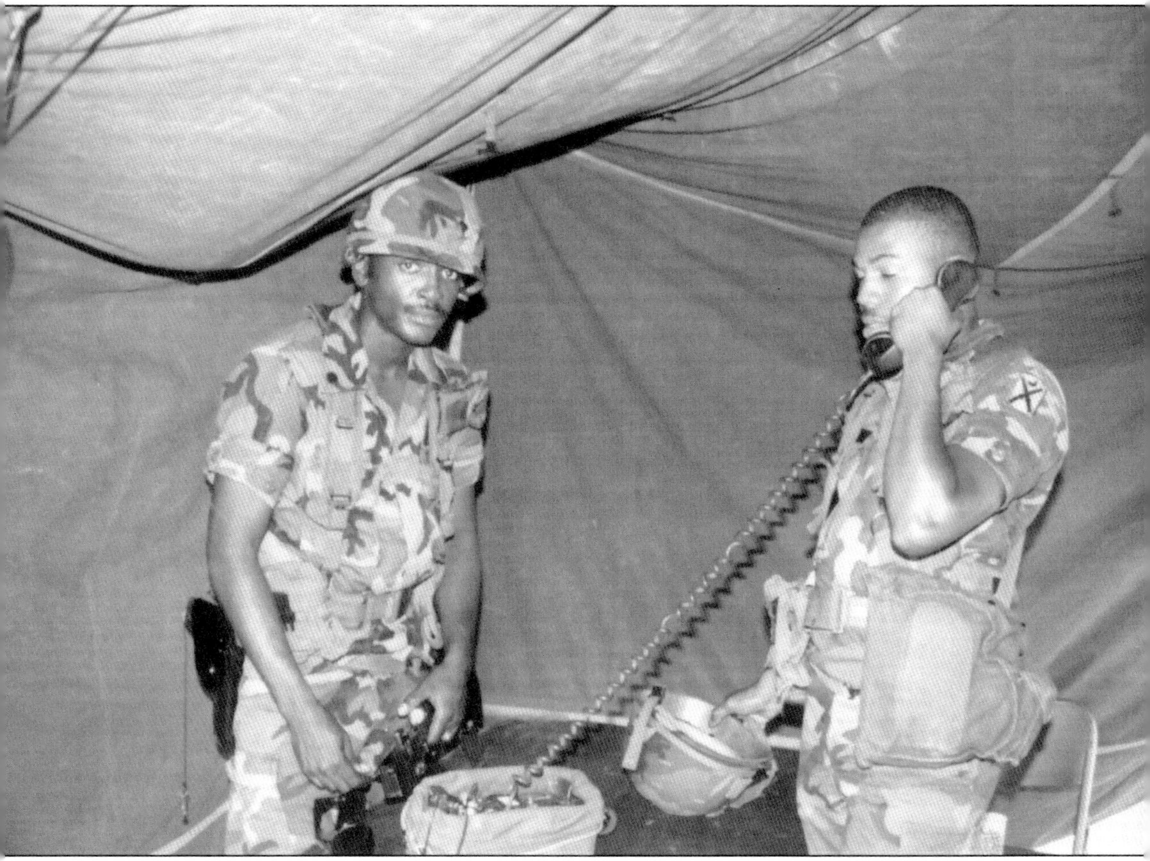

This photograph shows two of York's National Guardsmen demonstrating their field communications equipment during an open house at the York Armory in 1986. These open houses were a frequent occurrence during the 1980s, as the guardsmen sought new recruits and demonstrated their proficiency to the general public.

Eight

HOUSES

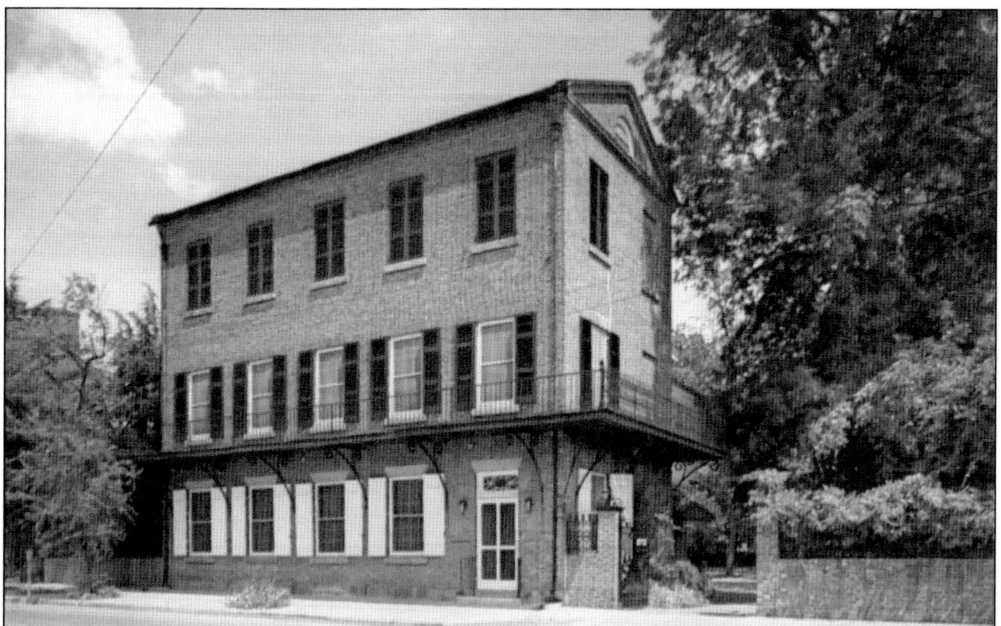

Robert Latta, a wealthy merchant from a Mecklenburg County, North Carolina, mercantile family, built this impressive three-story house at 17 South Congress Street in 1827 to house his dry goods store. Constructed of brick brought from England via Charleston, the Latta House occupies a 1.5-acre lot and remains one of the finest and most well-constructed homes in York. The south wall of the house contains a crack created by a Charleston earthquake in August 1886.

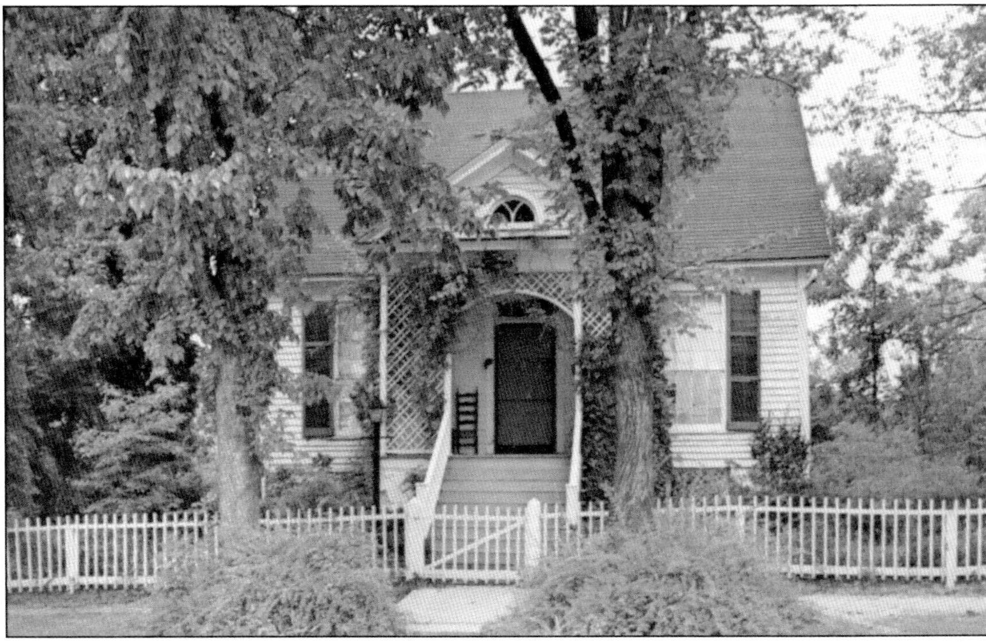

This image of the Gillam house in York comes from an early-20th-century postcard published by Colorama of Columbus, Georgia. The caption reads, "The Gillam house which dates to the Revolutionary period is built in the raised cottage style. Its basement called the Academy Room was used for an early school. It was also a distribution point for the refugees who flocked to York during the Confederate war."

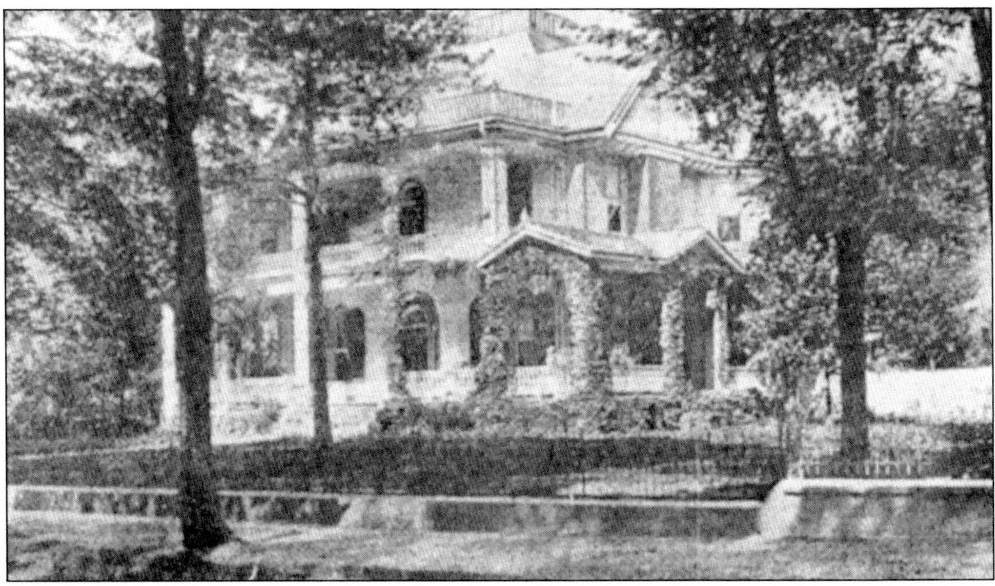

Joseph Herndon, born in Virginia in 1810, acquired this house at 103 North Congress Street around 1860. He and his wife, Amanda, had six children. The house was successively occupied by Joseph and Amanda's son Robert Joseph Herndon, followed by Robert Joseph's son Joseph McJunkin Herndon. Joseph McJunkin Herndon was the last Herndon owner, living in the house as late as 1970.

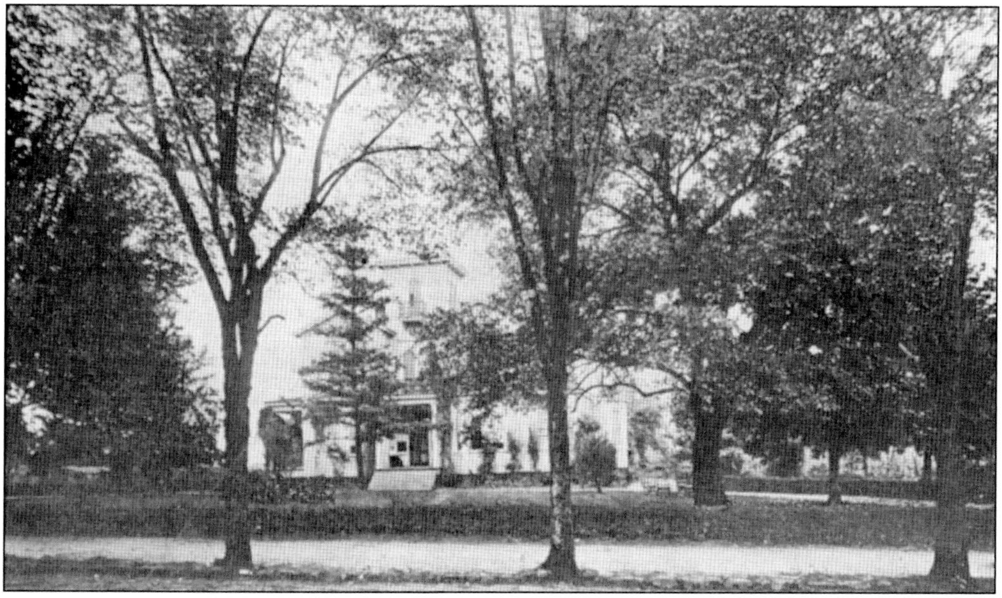

Martha Metts, widow of Walter Metts, lived in this house on North Congress Street near Madison Street in 1908. The house was demolished, and the York Winn-Dixie was built on the property by 1958. Whitesides' Cleaners now owns the former Winn-Dixie building.

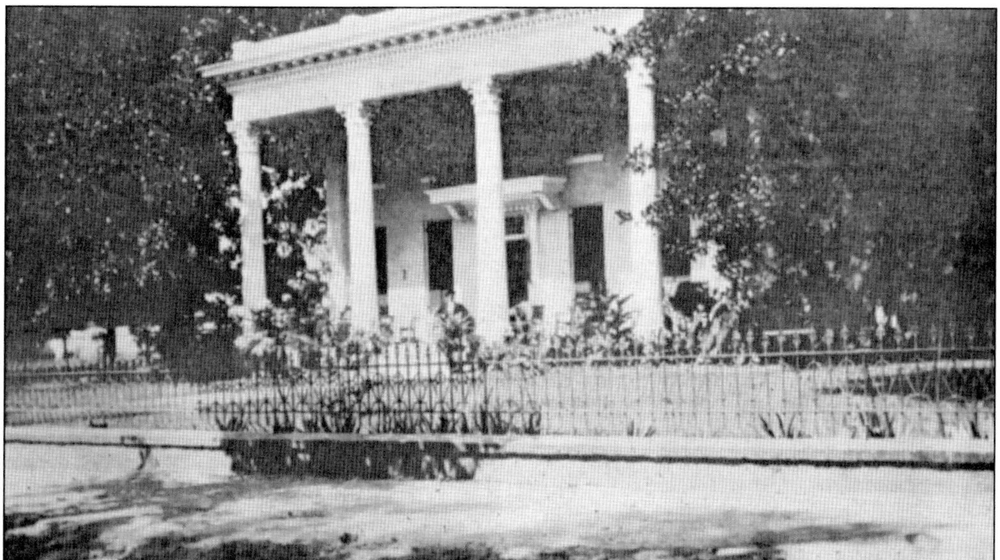

John R. McElwee owned this property at 109 North Congress Street until his death in 1847. Benjamin Neely purchased the property in 1849, and after his death in 1853, his wife, Elizabeth Ann Pearson Neely, occupied the house. Mrs. Neely deeded the house to Col. William H. McCorkle in July 1860. McCorkle served in the 12th South Carolina Regiment during the Civil War and was a York County probate judge. His son-in-law Benjamin Neely (B. N.) Moore lived in the house until his death in 1929. Moore was proprietor of Moore's Standard Warehouses and a cotton buyer who later became the president of York Loan and Savings Bank. He made extensive renovations to the Georgian-style home in the first quarter of the 19th century.

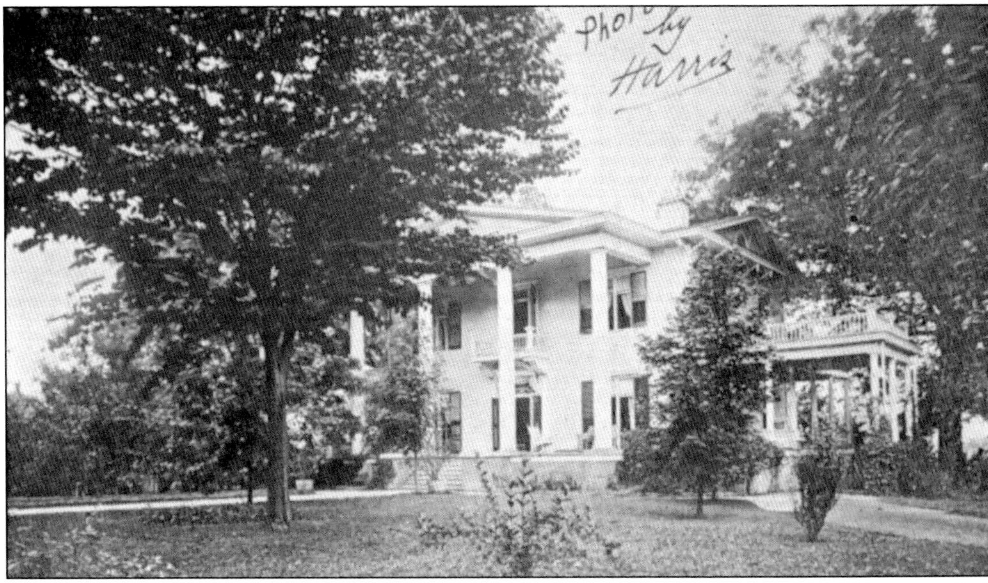

Elizabeth Ann Pearson Neely sold this plantation house on North Congress Street to Col. William Blackburn Wilson, a veteran of the 17th South Carolina Regiment, in 1869. His widow, Ann, sold the house to Samuel M. McNeel, president of the Loan and Savings Bank and Tavora Cotton Mills, in 1903. McNeel lived in this house with his wife, Theodora, and daughter Huldah. By 1975, the house had been demolished and the York County Health Department and Library were built on the property.

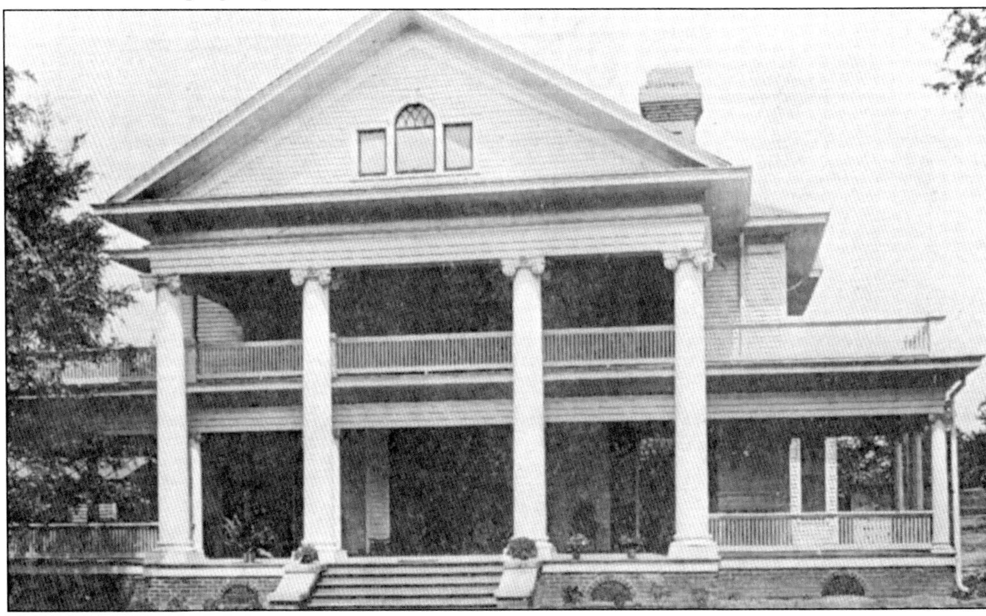

Yorkville lawyer and U.S. congressman David E. Finley owned this house on 111 North Congress Street with his wife, Bessie, and their eight children. Finley was elected to the Congress in 1890 and served terms in the House and the Senate until his death in 1917. His son David Edward Finley Jr. became the first director of the National Gallery of Art in Washington, D.C., in 1938 and was instrumental in founding the National Portrait Gallery and the National Trust for Historic Preservation.

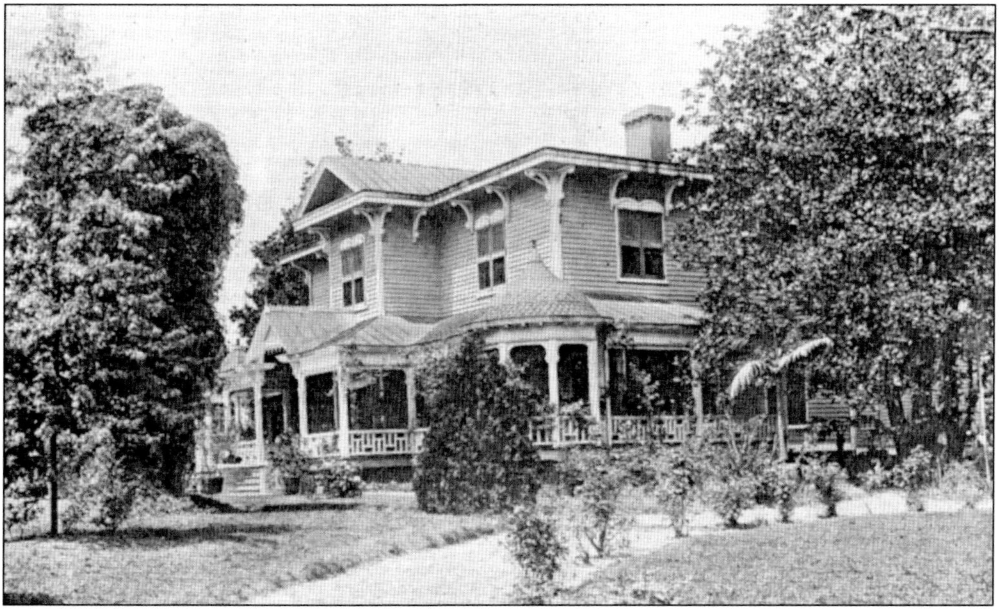

Located at 121 North Congress Street, this was one of the homes of Col. William Wright, first president of the Kings Mountain Railroad. He willed the Tuscan villa–style house and property to his wife, Mary, upon his death in 1857. After Mary died in 1862, their adopted niece, Margaret, wife of Judge Isaac Donnom (I. D.) Witherspoon, inherited the residence. The Witherspoons' daughter, Leslie, occupied the home until her death in 1959.

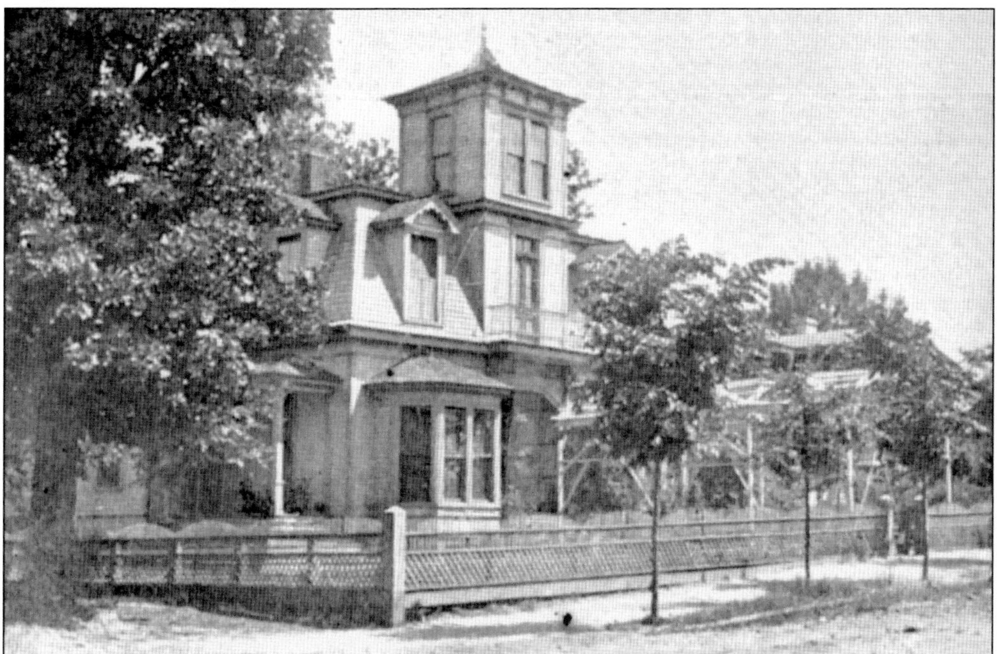

Dr. Adam Y. Cartwright, a Yorkville dentist, acquired this property on North Congress Street in 1893. Dr. Cartwright advertised his practice in 1912 as "surgeon dentist." He raised six children in the house after his wife's death in 1905 and also housed a number of boarders. By 1975, the house was no longer standing.

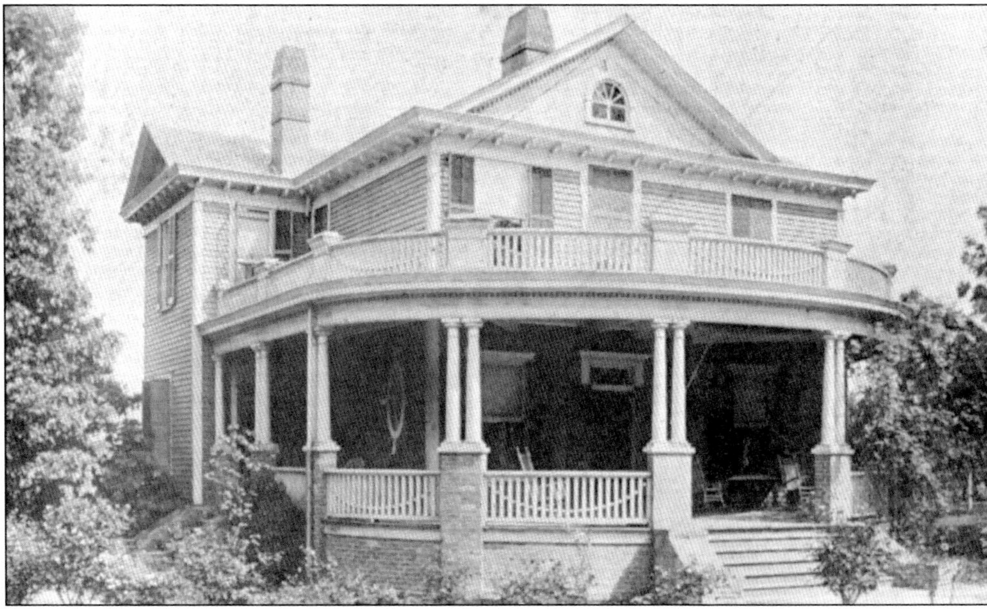

Henry and Marie C. Glenn lived in this house on North Congress Street from 1908 until at least 1912. Henry Glenn was a bookkeeper and farmer, and his wife lived in the house after his death.

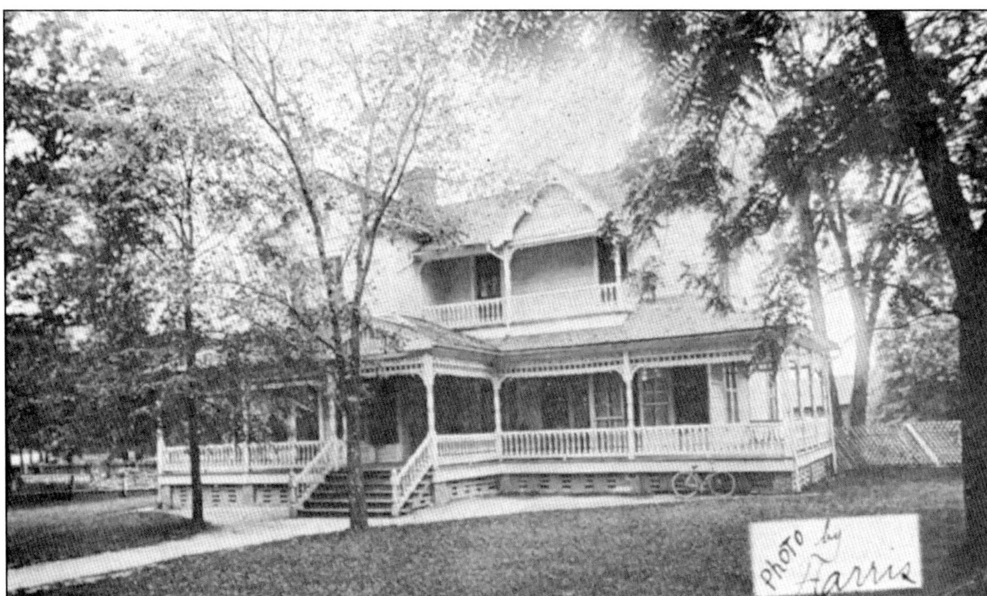

This Victorian home at 2 Kings Mountain Street was owned by Frank C. Riddle and was built around 1890. The family lived there until at least the 1920s, and the home was restored in 1989.

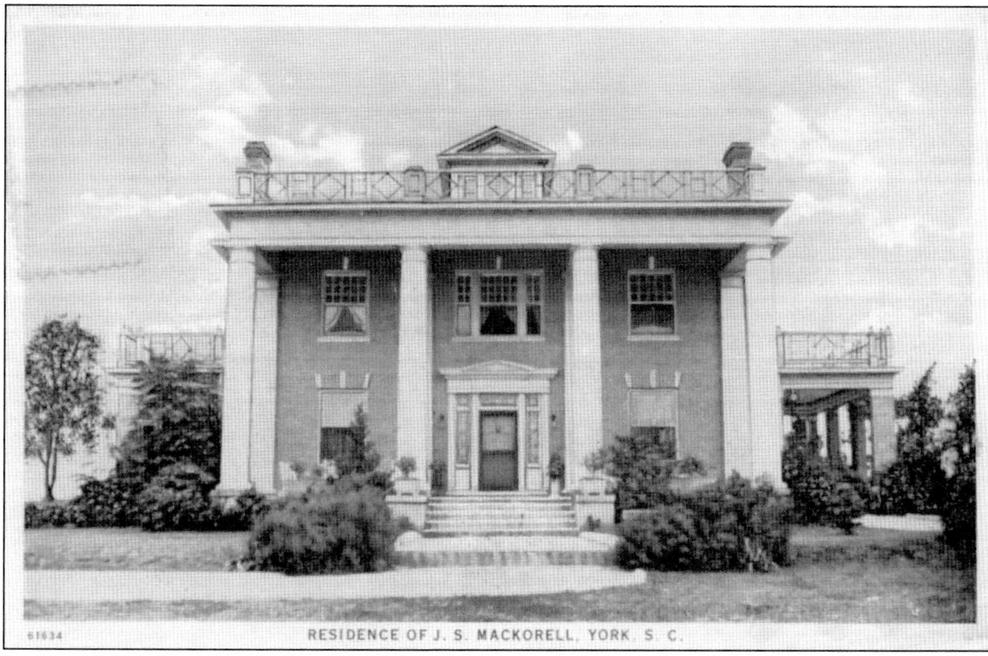

Jacob and Ophelia Mackorell resided at this three-story home on Kings Mountain Street with their three children for over 20 years. Jacob (J. S.) Mackorell and his brother, Robert, the sons of Irish immigrants, ran the Mackorell Brothers Wholesale Grocers store in York, "Manufacturers of Soda Water, Ginger Ale, Etc." Construction of the house began in 1917 and was finished in 1920.

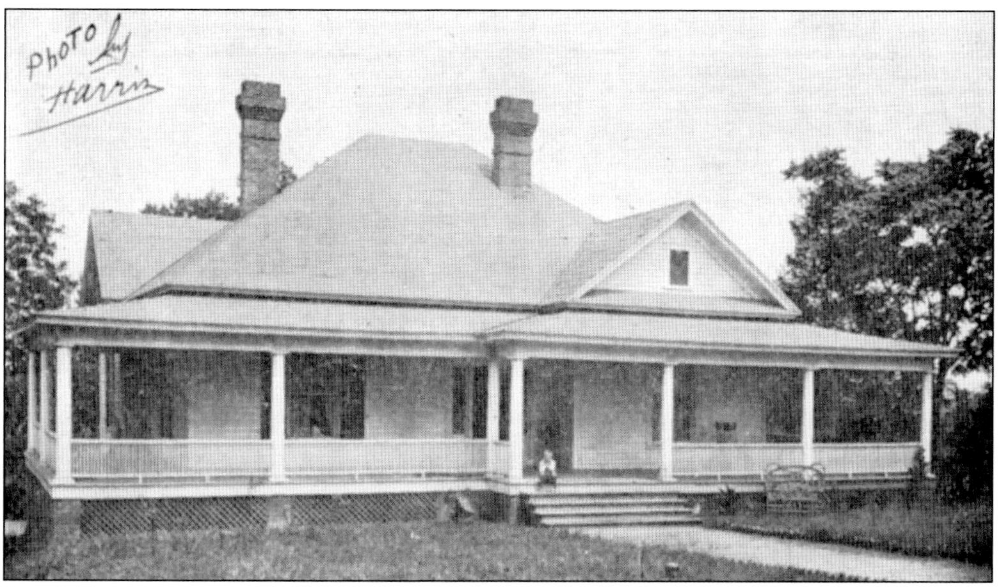

Joseph Harry Foster was a Yorkville lawyer in 1912. He left his law office at Gills Creek, Lancaster County, South Carolina, with his wife, Mary, and three children to set up a practice in York in the McNeel Building. The family lived in this house on Kings Mountain Street before moving to Rock Hill c. 1920.

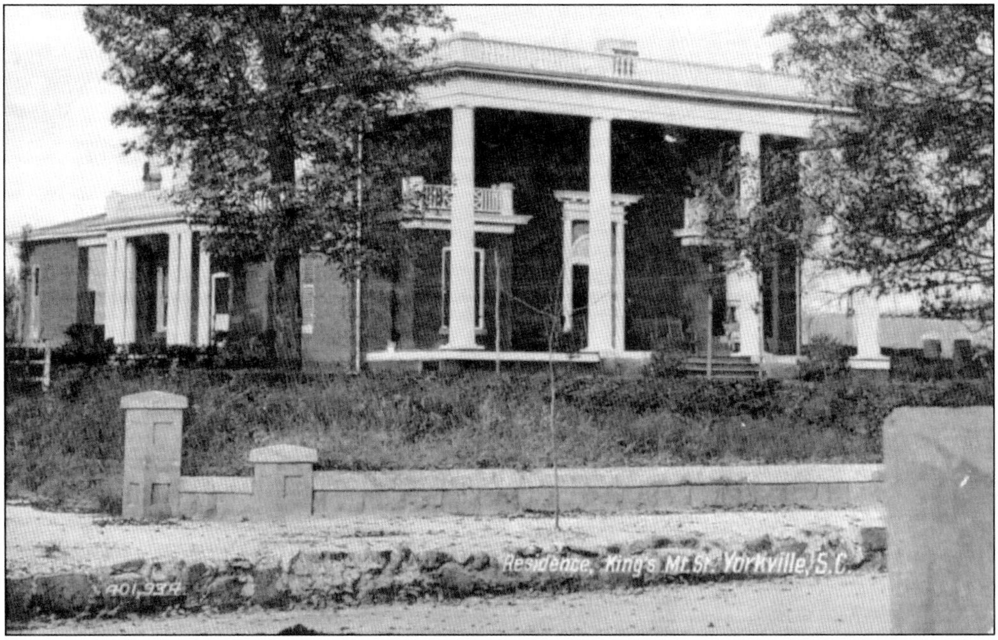

Robert Turner Allison built this Classical Revival–style house at 15 Kings Mountain Street about 1910 and lived here with his wife, Bessie, daughter, Ola, and son, Robert Jr. Allison was originally co-owner of Glenn and Allison, dealers in "vehicles, farm implements and live stock," but by 1912, he was proprietor of his own wagon and buggy business in Yorkville. He also built the Rock Barn on East Jefferson Street, the largest livery stable in York (later winter quarters for the Barnett Brothers Circus).

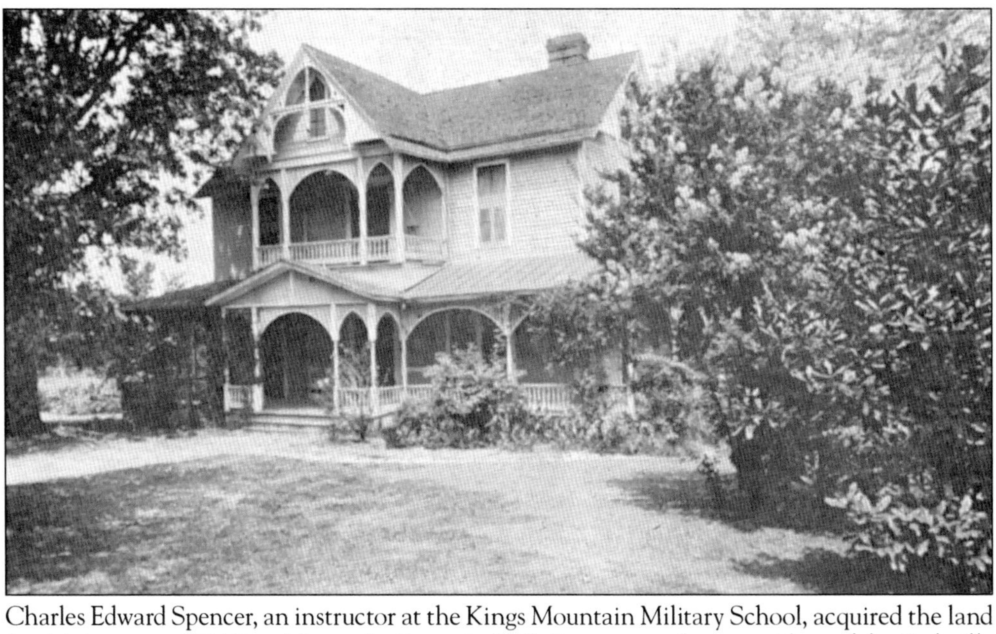

Charles Edward Spencer, an instructor at the Kings Mountain Military School, acquired the land for this house on 102 Kings Mountain Street in 1877. Spencer was later president of the Yorkville Monument Works and practiced law from about 1880 until his death in 1921.

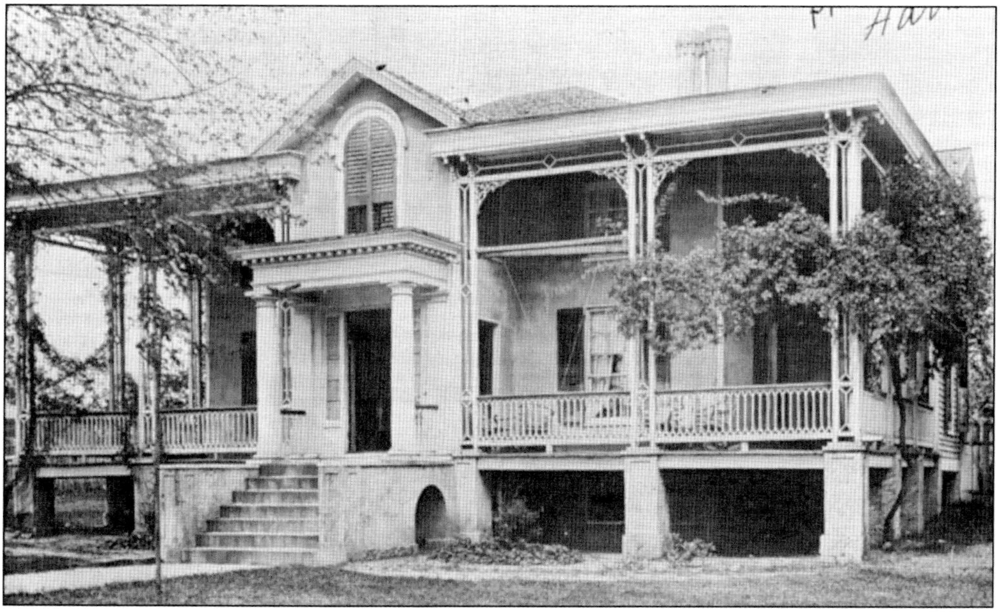

William Hambright Quinn purchased this New Orleans–style house at 216 Kings Mountain Street in 1881. His daughters Rachel and Betsey Quinn lived there when this photograph was taken around 1900. Their sister, Susan Wallace, moved in with Rachel and Betsey, both unmarried, after the death of her husband in 1904. The three sisters lived in the house until their respective deaths, the last being Susan in 1942.

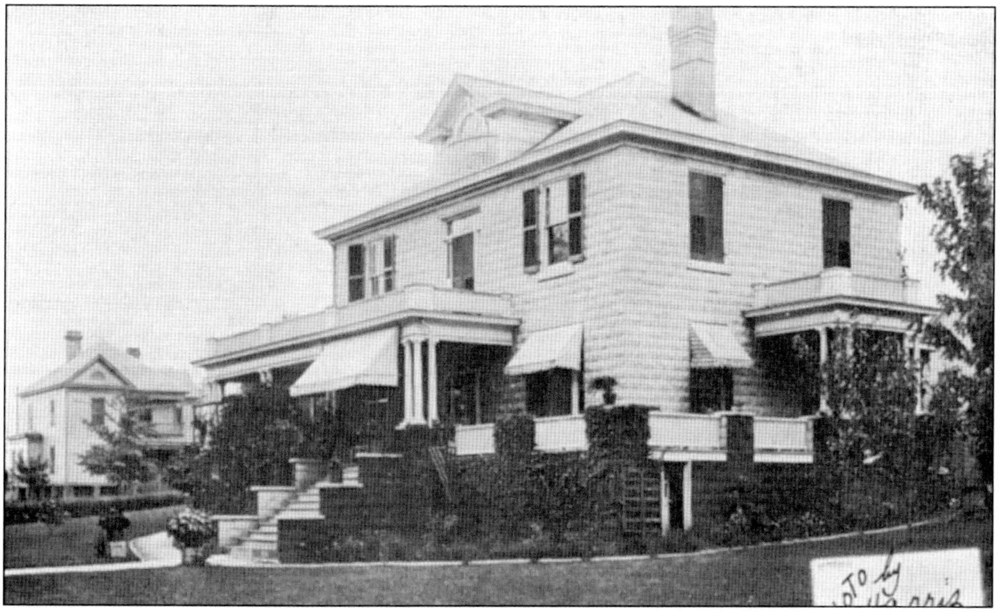

Oliver E. Wilkins moved from Gaffney, South Carolina, to York and built this house at 12 West Madison Street in 1906. The house is an example of the "Cape Cod Villa" style of Victorian architecture. Wilkins was president of the now-defunct First National Bank of York, originally located at the corner of East Liberty and South Congress Streets across from the courthouse. He and his wife, Lula, lived in the house with their two daughters. The house was purchased in the 1920s by the McConnell family.

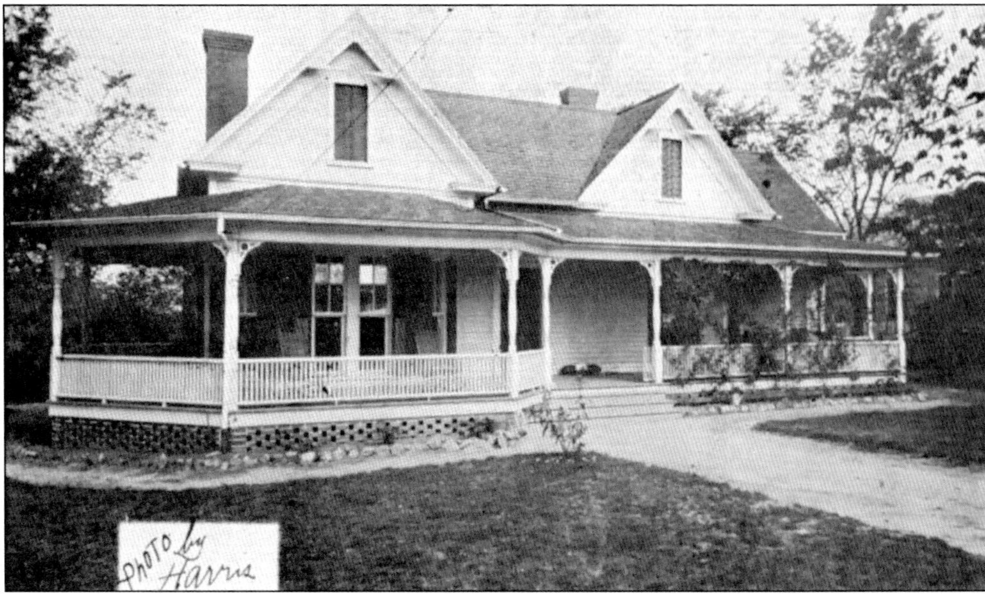

Lawyer and vice president of the Loan and Savings Bank, J. Steele Brice occupied this residence. He purchased the lot on Wright Avenue, formerly Cartwright Avenue, and was building a "cottage" there by 1894. His wife, Claudia, continued to live in the house after his death in 1923.

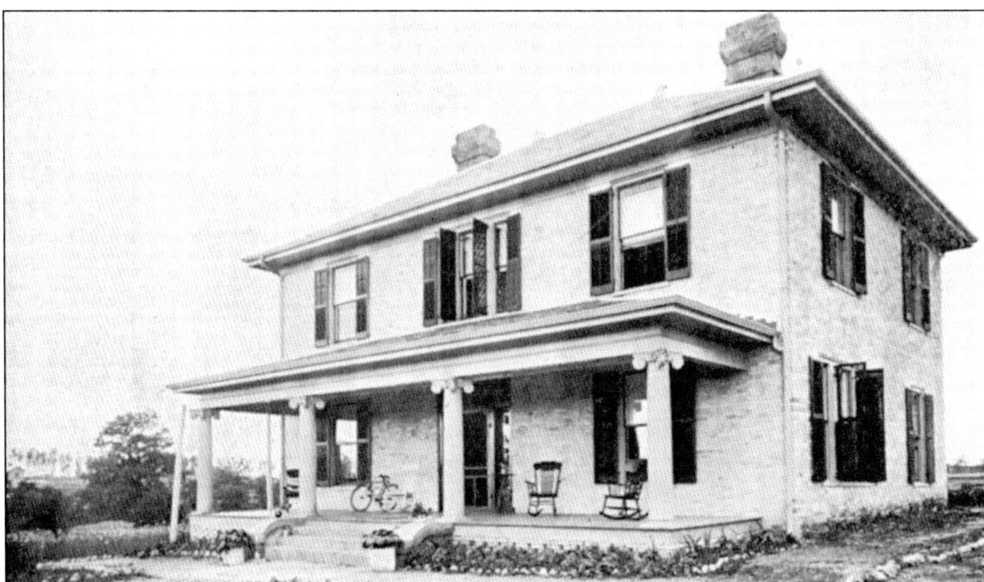

William Henry Herndon, son of Joseph Herndon, lived in this house at 202 West Madison Street in 1912. Herndon was a merchant in Yorkville, a "Dealer in Staple and Fancy Groceries." This Victorian brick house was built in 1907 and is currently owned by the mayor of York, Dr. J. Edward Lee.

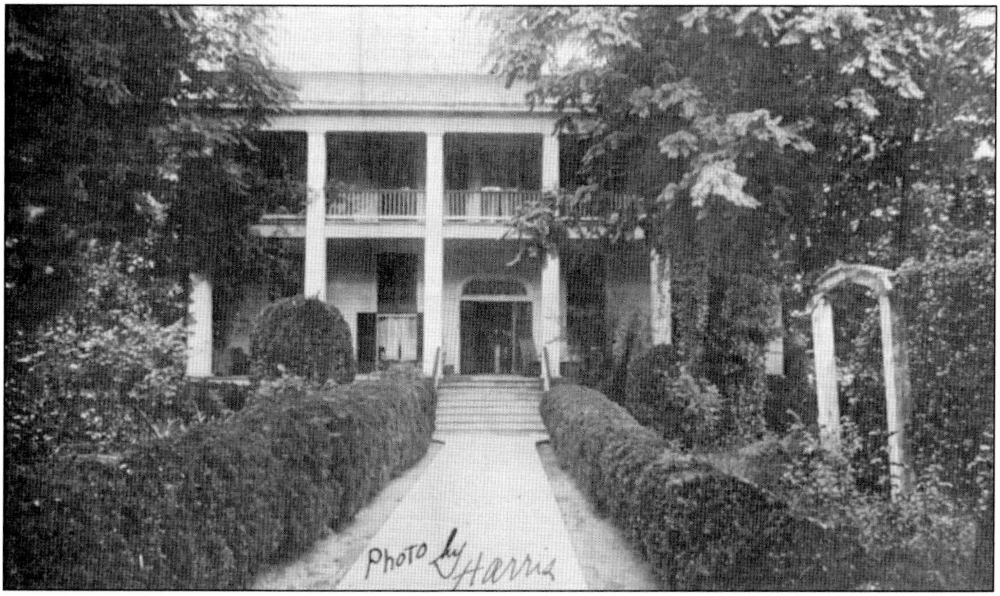

This house on 8 South Congress Street was built sometime before 1830 by Robert Clendenin, a Yorkville lawyer and South Carolina senator from York District (1816–1830). Dr. James Rufus Bratton purchased the house in 1847. Bratton was a surgeon in the Confederate army during the Civil War, and on April 27, 1865, Confederate president Jefferson Davis spent the night here as he fled west to escape Union troops. The house passed to Bratton's son, Dr. Rufus Andral Bratton, and was razed in 1956.

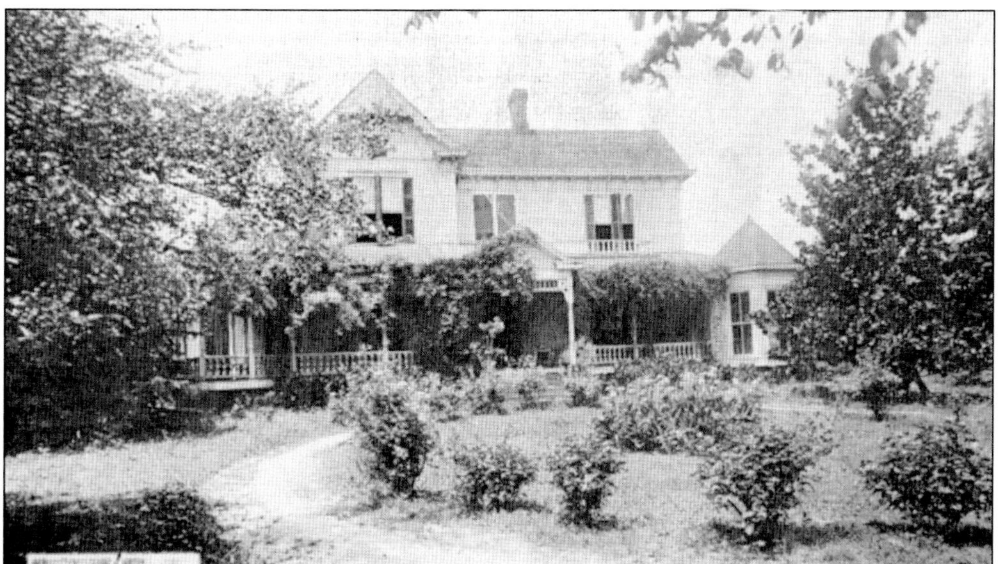

Dr. J. Harvey Witherspoon and his wife, Phoebe, moved to this home on South Congress Street by 1908, after Dr. Witherspoon retired from his medical practice, which he began about 1870. Phoebe Witherspoon resided at the house until her death in 1924.

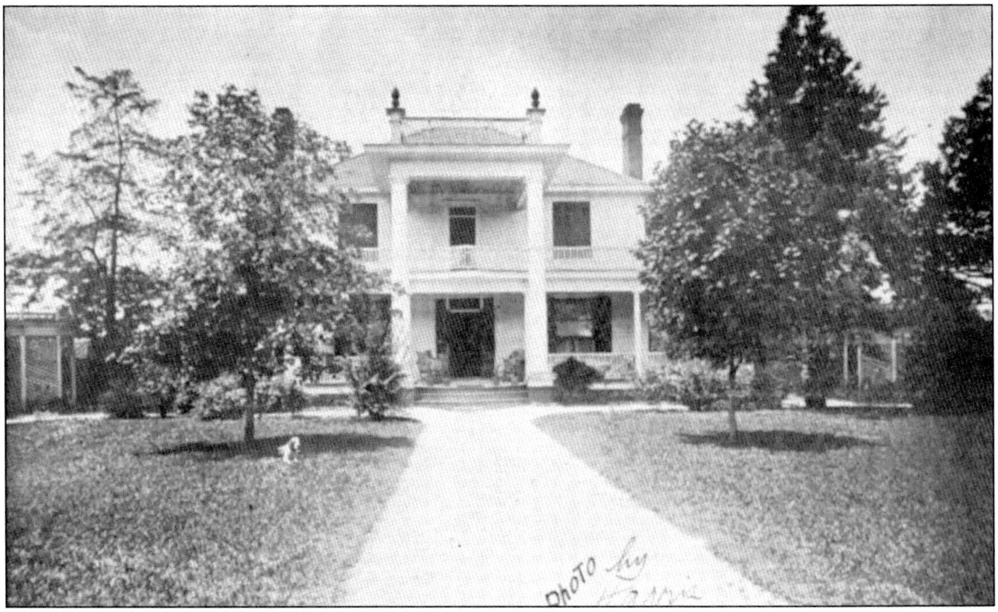

Monroe C. Willis, originally from Barnwell County, South Carolina, bought this lot on South Congress Street in 1888. He raised five children in this house with his wife, Fannie. Willis was proprietor of Yorkville Buggy Company for many years, but by 1920, he was head of the Church Home Orphanage, which moved north from Charleston in 1909 to the campus of the former Kings Mountain Military Academy.

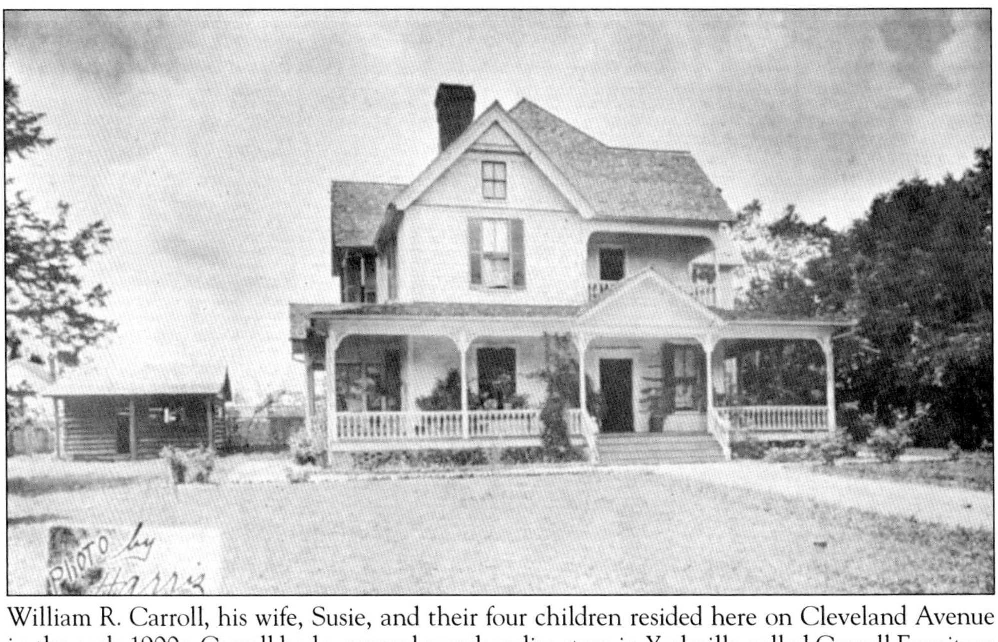

William R. Carroll, his wife, Susie, and their four children resided here on Cleveland Avenue in the early 1900s. Carroll had a general merchandise store in Yorkville called Carroll Furniture Company. After William's death in 1919, Susie remained in the home, and by 1930, her daughter, son-in-law, and grandchildren resided with her.

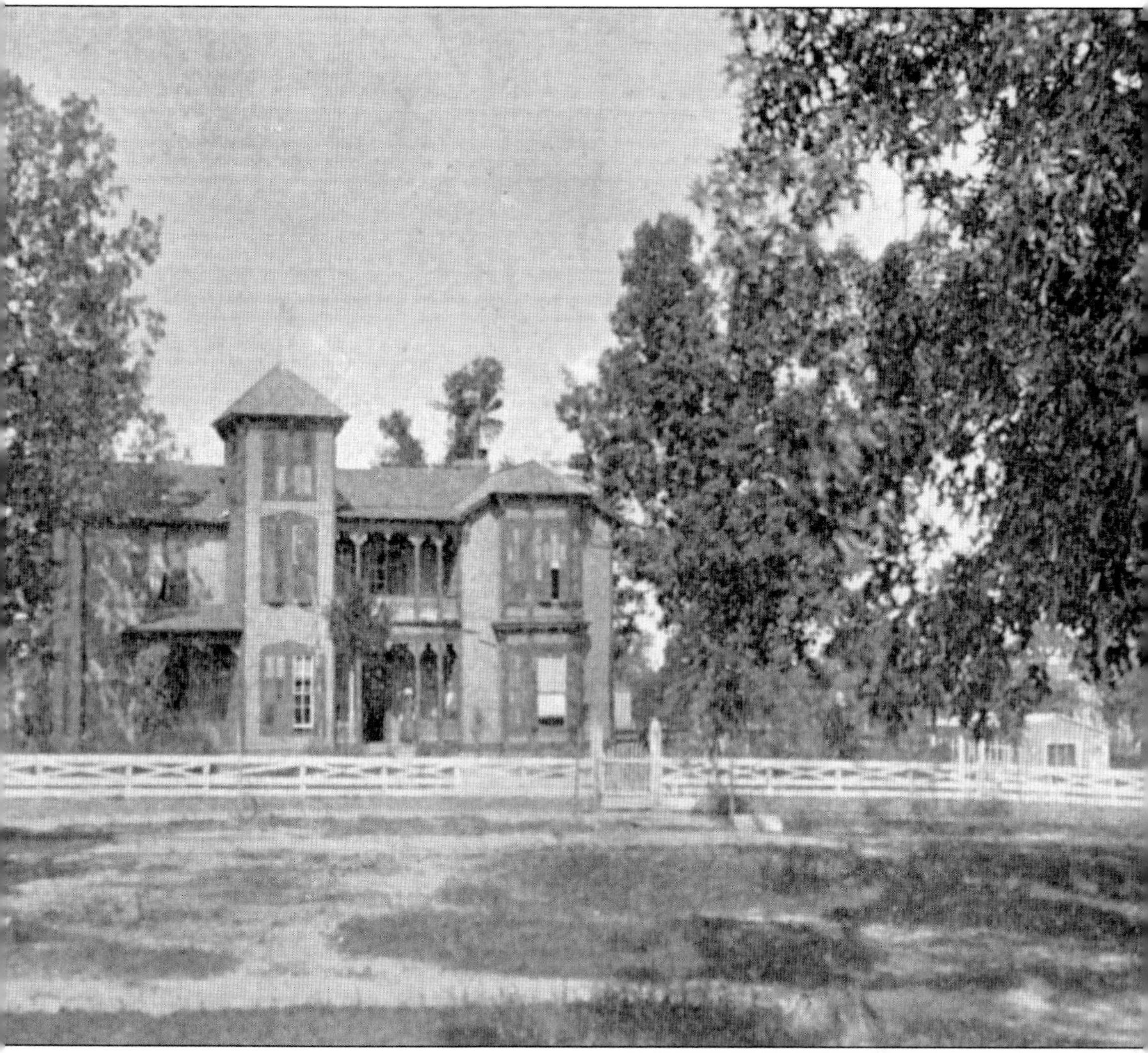

This house on 6 Cleveland Avenue was originally constructed *c.* 1815 by Judge William Smith, a U.S. congressman and senator, who sold it to Robert McCaw in 1852. Maj. James F. Hart—a Citadel graduate, lawyer, senator, and Confederate veteran—bought the house in 1870 and lived there with his wife, Margaret Jane, and their six children. Hart rebuilt the home in the Victorian style following a fire in 1881. After Hart's death in 1905, his son John R. Hart inherited the property. John Hart also practiced law and eventually became mayor of Yorkville.

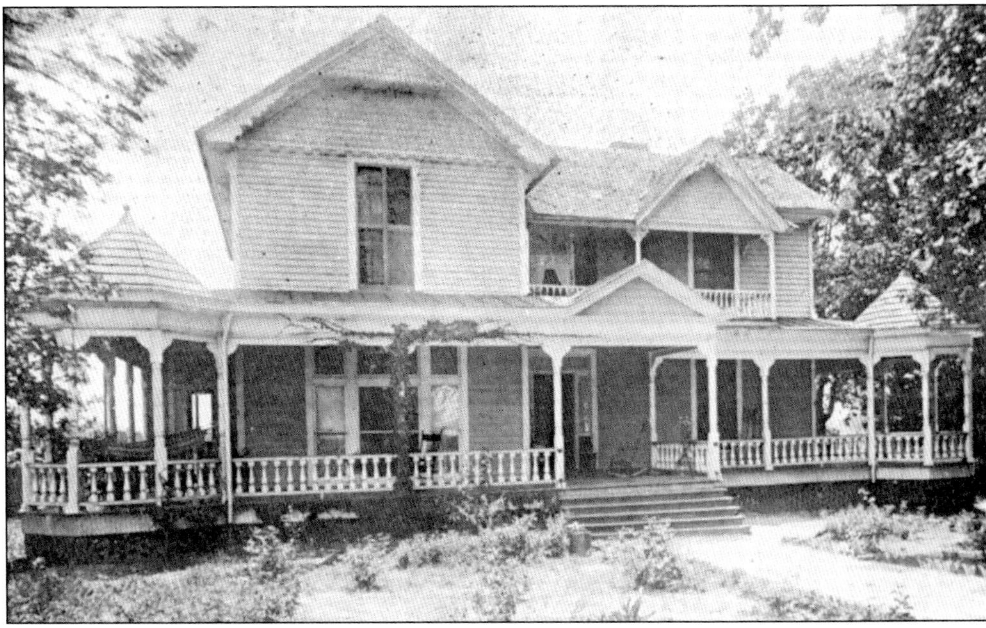

York County sheriff John R. Logan constructed this Victorian-style house at 334 East Liberty Street in 1889. He and his wife, Sally, raised six children in the home and had a number of boarders and servants as well. Logan was also co-owner of the J. J. Keller and Company lumberyard, and he reportedly spared no expense in constructing this house. Sally resided in the home after John's death in 1921.

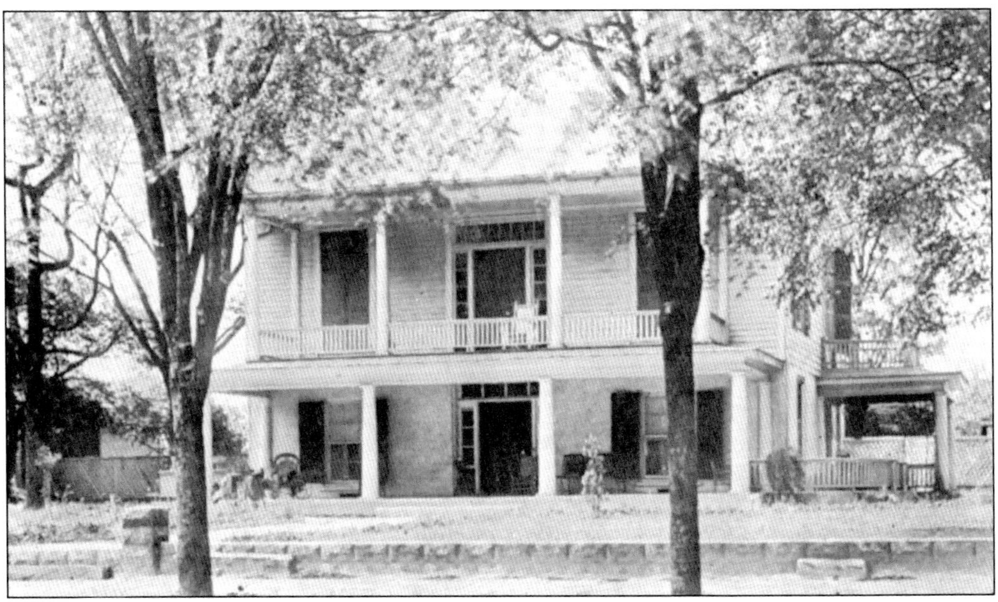

This house at 219 East Liberty Street is believed to be one of the three oldest in York, possibly the oldest. The core of the house dates to the late 1700s, and it was remodeled and added to during the 1840s. In the late 1850s, a builder named William D. Miller gave the house its current Greek Revival appearance. Robert J. Mackorell purchased the property in 1910 and lived here with his wife, Ella, and six children. Robert and his brother Jacob, the sons of Irish immigrants, ran the Mackorell Brothers Wholesale Grocers store in the early 1900s.

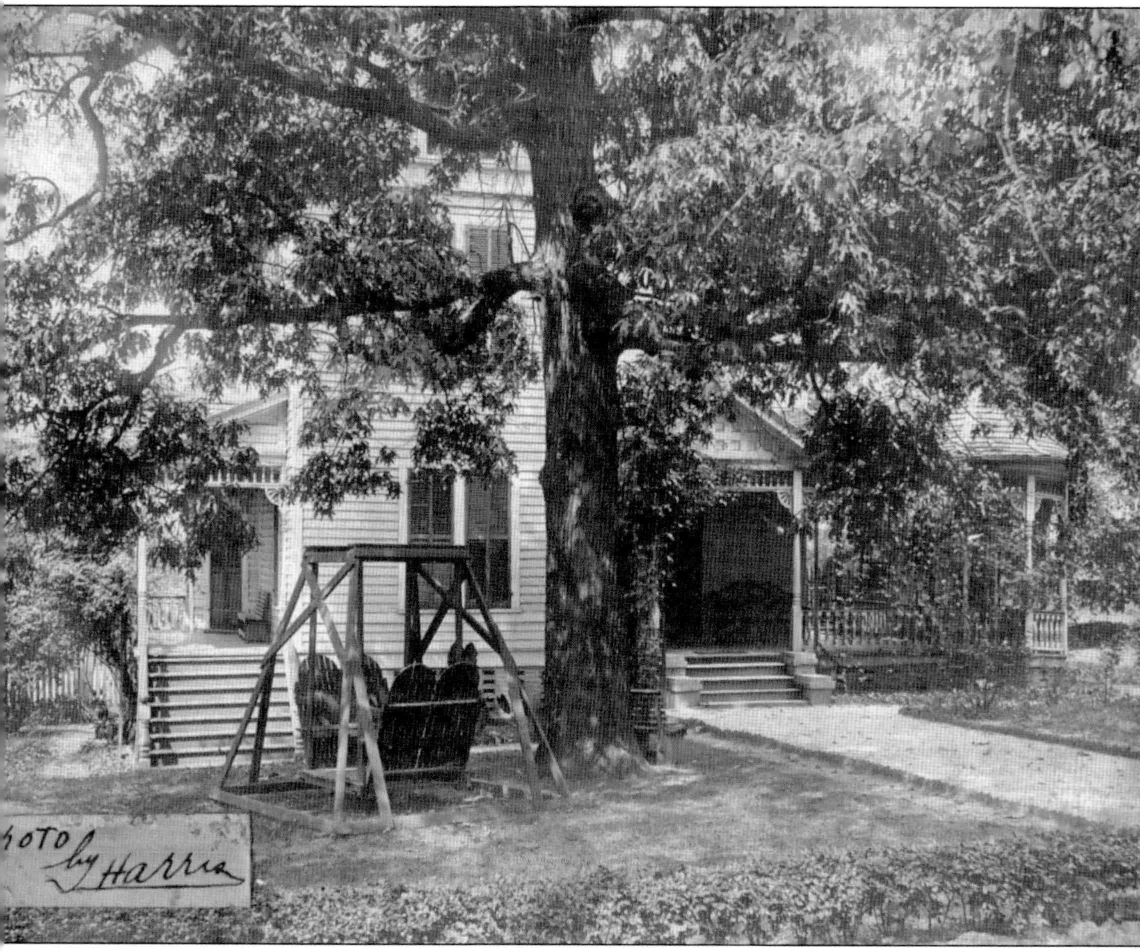

Col. William Wallace Lewis, a Yorkville lawyer, purchased a lot on 105 East Liberty Street in 1898 and built this Victorian-style house there in 1899. This photograph was taken about 1910. He and his wife, Anna, occupied the house with their three children. After Lewis's death in 1926, Anna lived in the home with their daughter Frances as late as 1930.

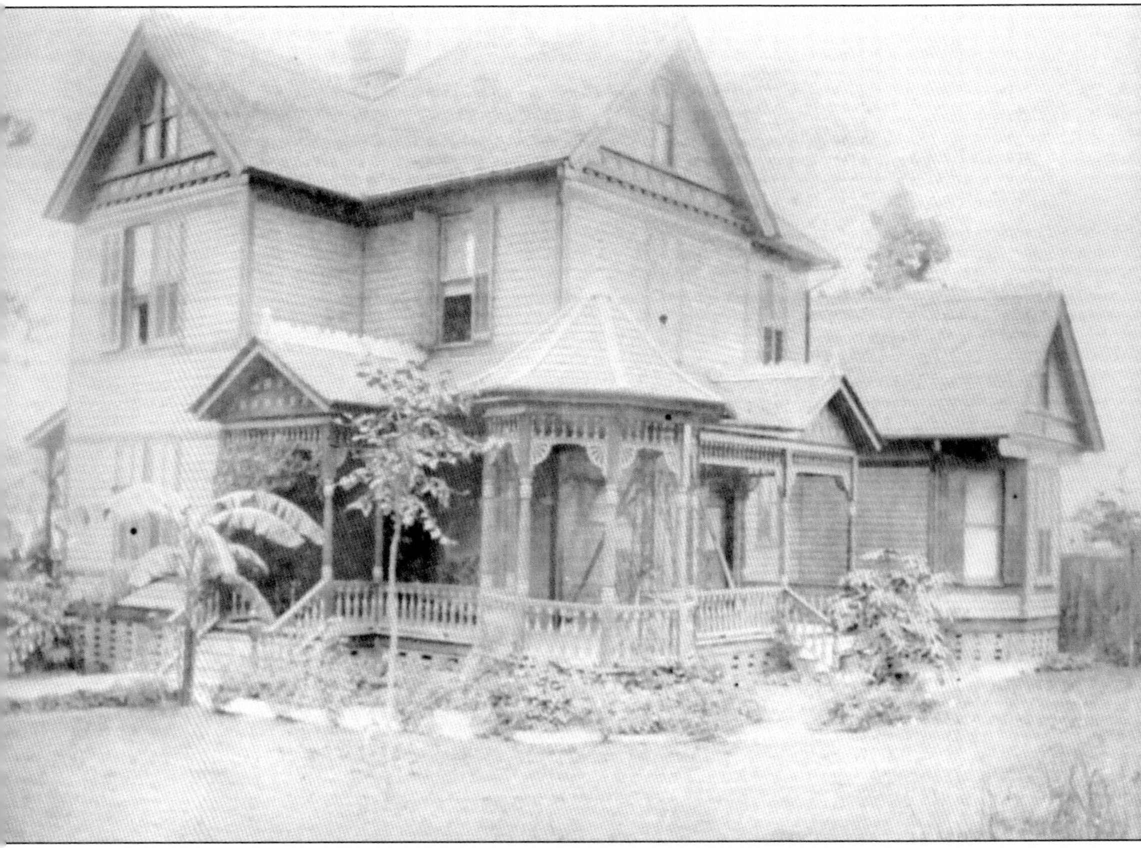

This second view of the William W. Lewis house shows more of the overall structure. This photograph appears to have been taken earlier than the one on page 99, not long after the house was completed.

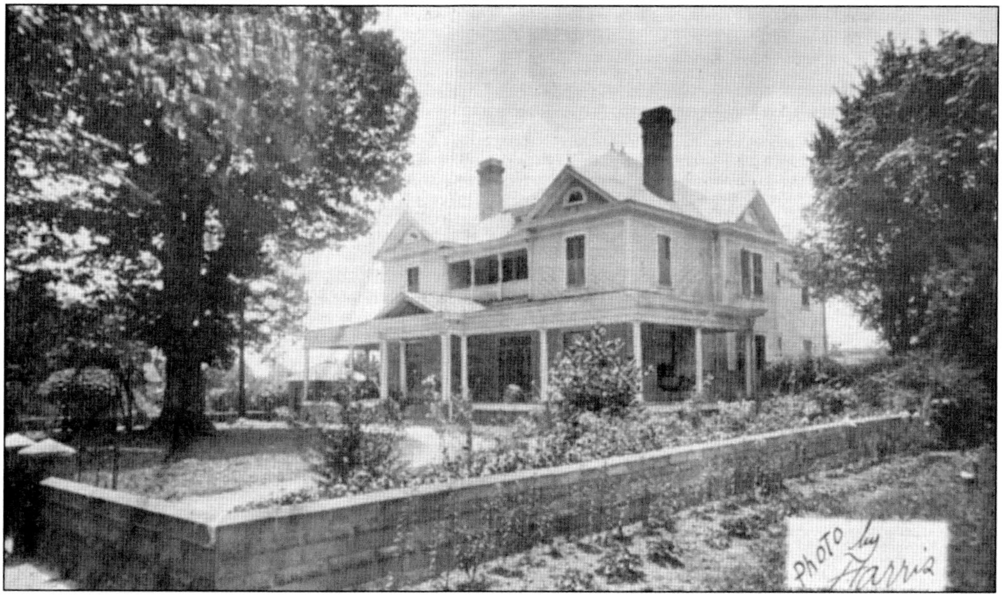

James M. Stroup was a merchant in Clover prior to moving his business to Yorkville. He acquired a lot on 206 East Liberty Street in 1899 and built this Colonial Revival–style home the following year. Stroup lived here with his wife, Harriet ("Hattie"), and their five children. Hattie Stroup lived in the home with her sons until her death in 1932.

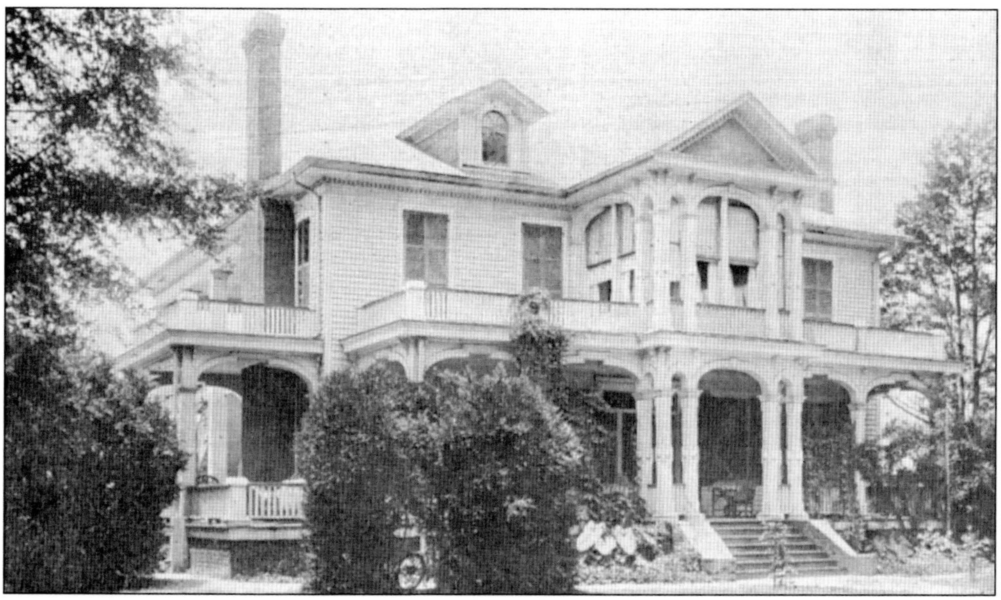

Dr. J. M. Lowry built this Tuscan villa–style house on 110 East Liberty Street in 1843. John R. Ashe acquired the property in 1885. After Ashe's death in 1901, his second wife, Sarah, raised their children in the home and also accepted a number of boarders for income. During this period, the house was the location of the York Tea Room, where businessmen ate family-style meals served at a large dining table. In the early 20th century, the house was referred to as the "Show Place of York."

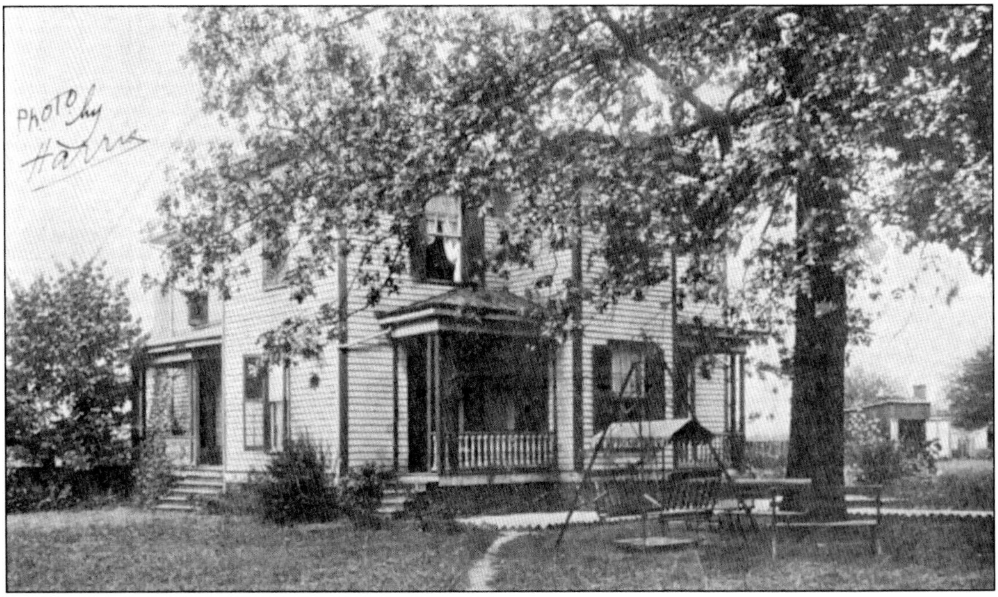

Robert Witherspoon and his wife, Sophia Bratton, moved from Brattonsville, south of Yorkville, to this home on East Liberty Street with their daughter Harriet around 1912. They resided here at least until the time of Robert's death in 1930.

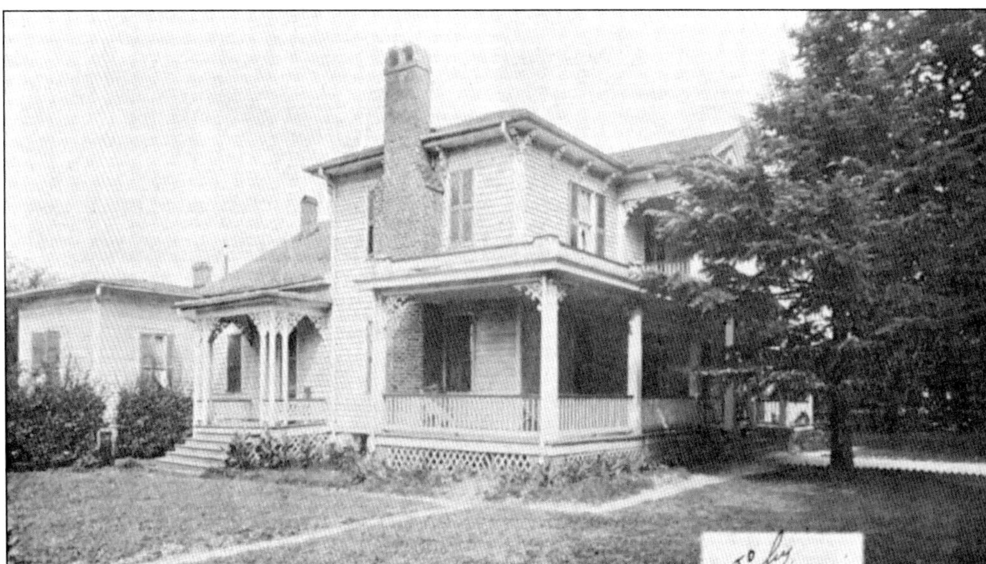

This house on East Liberty Street near College Street was the residence of William F. Marshall and his wife, Annie, in the first decade of the 20th century. Marshall was listed as a traveling salesman in the 1908–1909 city directory.

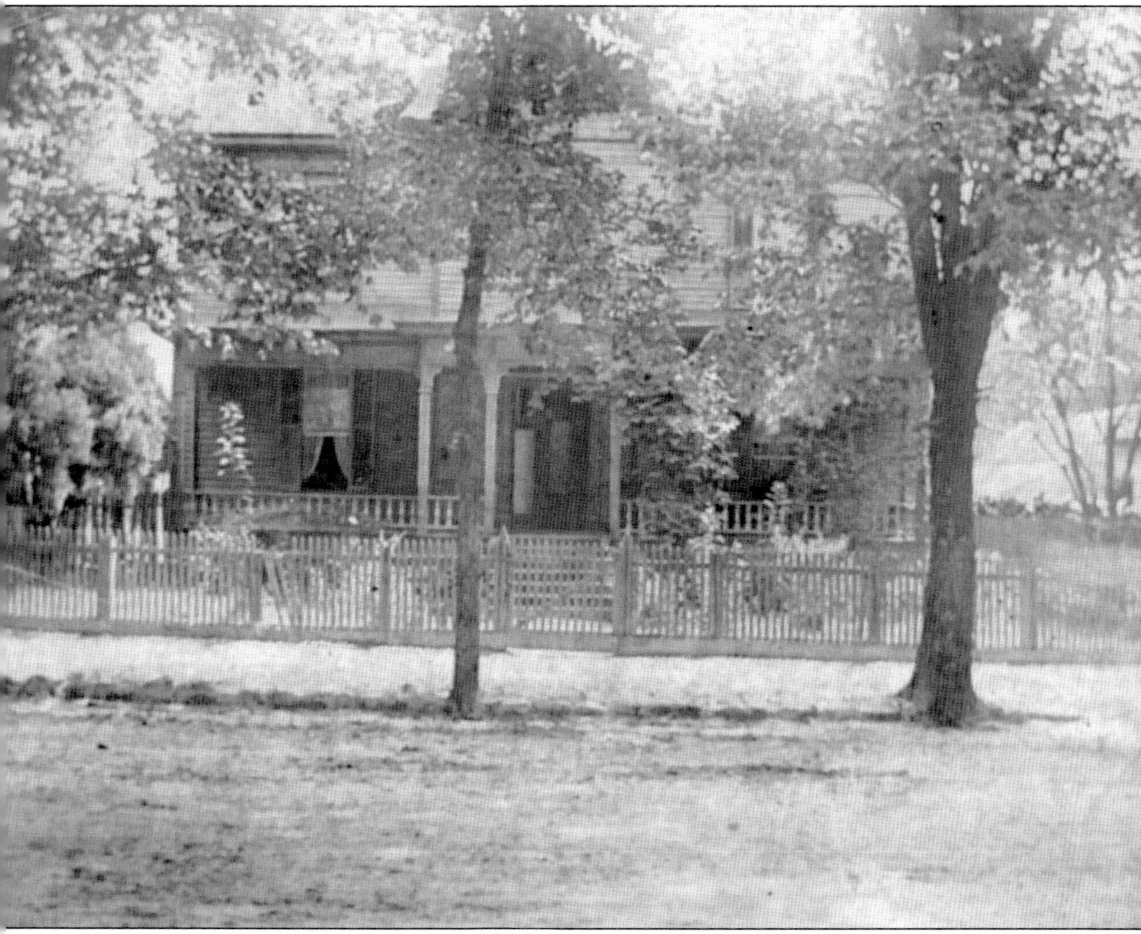

William Walker Jenkins owned this home near the corner of Congress and Madison Streets and operated a grocery store at the same location in the early 1900s. The house was located adjacent to the old ARP church manse and is no longer extant.

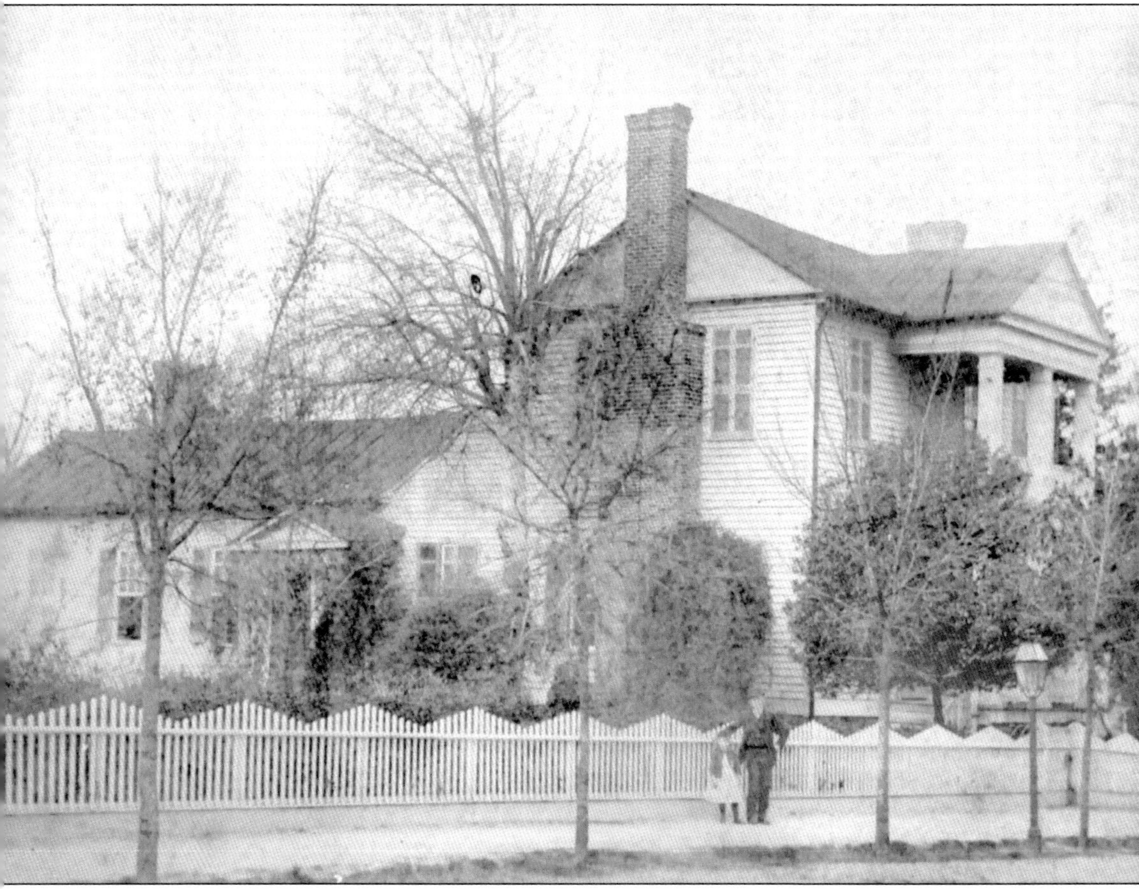

This house at 15 West Liberty Street was built in the 1820s by H. B. Hoover and later sold to Judge Isaac D. Witherspoon. The Witherspoon family inhabited the house for almost a century before selling it to John J. Hunter, one of the town's last surviving Confederate veterans. Hunter's daughter, Agnes Hunter Lawton, lived in the home until her death in the 1970s.

Nine

PEOPLE

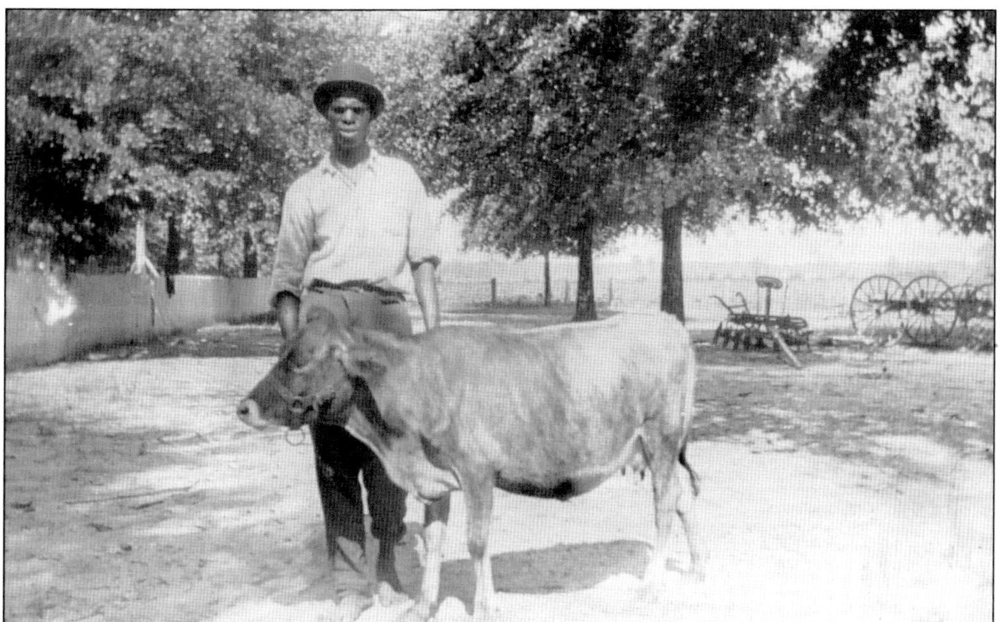

This photograph of an unidentified African American farmer with his cow was taken *c.* 1915. In the background are visible a group of mule- or horse-drawn agricultural implements, including a one-row plow, a disc harrow, and a wagon.

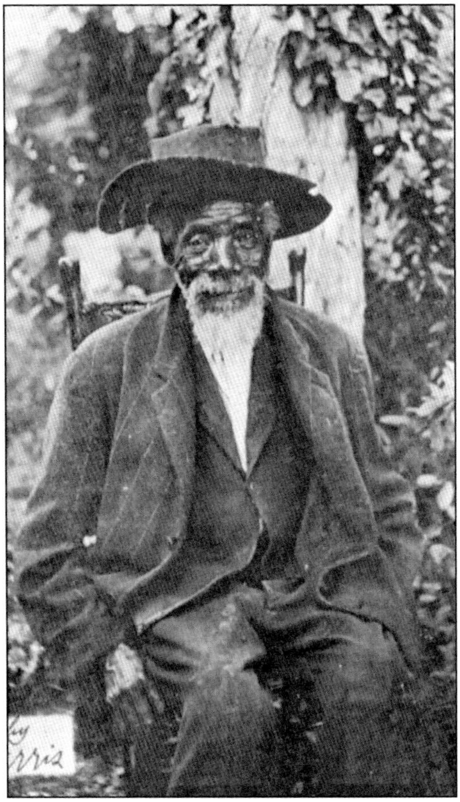

This photograph of an unidentified African American man appeared in the 1911–1912 Yorkville Graded School Annual Report with the title "Product of the Old South." The elderly gentleman was probably a former slave.

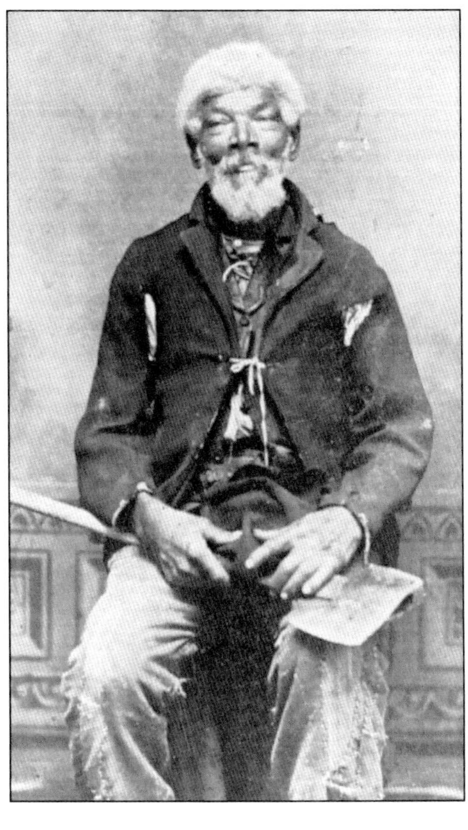

Another photograph of an unidentified African American, probably a former slave, also appeared in the 1911–1912 Yorkville Graded School Annual Report. This picture was entitled "Testimony to Yorkville's Healthfulness."

Frances Mary Witherspoon was born in 1843, the daughter of Isaac Donnom Witherspoon and Ann T. K. Reid of Yorkville. She married Henry R. Dickson, a widower and minister of the First Presbyterian Church, after 1870. Reverend Dickson died in 1877, and in 1883, she married Lewis D. Mason in New York. Frances, known as "Aunt Fannie" to her family, died in Connecticut in 1901.

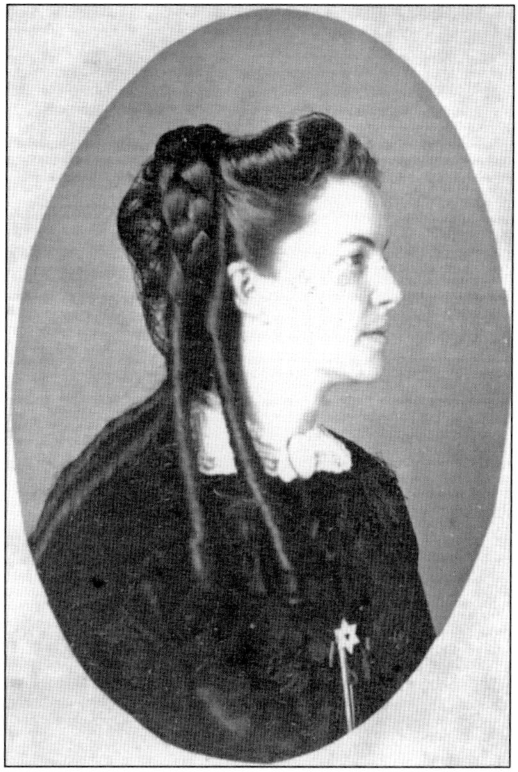

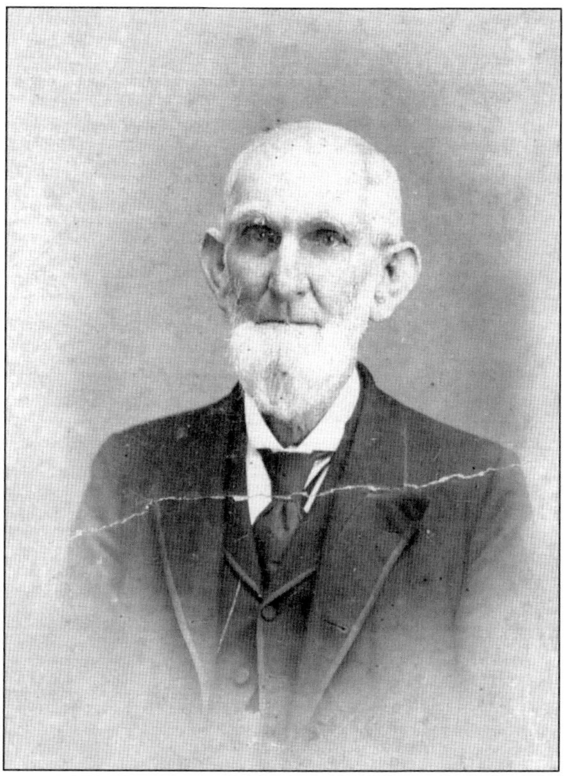

Dr. John Franklin Lindsay was born in York District in 1823. He attended the University of New York Medical School and was a local physician for many years. Dr. Lindsay was photographed by J. R. Schorb c. 1910.

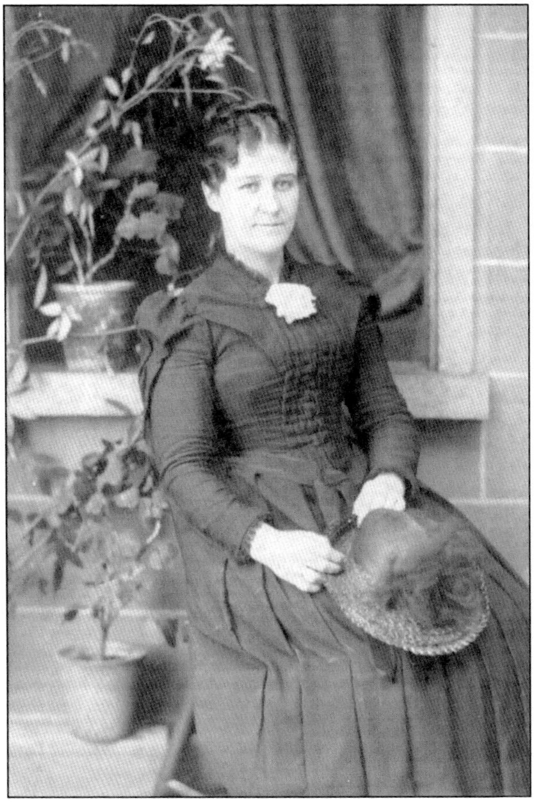

Catherine C. "Kitty" Dickson was born in August 1865, the daughter of Rev. Henry R. Dickson. She never married and lived with her aunt Ann McPheter until she died sometime before 1920. This photograph was taken by J. R. Schorb c. 1905.

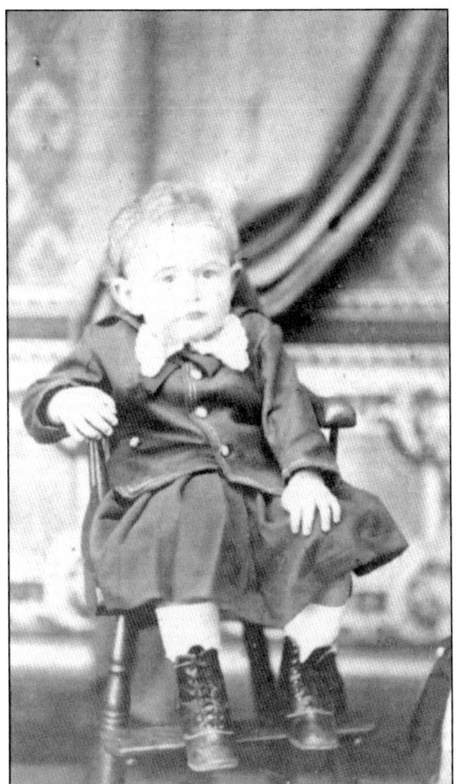

John Bratton Lowry (1849–1855) was the oldest child of John Thomas Lowry and Martha Elizabeth Bratton. He was photographed at the age of two years and four months by J. R. Schorb.

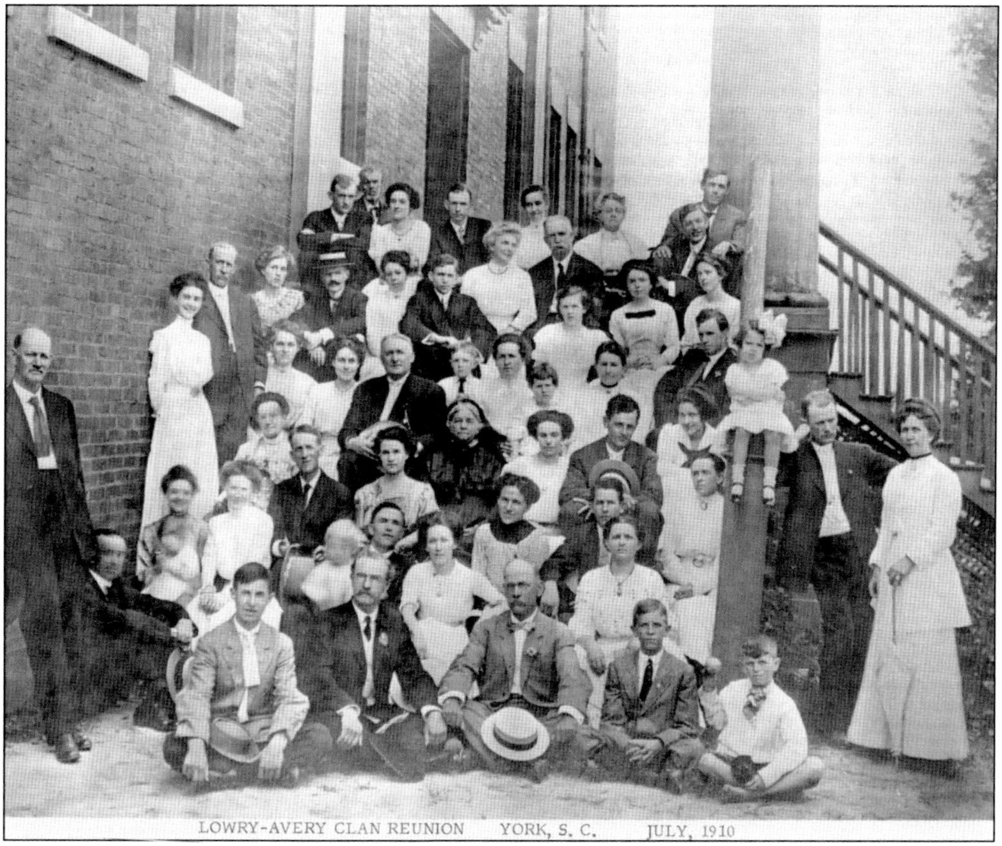

The Lowry-Avery Clan Reunion has been held in York every five years since 1910, except during World War I and World War II. This photograph shows the July 1910 gathering held at the Yorkville Graded School.

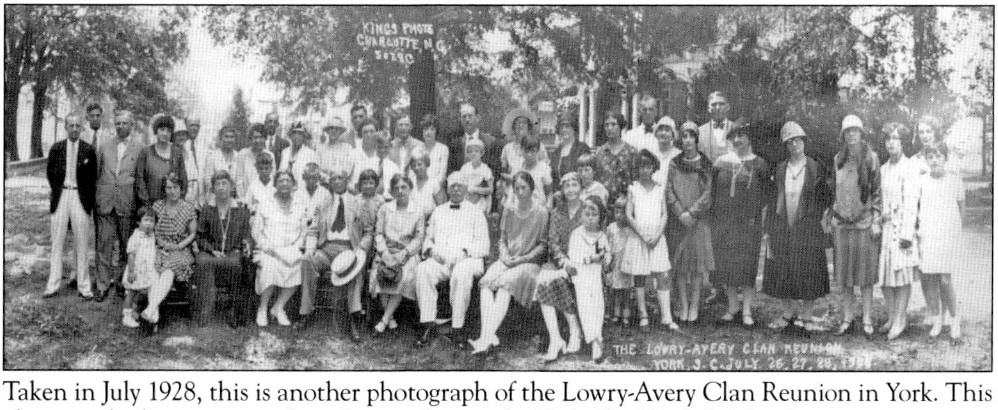

Taken in July 1928, this is another photograph of the Lowry-Avery Clan Reunion in York. This photograph also appears to have been taken at the Yorkville Graded School.

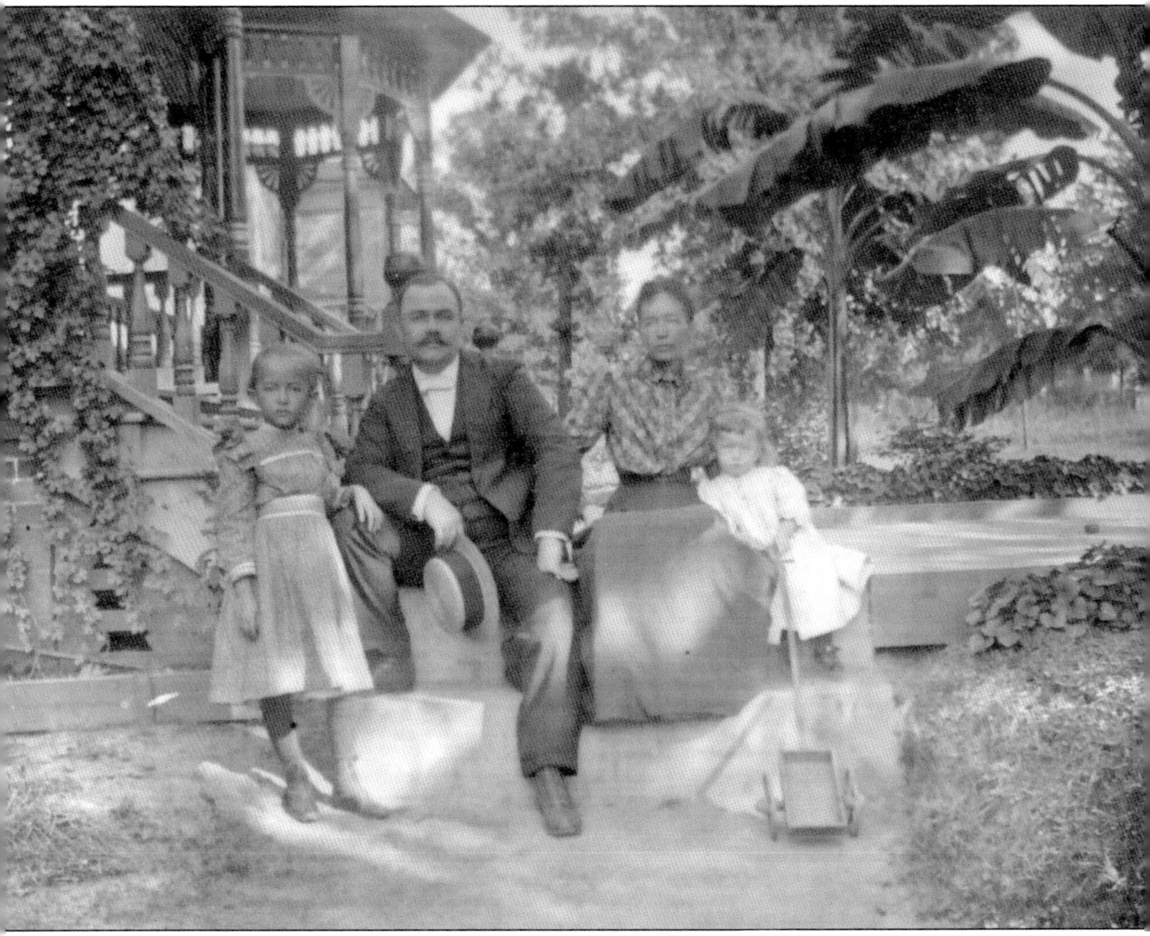

William Wallace Lewis (1866–1926) married Anna Kester Rawlinson (1860–1946) on December 31, 1890. They were the parents of six children, three of whom lived to adulthood. Pictured here at their home on 105 East Liberty Street *c.* 1898, the family is, from left to right, daughter Anna (who later married John Allison Latta); William W. Lewis; Lewis's wife, Anna Rawlinson Lewis; and daughter Frances Snow Lewis. Not pictured is son John Sumter Lewis, who attended South Carolina Military School in Charleston and later the Citadel.

Anna Kester Rawlinson Lewis (1893–1962) was about 20 months old when J. R. Schorb photographed her at his studio in Yorkville c. 1895. She was the second (and oldest living) child of Col. William Wallace Lewis and Anna Kester Rawlinson. In 1936, she married John Allison Latta (1857–1936).

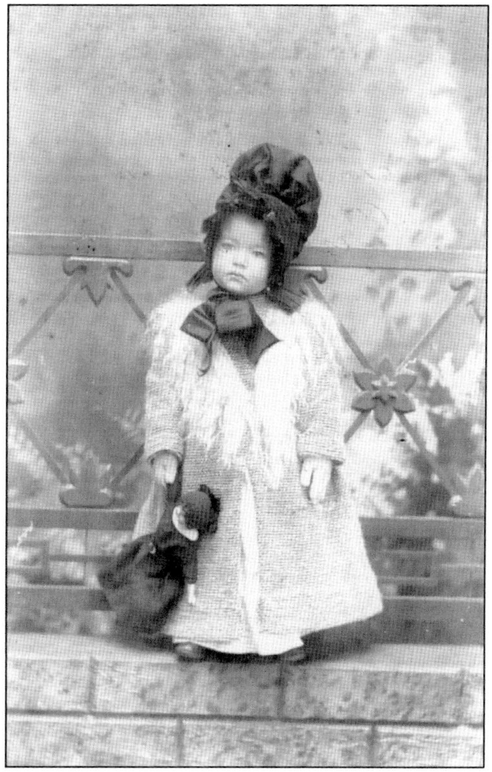

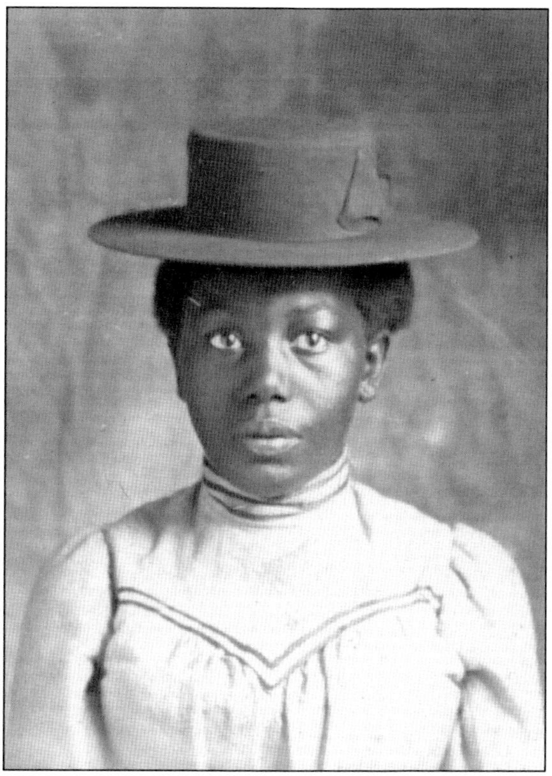

Nettie Love lived with the William W. Lewis family on East Liberty Street and cared for their children.

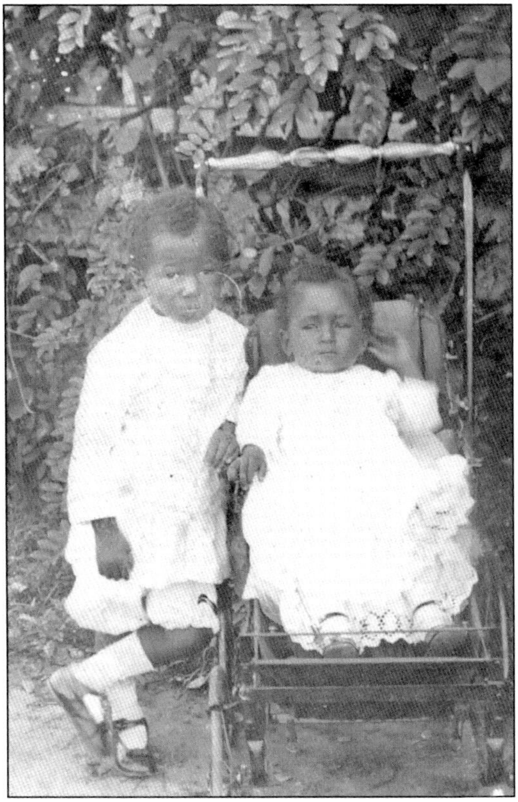

Fannie Johnson was the William W. Lewis family cook. This photograph shows two of her children.

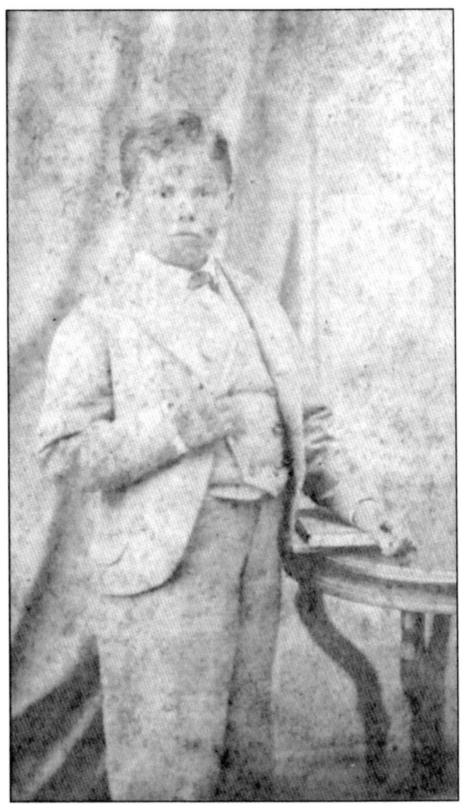

William Darby Glenn Sr. was born September 30, 1865. He was about 10 years old when photographer J. R. Schorb took this photograph. He went on to marry Ella Cynthia Carroll and died in 1911.

Ella Cynthia Carroll was born September 20, 1869, the daughter of Thaddeus Lamar Carroll and Martha Elizabeth Caldwell. This photograph was taken by T. B. McClain c. 1888. Ella married William Darby Glenn and died in 1957. They were the parents of four children.

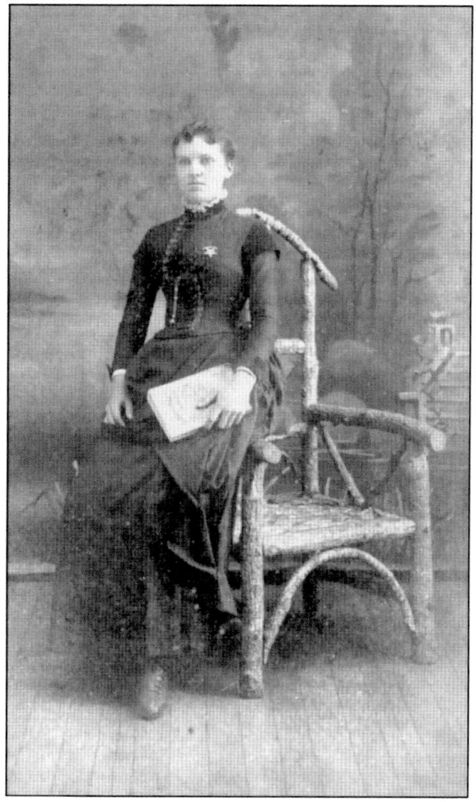

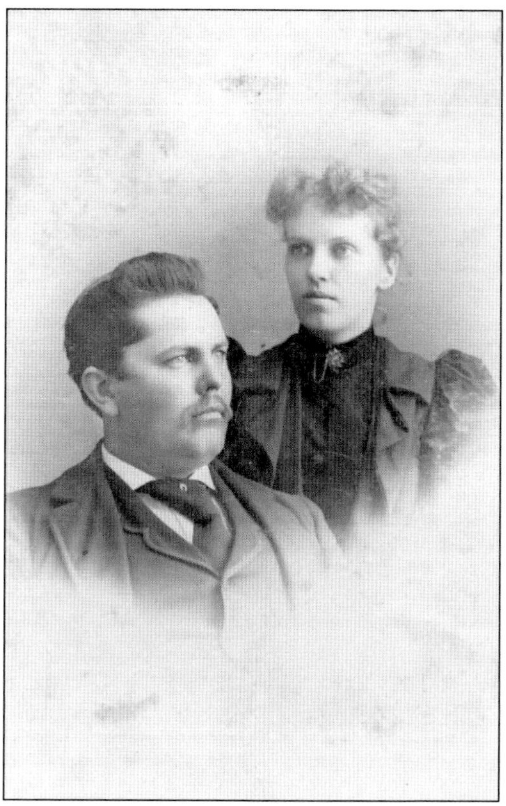

This studio photograph of William Darby Glenn and his wife, Ella Carroll Glenn, was taken in September 1893.

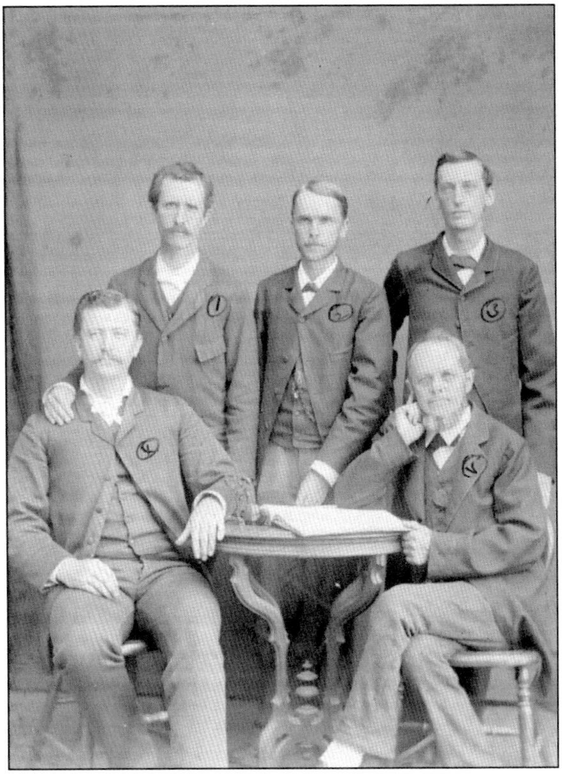

This photograph of five York businessmen was taken by J. R. Schorb in his studio *c.* 1900. The men are identified on the back of the photograph as, from left to right, (seated) John R. Ashe (1856–1901, operated the York Tea Room in his home on East Liberty Street) and J. R. Schorb (1818–1908); (standing) John Ashe Schorb, G. W. S. Hart (George Washington Seabrook Hart, 1851–1925, a Yorkville lawyer), and Baxter McClain (Thomas Baxter McClain, 1857–1932, a cotton manufacturer at the time of this photograph, later bookkeeper for the York County treasurer). Schorb was born in Neiderweilder, Germany, moved to Yorkville in 1853, and taught full-time at the Yorkville Female Academy and part-time at the Kings Mountain Military School. He became a professional photographer in 1869 with a studio on West Liberty Street, and he took many of the photographs reproduced in this book.

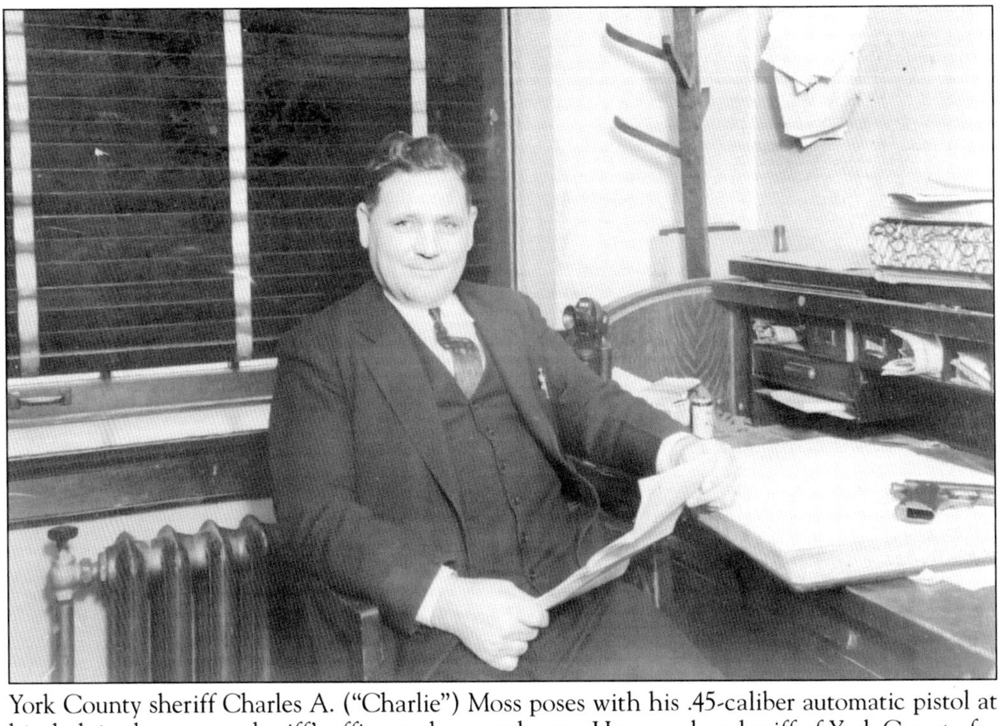

York County sheriff Charles A. ("Charlie") Moss poses with his .45-caliber automatic pistol at his desk in the county sheriff's office at the courthouse. He served as sheriff of York County for 22 years and died in office in 1956. (Courtesy Pat Guerry Hodnett.)

Pat Moss, granddaughter of Sheriff Charlie Moss, was standing in front of the booking room at the old jail on West Liberty Street when this photograph was taken c. 1945. (Courtesy Pat Guerry Hodnett.)

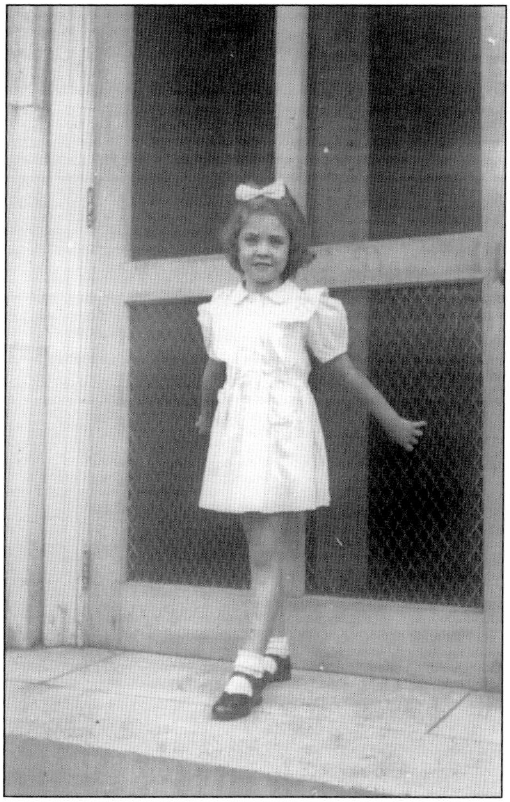

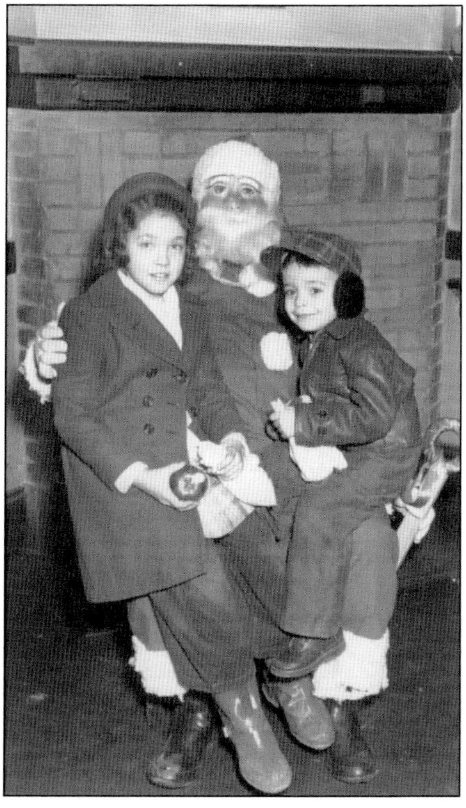

Pat Moss and her cousin Joey Oates visited Santa Claus in the York County Courthouse after the Christmas parade and tree lighting in 1949. The children enjoyed receiving white paper bags filled with goodies from Santa Claus (portrayed here by Sheriff Moss's son, Lewis Moss). (Courtesy Pat Guerry Hodnett.)

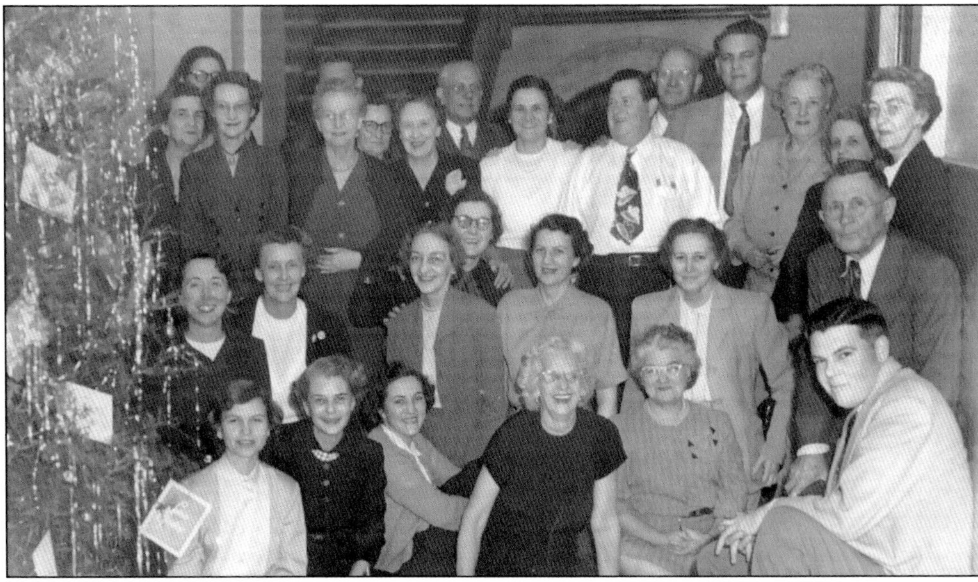

This photograph of a Christmas party was taken inside the York County Court House *c.* 1948. These are almost certainly employees and officers of the York County government.

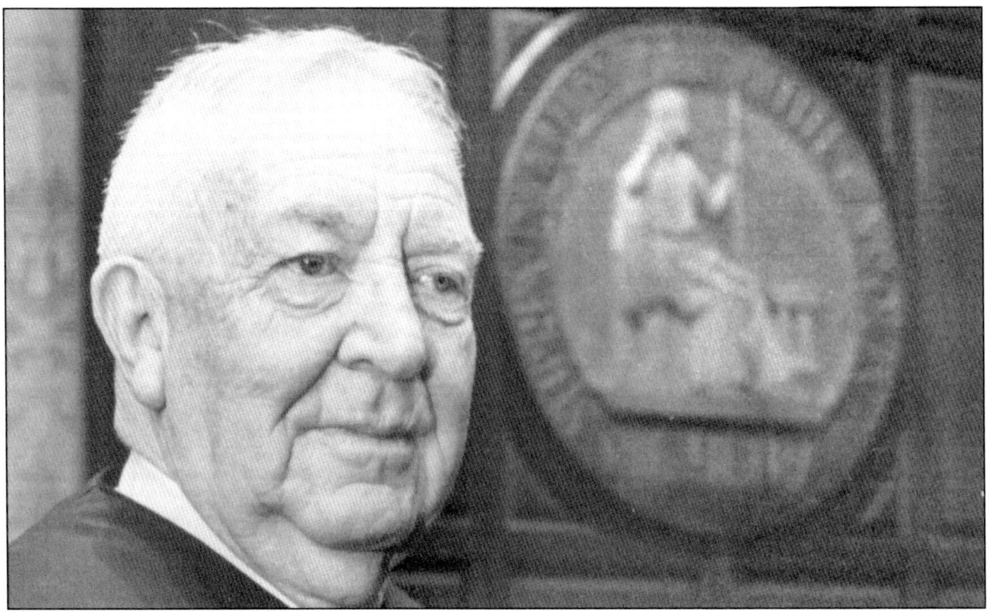

Joseph Rodney Moss (1903–1993) was born on the farm of his parents, James Lucius and Janie Ford Moss, in York County on July 15, 1903. He attended Erskine College and graduated from the University of South Carolina School of Law in 1927. Moss had a successful legal practice in York with John Hart and later his brother, James L. Moss Jr. In 1931, he married Rosa Dill, but she died in 1966 without issue. During his distinguished career, Moss served in the South Carolina Senate (1941–1948), the South Carolina Circuit Court Bench (1948–1956), and the South Carolina Supreme Court (1956–1975), serving as chief justice from 1966 until his retirement in 1975. Judge Moss was a lifelong member and ruling elder of York ARP Church, for which he helped lay the foundation as a youngster. This photograph was taken in October 1975, at the time of his retirement. The Moss Justice Center in York was named in honor of him.

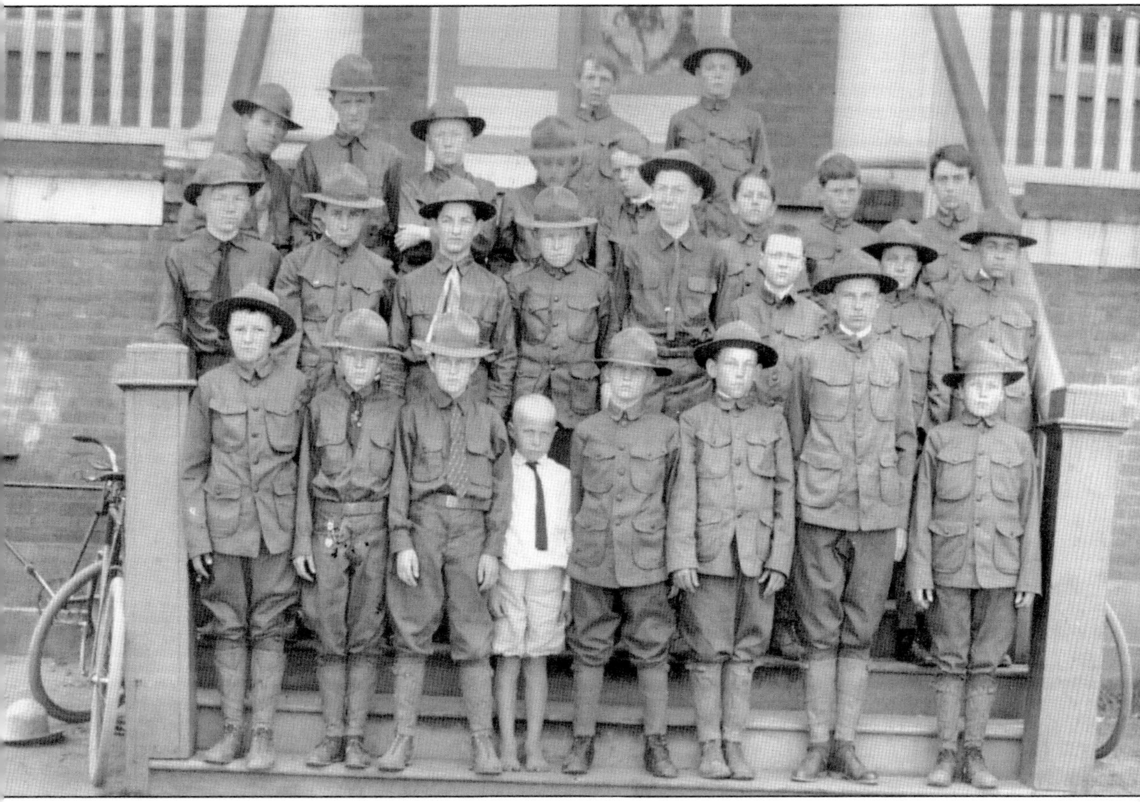

This photograph of the Yorkville Boy Scout troop was taken in 1914. The Boy Scouts of America organization was founded by William D. Boyce, a Chicago publisher, on February 8, 1910, to promote the social welfare of young men. The Boy Scouts went on to become the largest youth organization in the United States.

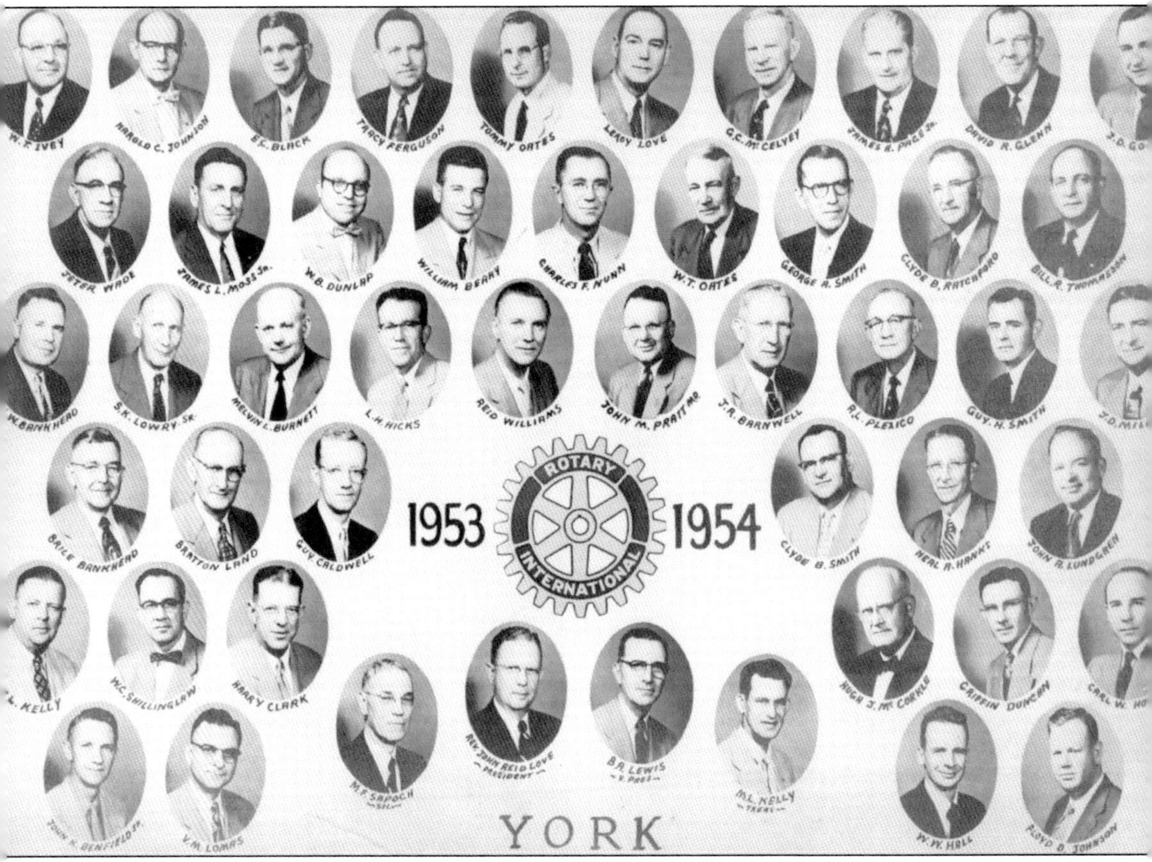

This collage of the York Rotary Club highlights the members for the calendar year 1953–1954. The first Rotary Club in America was formed in Chicago on February 23, 1905, by Paul P. Harris, an attorney. Meetings were rotated among members' offices, hence the name Rotary Club. In the decade that followed, Rotary Clubs were chartered all over the United States, and by 1921, Rotary Clubs had been formed on six continents. Rotary Clubs promote high ethical standards within all vocations. They also provide humanitarian service and build goodwill throughout the world.

Ten

The Circus

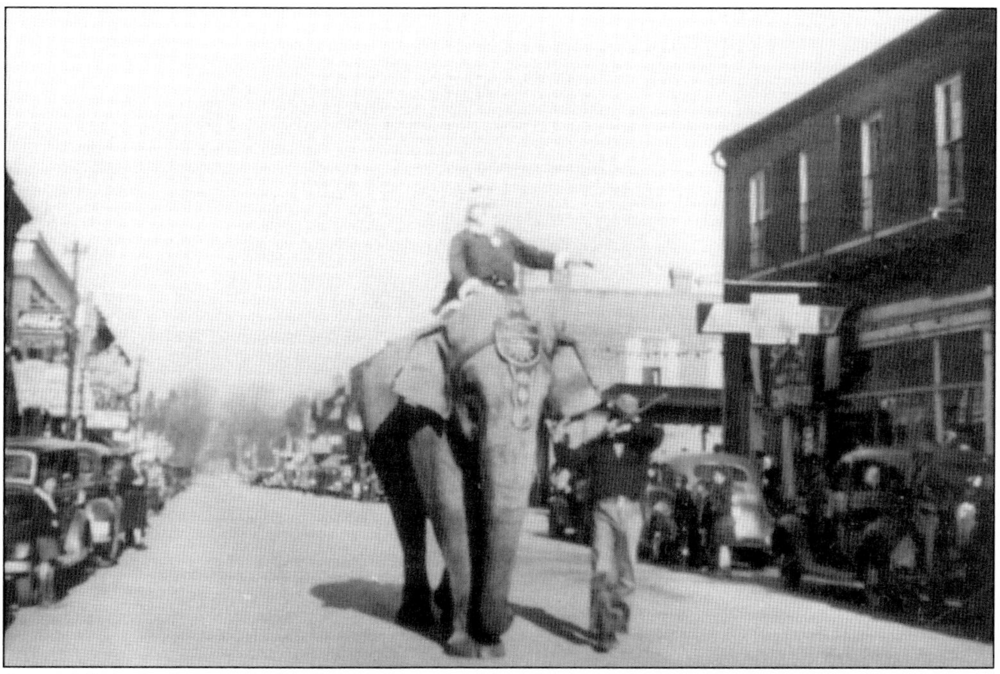

Santa Claus rode on an elephant, furnished by the Barnett Brothers Circus, in the annual Christmas parade in York *c.* 1940. The Barnett Brothers Circus, owned and operated by Ray W. Rogers, wintered in York in two buildings on East Jefferson Street from 1929 to 1944. The circus was very popular at that time and even inspired a group of local men, the Bennett brothers, to form their own circus.

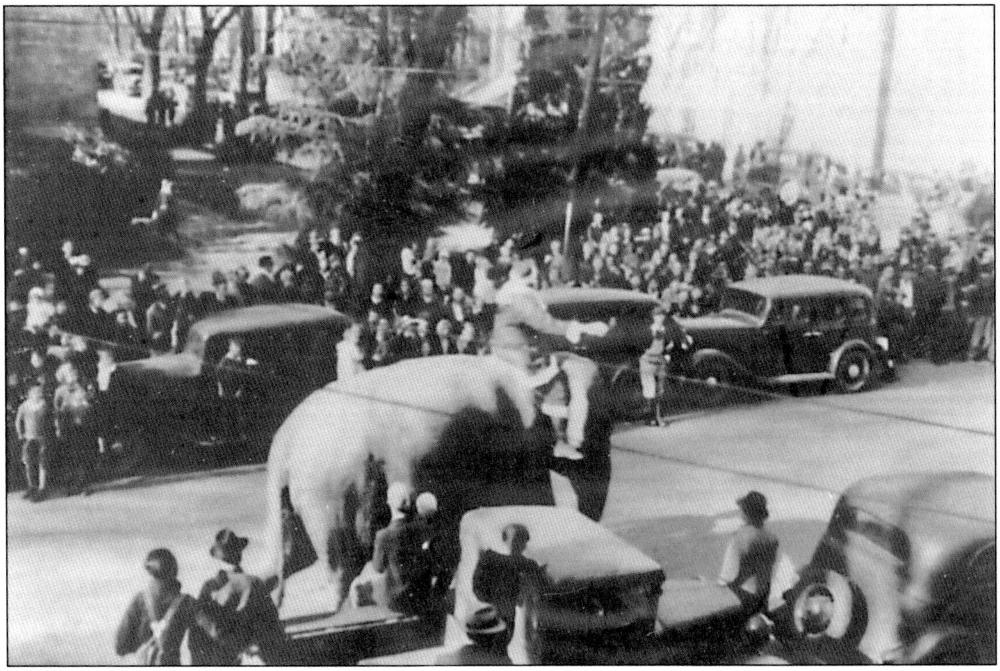

This photograph shows another view of Santa Claus riding the Barnett Brothers' elephant in the York Christmas parade, *c.* 1940.

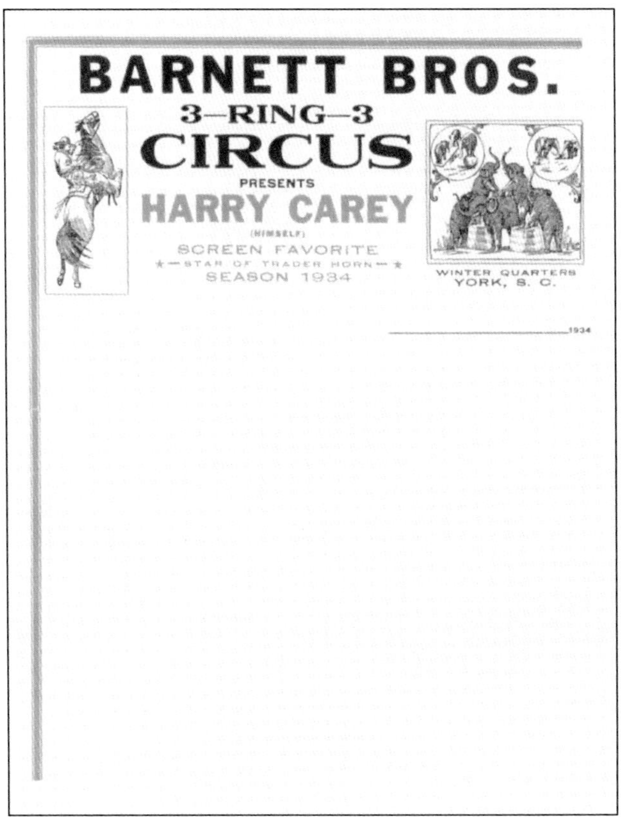

BARNETT BROS.
3—RING—3
CIRCUS
PRESENTS
HARRY CAREY
(HIMSELF)
SCREEN FAVORITE
★—STAR OF TRADER HORN—★
SEASON 1934

WINTER QUARTERS
YORK, S. C.

________________1934

This image shows the customized stationery used by the Barnett Brothers 3-Ring Circus in 1934. The circus at that time featured movie star Harry Carey, "screen favorite" and "star of Trader Horn." *Trader Horn* was a 1931 movie starring a young Harry Carey as explorer and adventurer Aloysius "Trader" Horn. In the movie, Carey searches for a young white girl (played by Edwina Booth) who was kidnapped by African natives and then became "the queen of their savage tribe," to quote from the movie trailer.

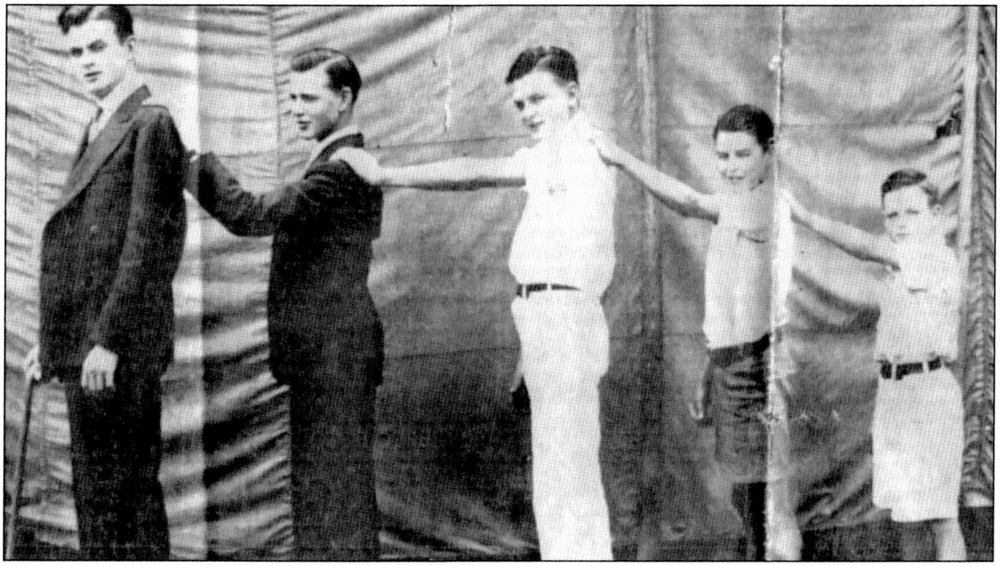

The Bennett Brothers Circus was named for the five sons of policeman C. P. Bennett of York and operated from 1930 to 1939. The Bennett brothers started their own circus in 1930 after seeing the Barnett Brothers Circus wintering in York. The oldest brother, Joe Bennett, was the manager and ringmaster. The Bennett Brothers are shown here in a picture from the *Charlotte Observer* dated October 17, 1937. From left to right, they are Joe, Charles, Bill, Stanley, and Douglas. A sixth brother, Orin, joined the circus after 1938. (Courtesy the *Charlotte Observer.*)

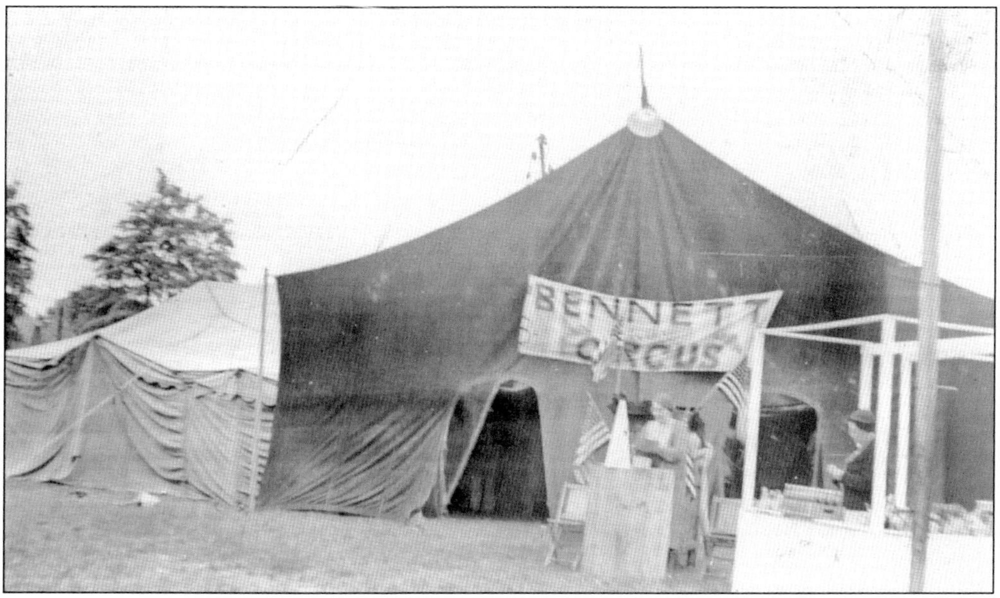

This image shows the Bennett Brothers Circus tent. The circus tent, which accommodated 700 people, was a gift from the owner and manager of the Barnett Brothers Circus, R. W. Rogers. The Bennett Brothers held performances at the circus lot on Lincoln Street in York. The Bennetts and about 20 other local youngsters performed in the circus.

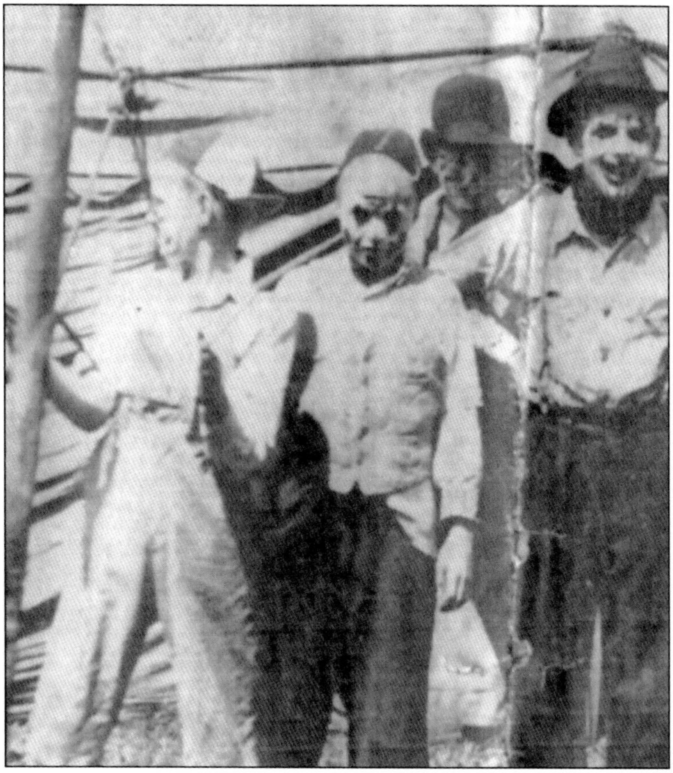

Some of the other young performers of the Bennett Brothers Circus are shown in this picture from the *Charlotte Observer* dated October 17, 1937. Admission to the Bennett Brothers Circus in the 1930s was 10¢ or 25¢, depending on the location of the seats. The show was complete with a band, standard circus ring, and peanut and soft drink vendors. (Courtesy the *Charlotte Observer.*)

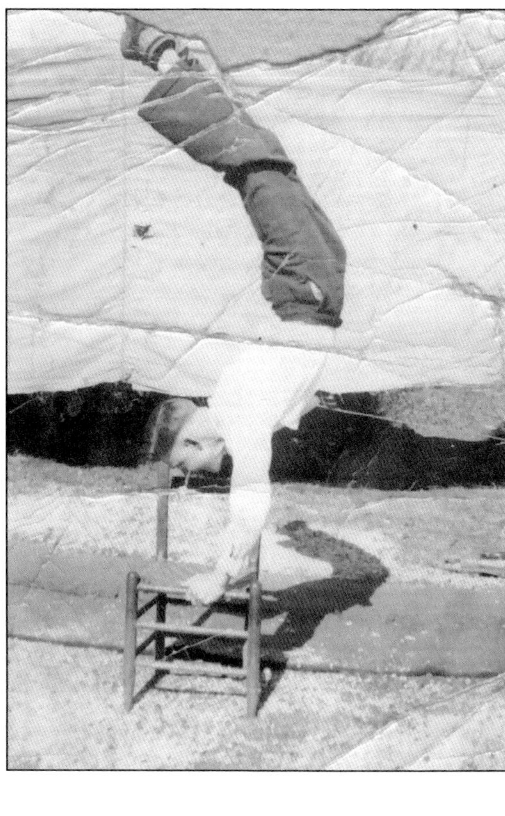

One of the young Bennett Brothers Circus performers demonstrates his skill in this photograph. The Bennett Brothers Circus show included acrobatics, balancing acts, rope spinning, tightwire acts, tumbling, and clowns. Occasionally they borrowed animals such as horses, elephants, or bison from the Barnett Brothers Circus. The Bennett Brothers made it big in York and eventually traveled to Rock Hill, Clover, and Sharon, but the circus closed after the outbreak of World War II.

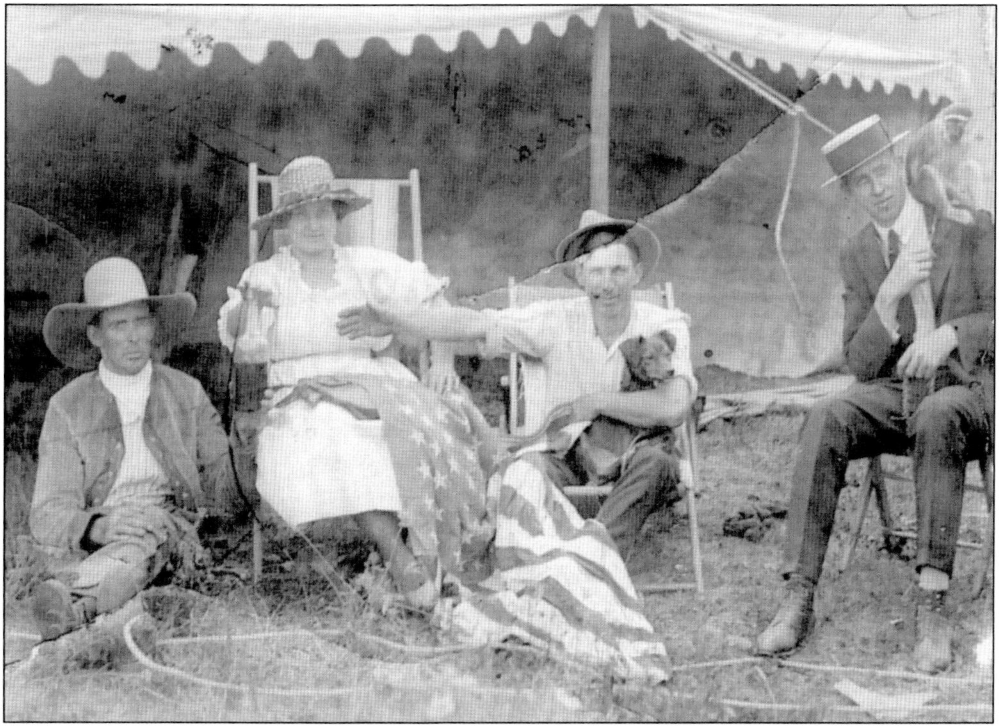

Walter Bell McGinnis was born July 15, 1889, in York and died August 29, 1950, in Camden, New Jersey. Walter was a member of the Barnett Brothers Circus all his life, and in 1925, he married Ella Louise Brack, who was also with the circus. In 1930, they were living in Mecklenburg County, North Carolina, with three children. Ella was a spinner at a cotton mill and Walter was a laborer with the circus/traveling show. In this photograph, Walter is second from the right, holding a dog. The other people in the image are unidentified.

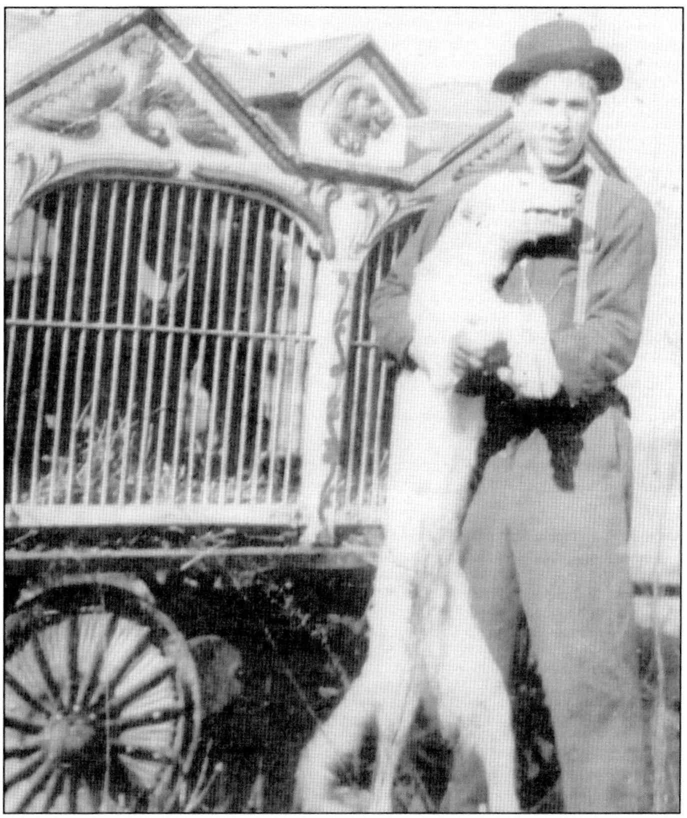

In this photograph, Walter McGinnis is once again shown holding one of the circus dogs.

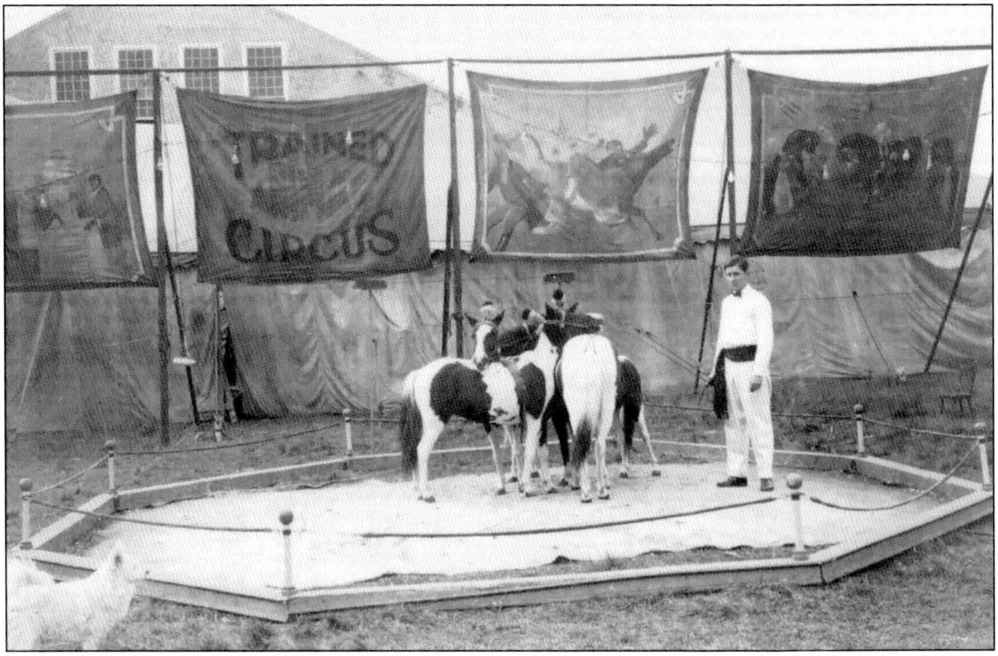

Among the most popular features of the Barnett Brothers 3-Ring Circus in the 1930s and 1940s were the animal acts. The circus featured a variety of trained animals that performed elaborate stunts. In this photograph, a trainer poses with his trained ponies and a dog. This was truly a "dog and pony show."

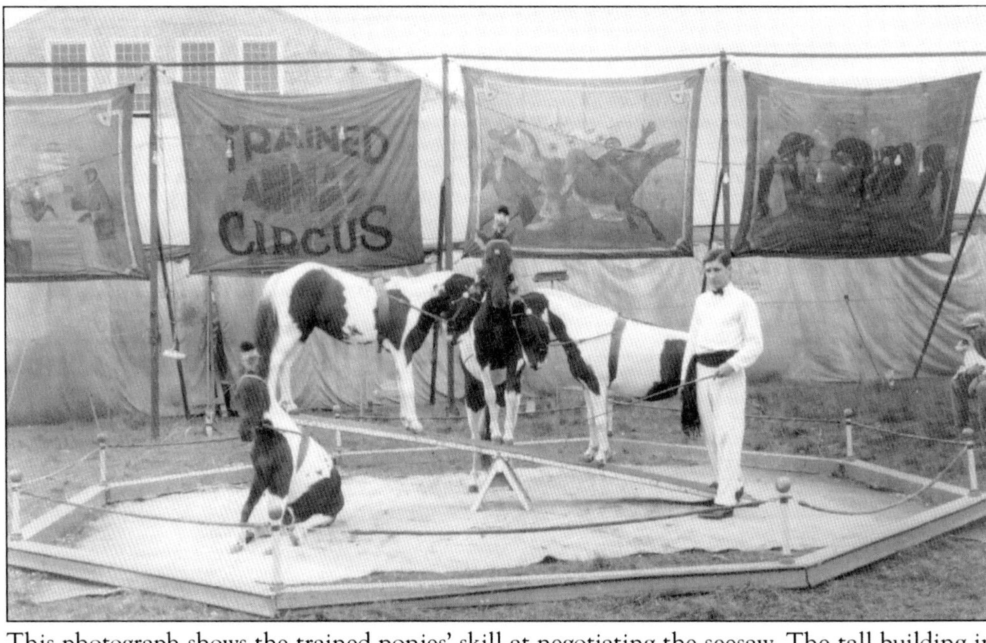

This photograph shows the trained ponies' skill at negotiating the seesaw. The tall building in the background is the Rock Barn on East Jefferson Street, which served as a barn for the larger and heavier animals while the circus wintered in York. The building is still in existence, but the roof was cut down and lowered in the 1980s. The Rock Barn was originally built as a livery stable and served as the National Guard armory in the late 1940s.

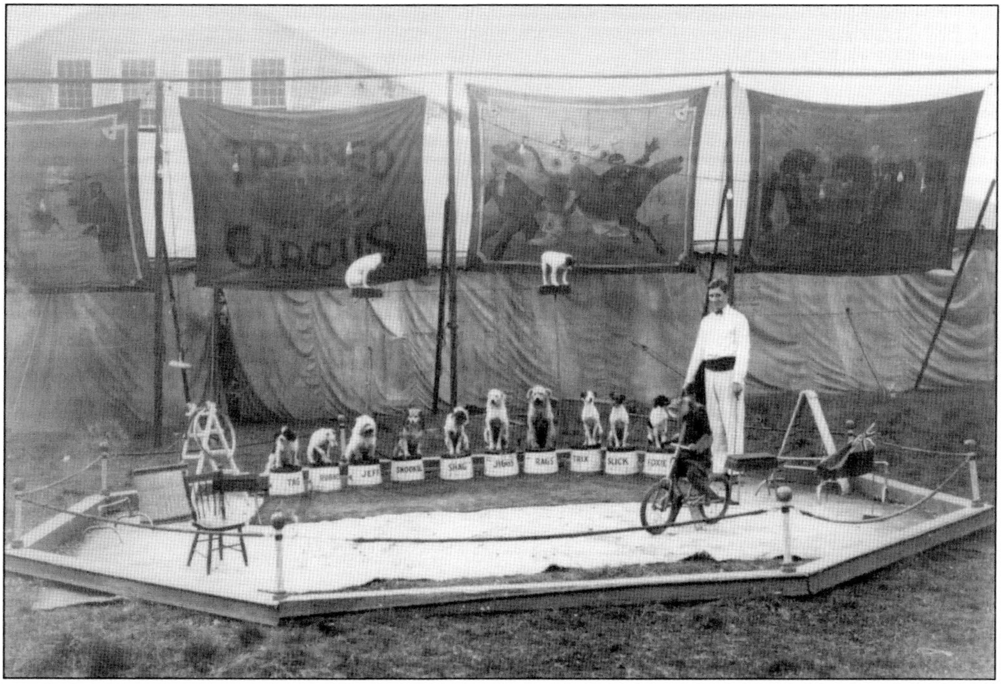

Another popular feature of the Barnett Brothers Circus was the trained dog act. Here the trainer puts 12 dogs through their paces (note their names on each stand) while a trained monkey rides by on his bicycle.

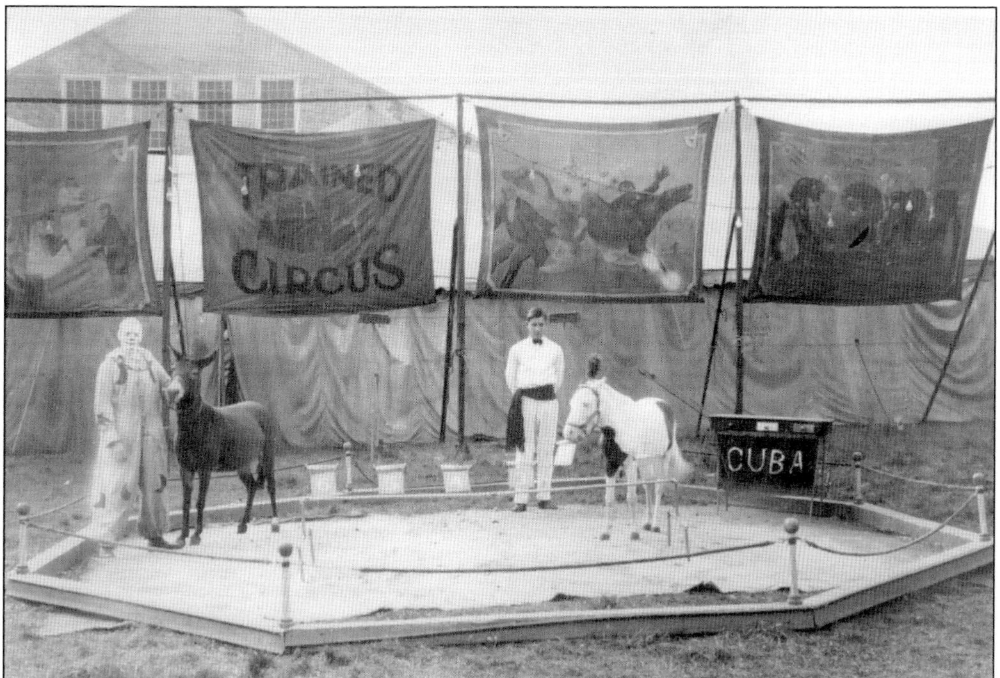

This last photograph shows the trainer with one of his ponies (right) and a clown with a donkey (left). Some type of trained bird is perched on the pony's head.

About the Authors

Michael C. Scoggins has lived most of his life in the McConnells community of York County, South Carolina. He has associate degrees from the University of South Carolina (Union) and York Technical College and a B.A. in history from Winthrop University, and he is currently pursuing his master's degree in history from Winthrop. Michael is employed as the staff historian for the Culture and Heritage Museums and is research director of the Southern Revolutionary War Institute at the McCelvey Center in York. He is the author or coauthor of five books on the American Revolution in the Southern colonies, is a frequent contributor to historical journals and magazines, and is editor of *The York County Genealogical and Historical Society Quarterly*.

Nancy Sambets is a native of Charleston, South Carolina. She received her B.A. in history from the College of Charleston and her master's degree in applied history (museum studies) from the University of South Carolina. Nancy has worked at several historic sites, museums, and archives throughout South Carolina, including Andrew Jackson State Park in Lancaster County. She is currently the archivist for the Culture and Heritage Museums and works at the Historical Center of York County in the McCelvey Center.

BIBLIOGRAPHY

Archives, Library, and Special Collections. Historical Center of York County, Culture and Heritage Museums, York, SC.

Catawba Regional Planning Council. *Historic Sites Survey York County*. Rev. ed. Rock Hill, SC: Catawba Regional Planning Council, 1977.

Hill Directory Company. *Hill's York (South Carolina) City Directory, 1970*. Richmond, VA: Hill Directory Company, 1970.

Lee, Edward, ed. *Yorkville to York*. Dallas, TX: Taylor Publishing Company for Yorkville Historical Society, 1998.

Miller, Ernest L, compiler. *Rock Hill and Yorkville South Carolina City Directory 1908–1909, Vol. I.* Asheville, NC: Piedmont Directory Co., Inc., 1908.

Moore, John Hammond, compiler and ed. *South Carolina in the 1880s: A Gazetteer*. Orangeburg, SC: Sandlapper Publishing, Inc., 1989.

Shankman, Arnold, E. Thomas Crowson, C. Jack Tucker, and Joel Nichols. *York County South Carolina: Its People and Its Heritage*. Norfolk, VA: The Donning Company for Rock Hill Area Chamber of Commerce, 1983.

United States Census, 1790–1930. Washington, D.C.: National Archives and Records Administration Microfilm. Historical Center of York County, Culture and Heritage Museums, York, SC.

White, William B., et. al. *First Presbyterian Church York, South Carolina*. Charlotte, NC: The Delmar Company, 1992.

Yorkville Enquirer newspaper (microfilm). Historical Center of York County, Culture and Heritage Museums, York, SC.

Yorkville Graded School Annual Report, 1911–1912.

Yorkville Graded School Annual Report, 1912–1913.

Yorkville Historical Society. *Welcome to Historic York, South Carolina: Walking Tour*. York, SC: Yorkville Historical Society, 2002.